Multiplan Models for Business

Douglas Ford Cobb
Gena Berg Cobb
Thomas B. Henderson

Que Corporation
Indianapolis

Library of Congress Catalog No.: LC 83-62487
ISBN 0-88022-037-6

Editorial Director
David F. Noble, Ph.D.

Editors
Jeannine Freudenberger, M.A.
Diane F. Brown, M.A.
Virginia D. Noble, M.L.S.

Managing Editor
Paul L. Mangin

Cover Design: Cargill Associates, Atlanta

About the Authors

Douglas Ford Cobb is General Manager of Software Products for Que Corporation. Mr. Cobb received his B.A., magna cum laude, from Williams College and his M.S. in accounting from New York University's Graduate School of Business Administration. He has worked for the firm of Arthur Andersen & Co. and was president of Cobb Associates, Inc., a Boston-based microcomputer consulting firm. Mr. Cobb is the co-author of *Spreadsheet Software: From VisiCalc to 1-2-3, SuperCalc SuperModels for Business, Using 1-2-3,* and *VisiCalc Models for Business,* all published by Que Corporation.

Gena Berg Cobb received her B.S. from the McIntire School of Commerce at the University of Virginia, where she graduated second in her class, and her M.B.A. from the Harvard Business School. Mrs. Cobb has worked in marketing management and held marketing research positions at American Digital Systems, Inc., and John Wiley & Sons, Inc., Publishers. Currently she is the Market Communications Manager for Que Corporation.

In addition to this book, Mrs. Cobb is the author of "A New Generation of Spreadsheet Software for Microcomputers," published in the *IBM PC Expansion & Software Guide* from Que Corporation. She is also co-author of *Spreadsheet Software: From VisiCalc to 1-2-3, SuperCalc SuperModels for Business, VisiCalc Models for Business,* and a proprietary research report on the use of personal computers in large organizations.

Thomas B. Henderson is Chairman of the Board of National Data Cable Company, Incorporated, an Indianapolis-based manufacturer of microcomputer cable assemblies, and President of G and H Associates, a software consulting firm.

An electronic spreadsheet expert and amateur mathematician, Mr. Henderson is the author of *The Osborne Portable Computer,* co-author of *Spreadsheet Software: From VisiCalc to 1-2-3,* and technical editor of *SuperCalc SuperModels for Business* and *VisiCalc Models for Business.* He has written numerous magazine articles on portable computing and a science fiction novel, *Six Seconds.*

Table of Contents

Introduction

Multiplan Models for Business is a book of models, or templates, for the electronic spreadsheet program Multiplan™. The book presents 20 models that show you creative ways to use Multiplan and your computer to help you run your business.

This book could be titled *Managing Your Business with Multiplan.* The business concepts behind each model are explained in the text so that you can learn new management techniques while you learn to use Multiplan. For example, some concepts covered by the text are net present value, ratio analysis, and cash flow management.

The models in this book range from fairly simple to very complex and cover topics from budgeting and financial statement preparation to managing accounts receivable. The text contains easy-to-follow instructions on how to set up and use the models. Each model is thoroughly illustrated so that you can easily follow along with the text.

Many of these models can be applied to your own business problems without modification, but some may need slight adaptation. Each model includes a section describing how the model can be modified to fit your needs.

Throughout *Multiplan Models for Business,* you will find innovative and creative techniques that can be used in your own models to "bend" Multiplan to fit your needs. These innovations are not limited to business applications for Multiplan; personal and home users as well can benefit from them.

The models in this book were created, tested, and documented to help you obtain maximum benefit from the Multiplan program. All Multiplan commands and functions are explained in the models so that even a novice can use them. The book also introduces a number of "tricks" that you can use to make Multiplan more powerful and flexible. You will not have to spend time to develop these features yourself because Multiplan has already done it. This book gives you sophisticated, adaptable models that you can use immediately. It will also give you new insights into the capabilities of Multiplan and help you become a Multiplan "pro" in a matter of days instead of the weeks it might take you on your own.

What Can You Do with Multiplan?

Spreadsheet programs like Multiplan are electronic replacements for the traditional financial modeling tools: the accountant's columnar pad, the pencil, and the calculator. In some ways, spreadsheet programs are to those tools what a word processor is to a typewriter. They offer dramatic improvements in ease of setting up and using financial models.

Because the computer's memory holds the spreadsheet programs while you set up the model, you are not bound by the physical limitations of the printed page. Are some of your formulas repeated across time? Use the spreadsheet's replicate function to project your assumptions quickly from one cell to another. Did you forget a row or a column? Simply insert it at the appropriate point. Is one of your assumptions or formulas incorrect, or is there a typographical error in one of your headings? Correct the error instantly with the edit command.

The act of building a spreadsheet model defines all the mathematical relationships in the model. Until you decide to change them, every sum, product, division, subtraction, average, and net present value will remain the same. Every time you enter data into the model, computations will be made at your command with no effort on your part. All of the computations will be calculated without math errors. Then next month, should you decide to use the model again, the formulas will still be set, ready to calculate at your command.

Even more important, spreadsheet software allows you to ask "What if...?" after your model has been developed. If you use paper, pencil, and calculator to build your models, then every change will require recalculating every relationship in the model. If the model has 100 formulas, and you change the first one, you must make 100 calculations by hand to flow the change through the entire model. When you use Multiplan, however, the same change requires pressing only a few keys! The program does the rest. This feature makes extensive "what if" analysis possible.

The versatility of Multiplan, SuperCalc™, VisiCalc®, and the other visible numeric processors makes them important tools for both small and large businesses. More and more companies of all sizes are using Multiplan and other spreadsheets to help speed and simplify financial analysis.

Spreadsheet programs are sometimes called planning tools, and one of their major uses is business planning. But thinking of spreadsheet programs only in this way ignores the spectacular abilities they have to solve other kinds of problems. Multiplan can be configured to solve almost any problem that formerly was attacked with a pad and pencil. Multiplan can be an auditing tool to assist accountants in the preparation of reports and financial statements; or it can analyze collections on accounts receivable, evaluate inventory stock level, and record employee performance. A well-designed spreadsheet program can even function as a limited accounting system for a small business, helping track disbursements into budget categories and monitor collections of accounts receivable.

Spreadsheet software can solve far more business problems than most people think. This book demonstrates the use of Multiplan for such diverse tasks as balancing a checkbook, evaluating investments in fixed assets, calculating depreciation, prepaying a loan, monitoring the activity of a line of credit, generating quotes, and preparing financial statements, as well as budgeting and forecasting.

The Table of Contents illustrates the broad range of models in this book. The models are grouped under seven categories: Cash Management, Debt Management, Fixed Asset Management, Working Capital Management, Financial Statements, Planning and

Budgeting, and Quote Preparation. These chapters cover the most important areas of financial business management.

Some of these sophisticated and flexible models can be combined with other Multiplan models to form Super-Multiplan models. For example, the Ratio Analyzer in Chapter 6 can be combined with the Interactive Income Statement and Balance Sheet in the same chapter, or with one of your own income statement/balance sheet models, to form a complete financial analysis system. The Cash Disbursements Spreadsheet in Chapter 2 can be combined with the Checkbook Balancer template in that chapter to build a comprehensive checkbook management model. In fact, the possibilities for combination are virtually limitless. Look for other ways to use these models with each other or with some of your own applications.

Who Should Use This Book?

Multiplan Models for Business should be used by anyone who owns, or is considering purchasing, the Multiplan program. Whether you are an experienced Multiplan user or a novice, this book will help you be more productive in your use of Multiplan.

A Note to Beginners

If you are new to Multiplan, you will appreciate the book's thorough, easy-to-understand explanations of Multiplan commands and concepts. For example, Chapter 1, "An Introduction to Multiplan," provides an overview of the important features of Multiplan. If you are just beginning Multiplan, you will probably want to start there.

The Managing Cash Flow section in Chapter 2 includes a discussion of "what if" analysis that will familiarize you with the technique that makes spreadsheet programs so popular.

The Statistics Calculator model in Chapter 7 explains the built-in Multiplan functions MAX, MIN, AVERAGE, STDEV, and COUNT.

Multiplan's IF-THEN-ELSE function is demonstrated and explained in the Budgeting for a New Venture section of Chapter 7. This simple example will prepare you for more advanced uses of the function in other models.

The LOOKUP function is used in the Quote Generator in Chapter 8. If you are not familiar with LOOKUP, this model will acquaint you with this useful Multiplan feature.

Multiplan's iterative recalculation feature is demonstrated in the Using Interactive Financial Statements section of Chapter 6. This model shows how to build an interactive balance sheet and income statement model that automatically recalculates to the correct solution.

Multiplan Models for Business will quickly bring you up to speed on Multiplan. While you are learning about the program, you will be building Multiplan models that will help you manage your business. Once you've learned the basics, *Multiplan Models for Business* will carry you on to more advanced concepts.

For Experienced Users

Professional users will appreciate *Multiplan Models for Business*'s explanations of the more advanced Multiplan features. For example, the ACRS Depreciation Calculator in Chapter 4 contains a complex LOOKUP table that uses conditional statements. This feature should suggest new ways that you can incorporate LOOKUP tables in your models.

The model also demonstrates a use for Multiplan's INDEX function. This function is ideally suited to building indexed tables that allow easy access to numeric data.

Multiplan's FIXED function is demonstrated in the Producing a Comprehensive Financial Statement section of Chapter 6. This model demonstrates a unique feature of Multiplan that makes it possible to link text and numbers in the same cell.

Sheet-to-sheet linking using the **X**ternal command is demonstrated in Chapter 2 in the Projecting Cash Flow section. This model includes an assumptions worksheet and a report worksheet that exchange data through a series of links. After using this model, you'll be an expert on sheet-to-sheet links.

A technique for automatically posting data to different columns is demonstrated in the Cash Disbursements Spreadsheet in Chapter 2. This posting technique can be applied to many types of models.

Only a few features of *Multiplan Models for Business* are mentioned above. Almost every model includes an innovation that will help you make better use of Multiplan.

What Do You Need to Use the Models in This Book?

The models in this book were developed on an IBM® Personal Computer with 64K of RAM memory and two disk drives. You will need at least that much memory and one disk drive to use the models. Some Multiplan models will barely fit on a 64K microcomputer. However, if you are fortunate enough to own a computer with more RAM, such as an IBM Personal Computer, you will be able to expand the models to make use of that extra memory.

Most of these models can be printed on a standard 80-column printer. If your printer is wider, or can print in a compressed type face, you'll be able to print all the models, even those using Multiplan's maximum width of 164 characters.

Although *Multiplan Models for Business* discusses many Multiplan functions, it is not a substitute for the Multiplan manual. Before you begin using the models in this book, take the time to read through the manual and practice using the program until you are familiar with its basic functions. The explanations in this book assume that you understand the concepts of rows, columns, and cells; the use of addition, subtraction, multiplication, and division in Multiplan; and the commands TRANSFER SAVE, TRANSFER LOAD, PRINT, COPY, FORMAT, DELETE, and INSERT.

Even if you don't own a computer, *Multiplan Models for Business* can show you ways you could use one. It can help you begin thinking about how to use a computer in your business.

Conventions Used in *Multiplan Models for Business*

A number of conventions, or standards, are employed in *Multiplan Models for Business* to help you use the models more effectively. Some of the more important conventions are discussed on the following pages.

The models in each chapter are arranged in order of difficulty—from simple to complex.

Each model is divided into sections. Typically, a model will have four sections: ASSUMPTIONS, SOLUTIONS, INSTRUCTIONS, and CONTENTS. Each section is labeled with a header and a sheet number.

A table of contents appears at the top of every model. Each listing in the table of contents includes the command GOTO NAME and the name of a section of the worksheet. We have assigned the names ASSUMPTIONS and SOLUTIONS to their areas of the model (or their equivalents). If you also choose to do this, you can move to these areas quickly using Multiplan's **G**oto command.

If you use Multiplan's **W**indow **T**itles command to lock the screen at the bottom of the contents section (usually around row 9 or 10), this section of the model will always be visible on the screen, giving you a permanent point of reference that will help you find your way through the models.

The model explanations in the text do not mention the contents or instructions sections. However, these sections can be valuable aids in building and using the models.

The explanations of the models are also divided into sections. The first section presents the business PRINCIPLES that lie behind the model; the second is a tour through THE MODEL; the third explains in detail the steps that must be taken in USING THE MODEL; and the last suggests possible MODIFICATIONS to the basic model. This structure should help you find the information you need.

Whenever you are asked to enter any information or type any commands, the text to be typed is shown in **a distinctive typeface**. Each command is presented exactly as it is to be typed, although the command may appear differently on the screen. For example, some typed letters will appear as a whole word followed by a comma.

Entering Cell References

Whether absolute, relative, or named, the cell references printed in the explanations of the models are presented in the same format that

Multiplan uses when you print the contents of a model. For example, look at this formula:

R5C1= I R1C2+9

The first symbol, R5C1, is the reference to the cell that contains the formula. The letter *I* indicates a cell format—in this case, I stands for Integer. Sometimes, the symbols L (LOCKED) and F2 (two digit format) are used. The final part of the formula represents the cell's contents.

Continuous Formatting

In all of the models, certain ranges of cells have been assigned the continuous format. This format allows text that is wider than a single column to cross the cell boundary into an adjacent blank cell. Without continuous labels, each cell will have to be filled individually.

In general, only the portions of the model that contain the text labels or headers have been assigned this format. Continuous labels are created by typing

FCCell Range) (TAB) (TAB)**C**(CR)

from the Multiplan main menu. This action changes the format of the designated cell range to accept continuous labels.

Recalculation

To set Multiplan so that recalculation is manual, use the command

Options**N**o(CR)

Unless you want Multiplan to recalculate every cell every time you change the contents of any cell, you must structure your models this way. If you do this, you'll need to use the recalculation control key that Multiplan recognizes on your computer to force recalculation. On the IBM Personal Computer, this is the F4 key; on other computers, the ! key performs the same task.

Model Size

Each model in this book fits into 64K of user memory, in many cases with room to spare. Three models, however, leave little room for expansion. These three large models are explained in the Projecting Cashflow, Quote Generator, and Using Interactive Finanacial Statements sections. To expand a model beyond memory is impossible; but, with Multiplan's sheet-linking capabilities (see above), two separate models can be linked together. If you need to expand one of the large models, you must find a way to split it into two linked models.

Conclusion

After you learn these conventions, the only thing that should keep you from realizing the full potential of Multiplan in your own business is a lack of imagination. Experiment with Multiplan to find new ways to use the program in your own environment. *Multiplan Models for Business* can be your springboard to even more imaginative applications for Multiplan.

Troubleshooting

We at QUE have made every effort to assure that the models work correctly. However, there is always a chance that errors will creep in when you build the models. We have found that many errors result from the following kinds of actions:

Using an incorrect range name spelling in a cell reference

Deleting from the worksheet a range on which other cells depend for information

Inserting rows and columns where absolute references exist

Changing the shape or size of a named range (this is especially dangerous when working with **X**ternally linked models)

Incorrectly placing parentheses in cell formulas

Multiplan Models Software

The Multiplan Models in this book are also available on diskette as *Multiplan Models for Business Software.* If you would like these models for your personal use, but don't want to spend the time to key them into your computer, you need *Multiplan Models Software.* You can buy *Multiplan Models Software* at your local computer or book store, or you can order directly from Que using the coupon at the front of this book. Formats are currently available for the IBM Personal Computer; the Apple II+® and IIe®; and CP/M® 8-inch single-sided, single-density diskettes. Other formats can be obtained by special request.

Keep in Touch

If you create a model that you think is unique and especially useful, QUE would like to hear from you. Call us in Indianapolis, at (317) 842-7162, and let us know what you are doing. We would also welcome any comments and suggestions that you have about *Multiplan Models for Business.*

Happy Modeling!

1

Introduction to Multiplan

Overview

Since its introduction in the summer of 1982, Multiplan has emerged as one of the biggest success stories in the microcomputer world. By the summer of 1983, Multiplan was one of the best-selling microcomputer programs. It was also in the top ten of the IBM PC market and the number two spreadsheet—behind 1-2-3.

Microsoft Corporation, one of the largest software companies in the microcomputer industry, publishes operating systems (such as MS-DOS and Xenix), languages (such as BASIC), and utility programs. Multiplan is the first major applications program published by Microsoft, but it undoubtedly will not be the last. A word-processing program, tentatively called Multi-Tool Word, has already been announced. Other applications programs will follow.

Multiplan owes its success to many factors. First, it is a powerful spreadsheet program. Its new functions and features meet most of the "wish list" desires of VisiCalc users. In addition, while many manufacturers of new-generation spreadsheets were ignoring the 8-bit, 64K market in favor of the IBM PC and its look-alikes, Microsoft decided to make Multiplan available on the Apple II and other 8-bit machines. Although this decision forced some compromises in program design (for example, Multiplan does not have the recalculative speed of VisiCalc or 1-2-3), it left Multiplan as the only superspreadsheet available for those machines.

The experienced VisiCalc or SuperCalc user will recognize most of Multiplan's features. In basic spreadsheeting capability, Multiplan is very similar to VisiCalc and SuperCalc. Like those programs, Multiplan uses a 254-row by 63-column spreadsheet. However, Multiplan numbers both rows and columns in the sheet. Thus cell address A1 in SuperCalc becomes cell R1C1 in Multiplan, and cell D5 becomes R5C4. Figure 1.1 shows a typical Multiplan spreadsheet.

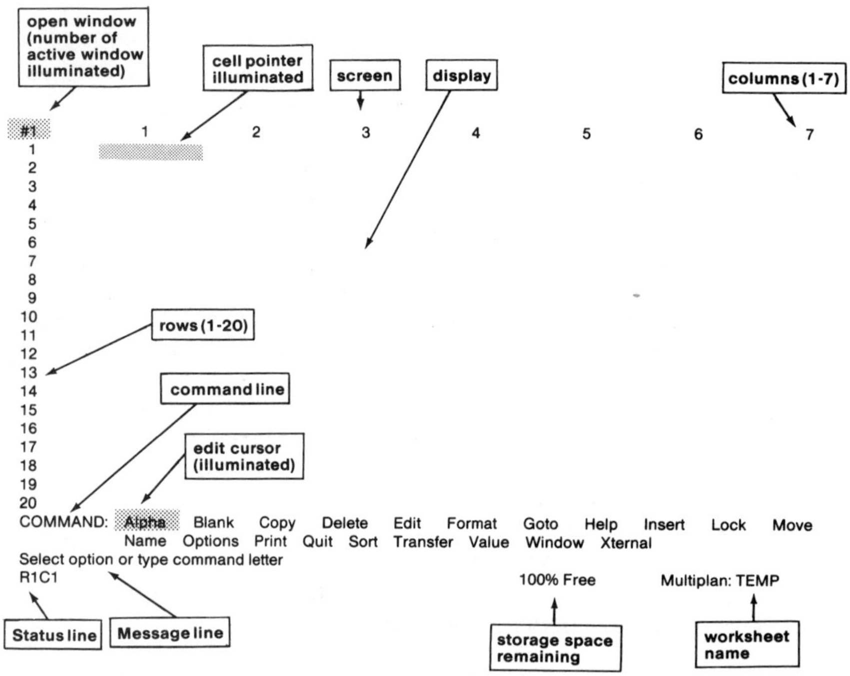

Figure 1.1
The Multiplan Worksheet

Multiplan's new method of stating cell coordinates does require some adjustment by the user. The serious spreadsheet user, however, will not be bothered by this small difference between the programs.

In fact, Microsoft has shown concern for former VisiCalc users by including a feature that reads a VisiCalc file directly into Multiplan with little effort. The directions for this translation are simple, and in our tests this function always worked perfectly.

User-Friendliness Features

Multiplan comes with extensive tutorials, a comprehensive manual, and a diskette that contains useful examples of Multiplan's unique functions. The program itself has on-line help available at a keystroke.

The Multiplan packaging and documentation provided by IBM are different from that provided by Microsoft. Microsoft packages Multiplan in a clear plastic box that doubles as a stand for the documentation. IBM uses a traditional three-ring binder. The IBM version of the documentation is slightly better than the Microsoft manual. Both manuals, however, are comprehensive and easily match any that the authors have seen.

The **H**elp command of Multiplan is keyed to respond to the current needs of the user. For example, if the help command was issued while the user was preparing to use the GOTO function, the resulting help screen would discuss the fine points of using GOTO. The user can then page forward or backward through the file one screen at a time, or choose to see a list of common application problems and their solutions.

The help files on diskette contain 25K of information. When the **H**elp command is chosen, the help screens do not provide examples of the commands, but summarize them well enough to be discerned by experienced users.

Multiplan comes with an extensive shirt-pocket guide that spans most topics of concern to the Multiplan user. It is the largest reference card we have seen thus far for any program.

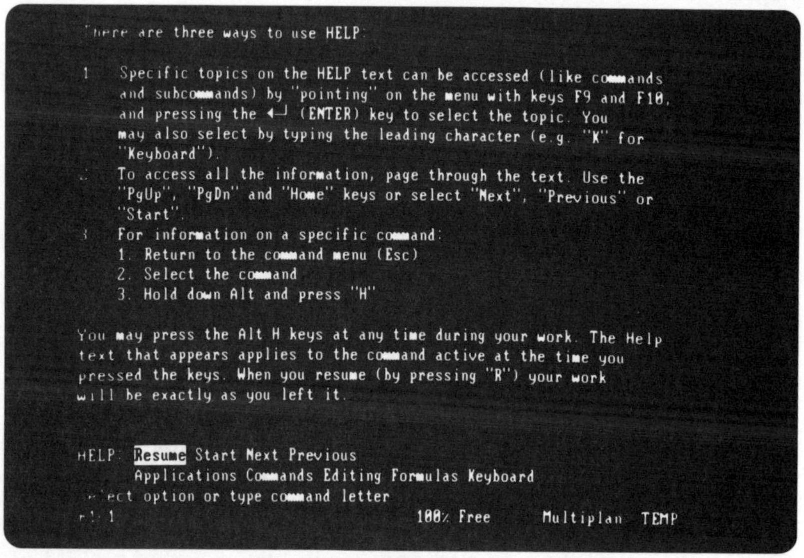

Figure 1.2
A Sample Screen

The Worksheet

Command Structures

Multiplan's commands are invoked directly without the use of any command signal. (Other spreadsheets, including VisiCalc and 1-2-3, use a 1 to initiate commands.) A command menu is always visible at the bottom of the screen, as shown in Figure 1.1. A command is invoked by selecting the first letter in its name. For example, to execute the Transfer command, the user would simply type T.

Multiplan uses a hierarchical command structure. Underlying most of the 20 first-level commands are secondary and tertiary commands with more specific meanings. Executing a given command may require the user to step down three levels into the command structure. For example, when you change a cell's format to Multiplan's "$" format, the following sequence of letters is required:

FC(TAB) (TAB)**$**(ENTER KEY)

Pressing the ESC key will cancel a command at any time. Unfortunately, instead of simply backing up one level to the next highest command, the ESC key returns the user to the top command level.

Entering labels and values into cells in Multiplan can be tricky. To enter a label, you would type A, for ALPHA, then the desired character string. Selecting V allows a value to be entered. Most spreadsheets do not require a signal for simple text and value entries. If you don't pay close attention, you can be quickly embedded within the command structure of Multiplan.

Error Messages

Multiplan goes well beyond the first-generation electronic spreadsheets by including a long list of descriptive error messages. They fully describe the nature of the difficulty and are much less insulting than the traditional cryptic ERROR, ?N?, or FORMULA ERROR. Of special interest are the #REF! message, which warns the user that a formula refers to a cell that doesn't exist, and the #DIV/0! message, which indicates that a division by zero has been attempted. Illegal or overflowing arithmetic is denoted by the #NUM! error message. These useful error messages are a major improvement over those used in the older spreadsheets.

Memory

Multiplan requires a minimum of 64K of RAM. On a 64K RAM system, only 15K of RAM is available for spreadsheet use. VisiCalc provides more than 30K in a similar configuration. Even though Muitiplan uses RAM memory very efficiently, 15K is enough memory for only a small model. When Multiplan is used with 128K of memory, 53K is available.

Multiplan uses overlay files to park unneeded sections of code on diskette. As the program runs, sections of code are swapped back and forth between RAM and the diskette. This swapping allows Multiplan to run in a 64K environment, but does slow the program down. The delays are more noticeable in computers with 64K than in computers with 128K because more of the Multiplan program is loaded into memory in a 128K system, reducing the need for disk swapping. On a computer equipped with 128K, the help files are the only part of the program that is not brought into memory.

Cell References

Like all electronic spreadsheets, Multiplan allows you to set up relationships between cells. In Multiplan these relationships can be established using three different techniques: absolute references, relative references, and name references. All three types of cell references are used in this book.

Absolute references indicate specific cell locations. These cell locations are given by stating the specific row and column coordinates of the cell. For example, if we wanted to define cell R1C1 as equal to cell R36C4, we would simply enter the reference R36C4 in cell R1C1. Absolute references are constant. When an absolute reference is copied, the resulting cell or cells contain the same absolute reference as the original.

Relative references are established by indicating the position of the cell being referred to in relation to the cell being defined. For example, if the contents of cell R36C4 are

RC[-1]

then R36C4 refers to R36C3, which is the cell that lies in the same row, but one position to the left of R36C4 (the phrase C[-1] can be translated as column-1). If the contents in R36C4 were

R[-16]C

cell R36C4 would refer to the cell 16 rows directly above itself, cell R20C4.

Relative references are easy to define and make copying convenient. However, because interpreting a relative reference requires adding and subtracting row or cell numbers, they can be difficult to understand. *Named references,* therefore, have many of the advantages of both relative and absolute references but are much easier to understand.

A *Named range* in Multiplan can be either a single cell or a rectangular area of any size. The names can be designed to describe the contents of the cell or the range being named, for example, SALES or TOTAL EMPLOYEES. Range names help users experienced in VisiCalc and SuperCalc to overcome the problems associated with Multiplan's row and column numbering conventions. Range names can also help new spreadsheet users. Formulas containing carefully selected names are easier to understand than formulas that use coordinates.

Named cell references are created by entering, into the cell being defined, the name of the cell being referred to. Multiplan also allows a single cell to refer to a named range of cells. Because names can be as long as 31 characters (without spaces), you can use whole words and phrases in cell names. Thus, Multiplan allows you to use common sense in creating names that are easy to understand and remember when used in formulas.

For example, if cell R36C4 is named SALES, Multiplan allows you to substitute the name SALES for the coordinates R36C4 in any equation anywhere on the current spreadsheet. The single named cell is treated the same way as the absolute cell reference.

Named ranges are treated differently from single cell names. The name command allows you to refer to a range of cells by a single name. The values in the cells that lie in that range can then be referred to both relatively and absolutely. If the range named consists of, for example, expense figures, the entire range can be used as an argument in a function or formula. The function SUM(EXPENSES) in our hypothetical range would total each cell that falls into the range. The equation 45+SUM(EXPENSES) would add 45 to the sum of the numbers in the cells called by the name EXPENSES.

Adjacent named ranges can also be used in arguments for functions and formulas in other adjacent areas. By rule, the areas must start and finish in either the same row or the same column.

For an example of adjacent range names and their effect, consider the following worksheet:

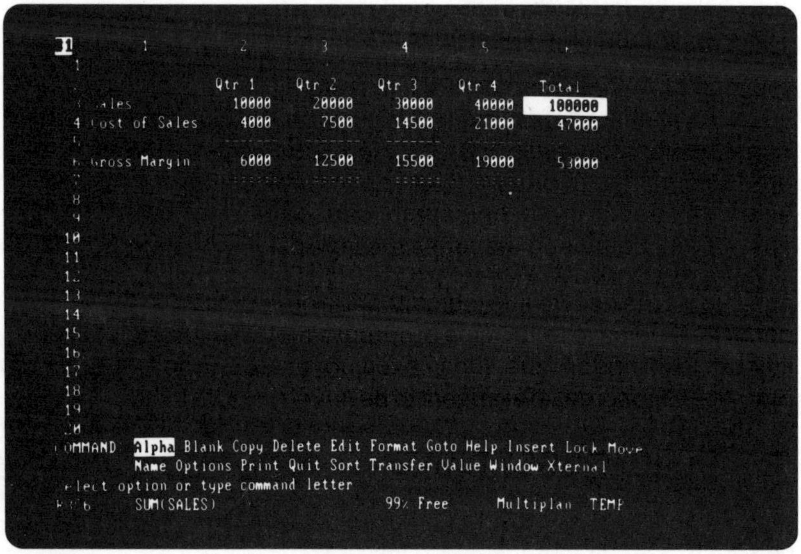

Figure 1.3

If the range R3C2:5 has been named SALES, then the first-year total can be derived from the function

R3C6 = SUM(SALES)

instead of

R3C6 = SUM(R3C2:5)

If the range R4C2:5 has been named COGS, the formula for Gross Margins in R6C2 could be

R6C2 = SALES-COGS

Actually, in the R6C2 formula, Multiplan is considering

R6C2 = R[-3]C-R[-2]C

not

R6C2 = R3C2-R4C2 or R6C2 = R3C2:4-R4C2:4

If the **C**opy command is used, the formula SALES-COGS will be copied relatively. For example, the formula SALES-COGS in cell R6C4 would be interpreted by Multiplan as

R6C4 = R[-3]C-R[-2]C

The Multiplan use of named references presents still other advantages. For example, if you refer to a blank cell by a name that has already been established, Multiplan will remind you of this mistake with the message

#Value!

If you misspell the name in a formula, Multiplan will place the ERROR message

#Name!

in the misspelled cell. As far as Multiplan understands, you have asked it to refer to a name that does not exist.

All the names in the current worksheet and the location(s) they refer to can be reviewed by typing N →. The names will appear on the screen one at a time, and their locations will scroll in sync with the names.

Sheet-to-Sheet Links

Multiplan allows several sheets to be linked together. Multiple sheet linking is probably the most exciting new feature of Multiplan because it helps to relieve the program's memory shortage problem and allows the user to link logically parts of several complex models.

The **X**ternal command manages the flow of information to and from external sheets. This command can copy data and establish permanent links to other sheets. Up to eight different dependency relationships can exist between worksheets on one diskette. The links can be made and broken at will. This allows much larger model systems to be built than could fit in RAM alone.

The uses for multiple sheet links are limited only by the imagination of the user. For example, for a four-sheet personal financial system, sheet 1 could contain an investment portfolio that is linked to the family budget on another sheet, which in turn is linked to a checkbook balancer that is linked to a year-to-date expense ledger.

In another example, the sales forecasts for four separate product lines (divisions, or stores) could be developed on four separate worksheets. A fifth sheet could consolidate these forecasts into a company-wide forecast.

Finally, suppose a company has three types of salary arrangements: hourly, salaried, and commission. Payroll expense records for each type could be recorded on different sheets, and a fourth sheet could be used to accumulate the total payroll expense.

Although Multiplan can support an unlimited number of single cell links between two worksheets, each link can directly join only two cells. For example, cell R1C1 on sheet A could refer to cell R1C1 on sheet B for its value, but could not access a lookup table or SUM range from sheet B. Links are established by using the **X**ternal **C**opy function, which extracts a value from the sheet to be linked to the one in use. The linked location on the current sheet can then be referred to as though it were any other cell location. The cell on the sheet in use that will be linked to the other one must be blank, or Multiplan will deliver the error message "Must Use Non-Blank Cell."

The **X**ternal function can pull the data from a cell in another sheet into the current cell, or it can establish a permanent link between those cells. But an **X**ternally linked cell cannot be a part of a cell formula.

A fairly serious limitation of Multiplan's sheet-linking functions is that the sheets that are linked to the present on-screen sheet may not be recalculated remotely. The linked sheet must be loaded as the current model before it can be recalculated. For example, if a set of worksheets is linked so that sheet C depends on sheet B, which in turn depends on sheet A,

A ===> B ===> C

and a change is made to sheet A that affects sheet C, the change will not be passed automatically from sheet A to sheet C through B. Sheet B has to be loaded into RAM and recalculated before sheet C will be correct.

Intersheet relationships must be carefully managed. For example, suppose that sheet A, in the example above, is a departmental expense budget and sheet C is the overall company budget. Suppose further that the divisional manager makes a change to sheet A, but does not take the time to load sheet B into memory before ending the session. Now suppose that the company president loads sheet C into the computer. Sheet C will not reflect the changes made to sheet A, and the company budget will be inaccurate.

One advantage offered by Multiplan is the ability to substitute the name of one file for another in a set of linked sheets. For example, suppose two sheets are linked. One, called COFINST, contains a company's financial statements. The other, called 483SUPRT, contains the company's trial balance and other supporting data for the month of April, 1983. Now suppose that a new sheet is created which contains the May, 1983, financial data. This sheet is identical to the April sheet, except that the May sheet contains new data. Multiplan allows the user to make COFINST look for its data on the sheet that contains the May data. This simple step replaces hours of work relinking the COFINST sheet with this new data sheet.

Another feature of the **X**ternal command is **X**ternal List, which lists all of the sheets that are linked to the sheet being viewed.

The Projecting Cashflow section of Chapter 2 demonstrates one use for Multiplan's **X**ternal command.

Advanced Lookup Tables

Multiplan's lookup tables are true tables rather than single rows or columns. For example, suppose you have a table with the column headings shown on the following page.

Using the employee number as the key variable, the user can LOOKUP name, age, length of service, or marital status. If age is the key variable, you can look up length of service or marital status. Name *cannot* be used as a key variable because the key variable must be numeric. To find the deduction status of Max Doe, the extended function would be

LOOKUP(1212,C1:C5)

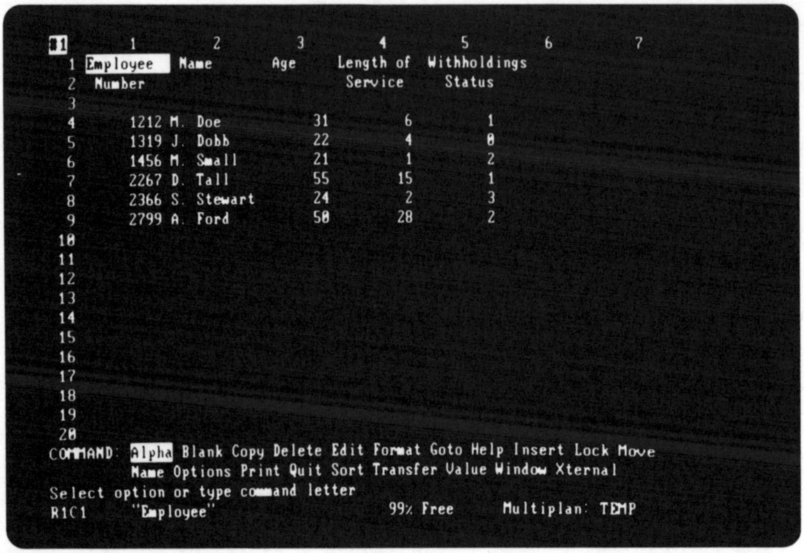

Figure 1.4

This formula says: Look up 1212 in column 1 and return the corresponding value from column 5. Notice that the table definition in this formula differs from that in VisiCalc and SuperCalc. Multiplan automatically determines the direction of the search from the shape of the table. If the table is square or higher than it is wide, the search proceeds down the columns. If the table is wider than it is high, the search will run across the rows.

Key variables must be in ascending order. This is true for all spreadsheets. Although this arrangement may appear to constrain a user's ability to change the key variable, the sort function (explained below) solves this problem.

Another limitation Multiplan shares with its first-generation counterparts is that two data items cannot share the same index in a lookup table. This limits Multiplan's usefulness as a true data manager. On the other hand, the LOOKUP function allows the user to retrieve information based on brackets or ranges, such as in a tax rate table, something few data managers can do easily.

Multiplan's LOOKUP function is demonstrated in the ACRS Depreciation Calculator in Chapter 4 and in the Quote model in Chapter 8.

Indexed Tables

The ability to retrieve information from an indexed table is another new information management feature of Multiplan. Unlike a lookup table, which allows the user to search a range of indexes for a data item, an indexed table requires the user to specify the exact coordinates of the data item being retrieved. For example, in Multiplan, the function INDEX(TABLENAME,2,3) returns the value located in row 2, column 3 (400) from the table shown below, called TABLENAME (see above for information on naming ranges). A table of rental rates for a skyscraper is one sample application of this feature in which one index represents the floor, and the other the location of the office space (North = 1, South = 2, and so on). The table is filled with rental rates for the various combinations of elevation and location. The rent of a particular unit can easily be determined by querying the table with the unit's floor and location.

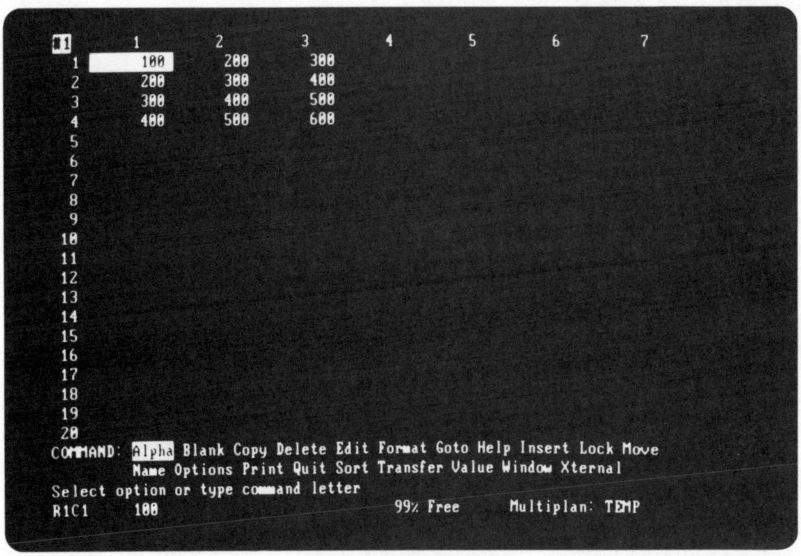

Figure 1.5

The ACRS Depreciation Calculator section of Chapter 4 shows one very useful application for the INDEX function.

Table 1.1

Multiplan Functions

ATAN(Value)
: Computes the arc tangent in radians of a given value

COLUMN( )
: Returns the number of the column in which the formula containing the COLUMN function appears

DELTA( )
: Computes the maximum of the absolute values of the cells from one iteration to the next

DOLLAR(Value)
: Same as Dollar and cents format. It embeds a dollar sign and places two digits to the right of the decimal point

EXP(Value)
: Calculates e to the power of the value

FIXED(Value,Number of Digits)
: Fixes precision in number of displayed digits and rounds

INDEX(Area,Subscripts)
: Calculates the value of a cell selected by subscripts from the rectangular area. Similar to Arrays in BASIC.

ITERCNT( )
: Displays the current iteration count during iteration phase

LEN(Text)
: Returns number of characters in a label

LN(Value)
: Calculates natural log of given value

LOG10(Value)
: Calculates the base 10 logarithm of the given value

Table 1.1 *(cont.)*

MID(Text Location,Start,Count)
Returns the portion of a label in Text Location, starting at the number of characters specified by Start, for as long as the Count.

MOD(Dividend,Divisor)
Returns the remainder of the dividend divided by the divisor

NPV(Rate,Range)
Calculates the net present value of the cash flows in the range, given the discount rate

ROUND(Value,Digits)
Rounds the value to the number of digits. Changes precision.

ROW( )
Returns the number of the row where the formula that contains the ROW function appears

SIGN(Value)
Returns a 1 if the sign of the value is +, 0 if negative

STDEV(Range)
Calculates the standard deviation of the range

VALUE(Text)
When using text that represents a value, it returns the number of that value. Example:

Value($23.00) returns 23

New Spreadsheet Functions

Multiplan offers a variety of new arithmetic, logical, and special functions. STDEV, for example, computes standard deviations. This function replaces the long formula used by SuperCalc to compute standard deviation. Early versions of Multiplan, before Version 1.06, had erors in the STDEV and SQRT (square root) functions, but they were quickly corrected. The STDEV function is used in the Statistics Calculator in Chapter 7.

Text Functions

Multiplan includes some interesting text functions that are similar to those of Microsoft's biggest-selling product, the Microsoft BASIC language. (Microsoft BASIC is the largest-selling microcomputer language in the world.)

The FIXED function converts a numeric entry to a text entry. For example, the entry "1234" can be converted to a text entry with the same appearance by using the function

FIXED(1234,0)

The zero in this formula specifies the number of decimals to be displayed. Converted numbers can be concatenated (linked together) with text to embed numerical data in the middle of sentences by using the concatenation operator &. For example, if cell R1C1 contains the number 100, the formula

"$"&FIXED(R1C1,2)&" per month"

would read

$100 per month

If R1C1 is changed to equal 200, the same formula yields

$200 per month

This extremely powerful function allows numeric data to be embedded directly in captions, labels, and even memos in the sheet. For example, most financial statements contain a caption like

Accounts receivable, less allowance for
doubtful accounts of $9567.75 in 1983 and $8352.11 in 1982

With the concatenation operator, the second two lines of this statement can be represented in Multiplan as

"doubtful accounts of $"&FIXED(9567.75,2)&"in 1983 and"
"$"&FIXED(8352.11,2)&"in 1982"

The FIXED function is used in the Comprehensive Financial Statements section of Chapter 6.

The MID function considers either text or a cell reference containing text and returns the specified portion of the total text string. For example, suppose that cell R1C1 (remember, both columns and rows are numbered in Multiplan) contains the text: Que Corporation. If cell R2C4 contains the text function MID(R1C1,5,4), the string "Corp" would be displayed in cell R2C4. An easier way of expressing what the MID function does in the example above is

```
MID(R1C1,5,4)
      |     ||
      |     |└ display the next number of characters
      |     └ go to the fifth position
      └ the text's location
```

One use for the MID function is demonstrated in the Quote Generator in Chapter 8.

Another text function, LN, simply returns the number of characters that are located in a cell. In the example above, R1C1 contains the text: Que Corporation. The LN(R1C1) function returns the number of characters in the cell; in this case, 15 characters (the space between Que and Corporation is counted as a character).

Multiplan allows text to serve as the object of a LOOKUP or IF function. Unlike some programs, there is no limit to the length of the string that can be returned. For example, the statement

> IF(R1C1=100,"Great job, sales department!","Better luck next time.")

places a congratulatory statement in the sheet if the condition was met, and a conciliatory statement if it was not. Multiplan's text LOOKUP capabilities are demonstrated in the Quote Generator in Chapter 8.

Other Functions

Multiplan offers two other unique functions: ROW() and COL(). These functions compute the current location of the cursor and insert the row or column number into the current cell. For example, if the cursor is in row 15, the ROW() function will return the number 15.

These functions can be used as shorthand to enter certain kinds of information into the spreadsheet. For example, if the cursor is in cell R3C4, the formula

1983+(COLUMN()-4)

enters the number 1983 into the cell. If the formula is replicated across the sheet, the cells in row 3 will automatically be labeled 1984, 1985, 1986, and so on.

Windows

Multiplan supports up to eight windows on the screen at one time, and each one is numbered as it is created. Windows can be set to scroll together (synchronized) or separately (unsynchronized), as in SuperCalc. The multiwindow option allows the user to view several different parts of a large worksheet at the same time.

Dividing a large Multiplan spreadsheet into windows that allow a view of summarizing areas lets you watch the recalculations as different parts of the spreadsheet change. The relationships take on an even stronger meaning when the windows are colored.

On some computers, including the IBM PC, Multiplan supports the use of color in windows created on the screen. As many as 16 border, 16 background, and 16 foreground colors may be chosen. Spreadsheet colors are selected through the command **W**indow **P**aint. An RGB monitor must be used with the 80-column version of Multiplan to support color; Multiplan will support color on a color television receiver in the 40-column mode only.

Each window may have its own color combination. Different colors can be selected to highlight important windows. For example, a red window might mark important summarizing figures, a green one could mark static costs, and blue could be used to mark departmental summaries, etc. The coloring possibilities also allow data entry personnel to discern rapidly which areas to change; in this environment, the color red could take on a "prohibited area" designation. When this feature is combined with the **L**ock command, the chance of accidental data loss is reduced even further.

Print Time Formatting

Multiplan offers several printing options for margins, number of lines per page, and height of printable area, as well as special options for printer codes. The options offered by Multiplan far exceed those available with any first-generation spreadsheet. The expanded printing formats produce reports that do not require extensive rework by a word-processing program. Multiplan also remembers the printing options chosen as defaults until the program is turned off. Each section of this book explains the special print formats used in the model being explained.

Text and Numeric Formatting

The **F**ormat command provides extensive formatting options for text or numbers/formulas in a cell. All of the basic VisiCalc formats are available, as well as additional formats.

In Multiplan, each cell possesses a set of formatting characteristics—the number of digits to be displayed, the justification of the contents, etc. This set of characteristics is the cell's *property sheet.* Because the property sheet contains all of the cell's formatting characteristics, it is possible in Multiplan to change all of the characteristics of a cell with a single command. Figure 1.6 illustrates a property sheet as displayed after the command **F**ormat **C**ell has been issued.

Text may be aligned in a cell as centered or left- or right-justified. It may also exceed the column width to provide larger-than-cell-width labels. This is accomplished with the **F**ormat **C**ell **C**ontinuous command.

Numbers may be formatted to have a fixed number of significant digits. Like SuperCalc², Multiplan offers a wide range of possible formats, including floating dollar signs, commas, asterisks (or other graphics characters), exponents, integers, and percentages. Table 1.2 illustrates all of the formats available for Multiplan.

Table 1.2
Multiplan Formats

	Format	Displays	As
Alignments:			
FCtr	(Center cell contents format)	John	John
FGen	(Right alignment)	John	John
FLeft	(Left justify)	John	John
FRight	(Right justify)	John	John
Formats:			
Cont	(Cross cell boundary with label)	Departm	Department of Revenue
Exp	(Scientific notation format)	67000	6.7E4
Fix	(Fixed precision format)	2.345	2.3†
Gen	(Numbers w/most significant digits)	6.7E4	67000
Int	(Integer)	2.345	2
$	(Dollars and cents, embedded $)	67000	$67000
*	(Bar graph)	2.345	**
%	(Percent format, embedded %, value *100)	.478	47.8%

†With precision fixed at one significant digit

Where possible, we have used the "$" option to format cells containing dollars. Multiplan, however, requires that numbers displayed in the "$" format also display two digits (cents) to the right of the decimal point. Thus, formatting a cell to "$" can add as many as four characters to the length of the cell contents. For example, the number

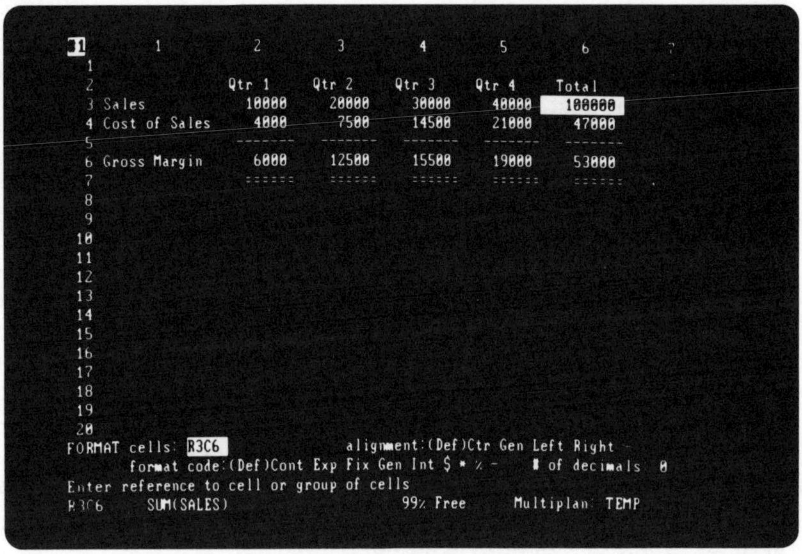

Figure 1.6

12,345

(displayed in comma format) would become

$12,345.00

in dollar format. This characteristic of Multiplan means that you usually must widen the columns on your worksheet to display "$" numbers. In some cases we have done this; in others, we have selected the comma format over the "$" format.

Locking Cells

Multiplan allows cells to be locked or unlocked. Cells that are locked cannot be written to or erased unless they are deliberately unlocked. Multiplan allows entire regions to be locked or unlocked by specifying the region's name or cell coordinates. Locking prevents erroneous operator entry on formulas or unchanging factors.

We usually lock the cells in our worksheets that contain formulas. Since these cells are not used for data entry, it is not inconvenient to lock them, and doing so protects them against being accidentally erased. We suggest that you do the same.

Sorting

Multiplan can sort columns and tables of data within the spreadsheet. The user must specify the range to be sorted (one or more columns of data), the column by which the sort is to be performed (the sorting key), and whether the sort is to be in ascending or descending order. Sorting can be performed either numerically or alphabetically. This sorting capability, when combined with LOOKUP, allows Multiplan to function as a simple list-management program. Although Multiplan has sort capabilities, they are cumbersome and difficult to use in the context of a data base. Despite this drawback, the **S**ort feature is a useful tool

Sorting also enhances the table arrays and string functions of Multiplan. Areas can be entered, sorted, then referenced in formulas. The Quote model in Chapter 7 shows one application for the sort command.

Recalculation

Most spreadsheets use a simple linear form of recalculation. Recalculation begins at the upper left corner of the spreadsheet (cell A1) and proceeds either row by row or column by column through the sheet. The user must be careful to build dependencies in the worksheet to avoid forward references (a cell whose value depends on other cells below it in the recalculation order) and circular references (two or more cells defined by each other) that can create calculation nightmares.

Multiplan addresses this limitation of the first generation. Like 1-2-3 and ProCalc, Multiplan uses a *natural* mode of recalculation. Natural recalculation begins by discerning the most fundamental cell in the sheet (that is, the cell on which the most other cells are based). This cell is evaluated first. Next, the program searches for the second most basic formula in the sheet and evaluates it. This process continues until the entire worksheet is recomputed.

Accompanying natural recalculation in Multiplan is the ability to perform iterative calculations. The number of iterations can also be determined by a predefined limit of change in a given cell. For example, you may want the sheet to continue recalculating until the total change in all of the values in the sheet is less than .001 from one recalculation to the next. Iterative calculation helps to relieve the problem of circular references.

These two new features help to simplify the design and use of complex spreadsheets. With the new programs, the user does not have to be as careful about planning the locations of the various sections of models. The computer can manage the order of recalculation.

Summary

Multiplan offers extensive capabilities that should satisfy the most demanding spreadsheeter. Its extensive features allow a large amount of data to be linked relationally. Although a sacrifice of speed is initially encountered in model development, Multiplan offers very sophisticated operations once the model is in place.

Multiplan is close to being the ultimate spreadsheet program. It also comes close to the limits of usability with its large number of functions, formatting options, and commands. Multiplan's features, however, far outweigh its minor flaws. It represents very high quality in a spreadsheet format.

2
Cash Management

Balancing the Checkbook

Tracking Cash Disbursements

Managing Cash Flow

Projecting Cash Flow

Balancing the Checkbook

When was the last time you opened your monthly bank statement and found that the ending balance agreed with your checkbook balance? Maybe never? Every business faces the frustrating chore of reconciling its checkbook to a bank statement at least once a month. Many businesses must reconcile more than one account. This boring and repetitive job always seems to require more time than it is worth. But, because the bank statement serves as the only check against in-house records, the job must be done. Let's see how Multiplan can help streamline the checkbook-balancing process.

Principles

The disparity between your balance according to the bank and your checkbook balance can occur for one of three primary reasons. The most common one is that either you or the bank made a mistake in recording a check or a deposit, or in computing the balance, or both. Whatever your situation, the error must be corrected so that both sets of records are accurate and in agreement.

A second possible difference arises from bank-initiated charges or credits, such as a monthly service charge. If your cash is in a NOW account, you will also show a credit for interest earned on your monthly statement. These charges and credits must be entered into your records before the books will balance.

The third common cause of discrepancies is time. Often a delay of one or more days occurs between the date you write a check and the date it is charged against your account. Some banks will not credit your account until a deposit has cleared at another bank, which may take several days. These timing differences have specific names: outstanding checks and deposits in transit. You

```
        1          2          3          4          5          6          7          8
 1 ==========================================================================================
 2 CHECKBOOK                                              Copyright (C) QUE Corp. 1983
 3 ==========================================================================================
 4
 5          For CHECK DATA (G)oto (N)ame 'CHECKDATA'
 6          For PREVIOUSLY OUTSTANDING ITEMS (G)oto (N)ame 'OUTSTANDING'
 7          For RECONCILIATION (G)oto (N)ame 'RECONCILIATION'
 8          For INSTRUCTIONS (G)oto (N)ame 'INSTRUCTIONS'
 9 ==========================================================================================
10 CHECK DATA (Continues to row 58)                                               Sheet 1.1
11 ==========================================================================================
12
13          Check                                      Check     Deposit    Running
14 Date     Number         Description                Amount    Amount     Balance
15 ----     ------    ---------------------------    --------  --------   --------
16 8-1                Opening Balance                                       443.01
17 8-2      1005      Dividend                          440.00  12500.00  12503.01
18 8-2      1006      CEB for Travel                    234.15            12268.86
19 8-3      1007      CEB Salary                       1200.00            11068.86
20 8-4      1008      A Trade Paper Subscription         25.00            11043.86
21 8-5      1009      A Magazine Subscription            40.00            11003.86
22 8-8      1010      My Health Insurance Co.            55.87            10947.99
23 8-10     1011      Void                                0.00            10947.99
24 8-11     1012      Lawyer                             55.00            10892.99
25 8-14     1013      Postage                            30.35            10862.64
26 8-14     1014      Vendor 1                         2550.00             8312.64
27 8-17     1015      Vendor 2                         2556.00             5756.64
28 8-17     1016      FAB Salary                       1303.33             4453.31
29 8-17     1017      Void                                0.00             4453.31
30 8-20     1018      Accountants                       975.00             3478.31
31 8-21     1019      Landlord                          311.67             3166.64
32 8-22     1020      Office Supply Store                10.00             3156.64
33 8-24     1021      Postage                            40.00             3116.64
34 8-25     1022  ①   Vendor 2                         2335.00   3000.00   3781.64  ②
35 8-25     1023      Vendor 4                          288.75    110.00   3602.89
36 8-27     1024      Landlord                           13.07             3589.82
37 8-29     1025      Consultant                        150.00             3439.82
38 8-30     1026      Vendor 7                         2164.00             1275.82
39          1027                                                           1275.82
40          1028                                                           1275.82
41          1029                                                           1275.82
42          1030                                                           1275.82
43          1031                                                           1275.82
44          1032                                                           1275.82
45          1033                                                           1275.82
46          1034                                                           1275.82
47          1035                                                           1275.82
48          1036                                                           1275.82
49          1037                                                           1275.82
50          1038                                                           1275.82
51          1039                                                           1275.82
52          1040                                                           1275.82
53          1041                                                           1275.82
54          1042                                                           1275.82
55          1043                                                           1275.82
56          1044                                                           1275.82
57                    End of Period Book Balance:                          1275.82
58
59
```

```
        9          10         11          12         13
 1
 2
 3
 4
 5
 6
 7
 8
 9 ====================================
10 CODING DATA
11 ==================================
12                                     Deposits
13    Outstanding         OS             in
14  Checks  Deposits   Checks        Transit
15 -------- --------  --------      --------
16
17
18
19
20
21       1             40.00
22
23
24
25
26
27
28
29                                ③
30
31
32
33
34
35                1                 110.00
36
37                                                ④
38
39
40
41
42
43
44
45
46
47
48
49
50
51
52
53
54
55
56
57
58
59
```

```
           1        2         3         4         5         6         7         8
60 ===========================================================================
61 PREVIOUSLY OUTSTANDING ITEMS                                      Sheet 2.1
62 ===========================================================================
63
64          Check                                       Check     Deposit
65 Date     Number          Description                 Amount    Amount
66 ----     ------   --------------------------   --------  --------
67 6-5      955      Office Supply Store           100.00
68 7-12     967      Landlord                      345.67
69 7-17     990      Accountant                    200.00
70 7-15     1002     Parking Garage                112.00
71
72
73
74 ===========================================================================
75 RECONCILIATION                                                    Sheet 3.1
76 ===========================================================================
77
78          Ending Book Balance:                              1275.82 (7)
79          Bank Charges and/or Credits                          5.00
80                                                            -------
81          Adjusted Book Balance                             1270.82 (8)
82
83          Outstanding Checks                                 140.00 (9)
84          Deposits in Transit                                110.00 (10)
85          Adjustments to Bank Balance                          0.00
86                                                            -------
87          Bank Balance                                      1300.82 (11)
88                                                            =======
89
90 ===========================================================================
91 INSTRUCTIONS                                                      Sheet 4.1
92 ===========================================================================
93
94          1) Enter CHECK DATA and PREVIOUSLY OUTSTANDING ITEMS
95          2) At end of month, CODE Outstanding Checks and Deposits
96          3) Recalculate by typing: F4 or !
97          4) SAVE by typing: TSB:CHECKBK (CR)
98          5) PRINT by typing: PP
```

```
         9         10          11          12          13
60
61
62
63
64
65
66                                      Deposits
67     Outstanding          OS            in
68   Checks  Deposits    Checks      Transit
69   -------- --------  --------   --------
70          1            100.00⑤           ⑥
71
72
73
74
75
76
77
78
79
80
81
82
83
84
85
86
87
88
89
90
91
92
93
94
95
96
97
98
```

BALANCING THE CHECKBOOK

NUMBER	LOCATION(S)	FORMULA
1	R18:56C2	R[-1]C+1
2	R17:57C8	R[-1]C-CHECK+DEPOSIT
3	R17:56C11	IF(CHECKSOUT=1,CHECK,"")
4	R17:56C12	IF(DEPOSITSOUT=1,DEPOSIT,"")
5	R67:73C11	IF(CHECKSOUT=1,CHECK,"")
6	R67:73C12	IF(DEPOSITSOUT=1,DEPOSIT,"")
7	R78C7	R57C8
8	R81C7	R78C7-R79C7
9	R83C8	SUM(OSCHECKS)
10	R84C7	SUM(DEPINTRANSIT)
11	R87C7	R81C7-R84C7+R83C7+R85C7

must identify these items and make adjustments for them before your checkbook will agree with the bank statement. This can be a time-consuming task, but the Checkbook Balancer can make the job easier.

The Model

This model has four sections: CHECK DATA, CODING DATA, PREVIOUSLY OUTSTANDING ITEMS, and RECONCILIATION. The CHECK DATA section begins at row 10. Column 1 displays the dates of all checks entered in the period. The check numbers are recorded in column 2. Notice that cell R18C2 is defined as +R[-1]C+1, cell R19C2 as +R[-1]C=1, and so on. With this arrangement, the model can number the checks on a spreadsheet automatically, saving input time.

CHECKBK: Locations of Named Cells and Ranges

Description	Location	Name
CHECK DATA	R11C1	CHECKDATA
CODING DATA	R11C10	CODE
Check Amount	R16:73C6	CHECK
Deposit Amount	R16:73C7	DEPOSIT
Outstanding Checks (Code)	R16:73C9	CHECKSOUT
Outstanding Deposits (Code)	R16:73C10	DEPOSITSOUT
Outstanding Checks (Amount)	R16:73C11	OSCHECKS
Deposits in Transit (Amount)	R16:73C12	DEPINTRANSIT
PREVIOUSLY OUTSTANDING ITEMS	R62C1	OUTSTANDING
RECONCILIATION	R76C1	RECONCILIATION
INSTRUCTIONS	R92C1	INSTRUCTIONS

Columns 3, 4, and 5 provide space for a description of each check. Column 6 contains the check amounts, and column 7 shows the amounts of any deposits made.

The running balance in the account is computed in column 8. The formula in cell R17C8

R17C8 F2 = R16C8-R17C6+R17C7

or

R17C8 F2 = R[-1]C-CHECK+DEPOSIT

is typical of the cells in this column.

CODING DATA, the second section of the model, begins at cell R10C9. Columns 9 and 10 code outstanding checks and deposits in transit for adjustment. If a check listed at the left is not reflected in the bank statement, the check should be recorded as outstanding by inserting a 1 in column 9. To code a deposit as outstanding at the end of the period, insert a 1 in column 10. Check or deposit amounts coded in this manner will automatically appear in column 11 or 12, respectively, after the model has been recalculated. This automatic entry is achieved by using an IF statement in the cells in columns 11 and 12. For example, the formula for cell R17C11 is

R17C11 F2 = IF(R17C9=1,R17C6,"")

or

R17C11 F2 = IF(CHECKSOUT=1,CHECK,"")

The double quotation marks in the range name formula above render a cell blank unless the CHECKSOUT column, column 9, contains a 1. The blank caused by the double quotation marks could also be changed to the label "OK".

The same relationship is used for the other cells in these two columns. Take the time to become familiar with this method of coding. It can be very useful in models where certain items in a series must be isolated for special treatment. Automatic entry is also used in the Cash Disbursements Spreadsheet model.

PREVIOUSLY OUTSTANDING ITEMS, the third section of the model, begins at cell R61C1. This section accounts for checks that are outstanding for more than one month.

RECONCILIATION, the fourth part of the model, begins at cell R75C1. Notice that its components are the same as those discussed above: bank initiated charges and credits, outstanding checks and deposits in transit, and adjustments to the bank balance. Cells R83C7 and R84C7 total the outstanding checks and deposits in columns 8 and 9, respectively, using the formulas

R83C7 F2 = SUM(R16C11:R73C11)

or

R83C7 F2 = SUM(OSCHECKS)

and

R84C7 F2 = SUM(R16C12:R73C12)

or

R84C7 F2 = SUM(DEPINTRANSIT)

Cell R79C7 is an input cell. You supply the proper amounts for bank credits and charges when the bank statement is received. Cell R85C7 will be used infrequently, but it is needed for error adjustment.

Using the Model

Begin by calling the model from disk. Move the cursor to cell R17C2 and input the first check number for the new month. If the last check written for the preceding month was number 1004, then 1005 should be entered in cell R17C2. Now recalculate by typing F4 or ! and note how the check numbers are replicated down column 2 in ascending numerical order.

Move the cursor to cell R16C8 and input the last period's closing balance according to your checkbook. If you have not yet reconciled the account for last month, you may leave this cell blank for now and fill it in after the reconciliation is completed. Note, however, that until the cell is filled in, the running balance column will not be up to date. If you post your unreconciled balance to this cell, you may need to make an adjustment to it after completing the prior month's reconciliation.

When you receive the bank statement for the prior month's activity, fill in the PREVIOUSLY OUTSTANDING section of the model.

Examine the statement, looking for outstanding checks and deposits. Move the cursor to cell R67C1 and post each outstanding item just as you would a newly written check. Be aware, however, that these items are not included in the running total. This part of the model holds the checks and deposits only until they clear on a subsequent statement.

The model is now configured for a new month. As you write checks, input the information as you would in a manual checkbook—date, description, and amount. If a check is voided, type 0 into the amount column for that check number. Post deposits in column 7 as you make them throughout the month.

At the end of the month, be sure to save the just-completed worksheet by typing **TSB:CHECKBK1** (CR). You may use any file name you desire instead of CHECKBK1. A descriptive file name will help you remember where you stored your data. For example, September's check register may be saved as "Chkbk983," an abbreviation for "Checkbook 9/83."

When you receive a bank statement, call up from disk the checkbook file for the month covered by the statement. Compare the statement with the check register and code any outstanding checks or deposits in transit, using a 1 in column 9 for checks, and a 1 in column 10 for deposits. Note whether any items in the PREVIOUSLY OUTSTANDING section are still outstanding on this statement and code them as explained above. Be sure to blank the cells that contain information about any checks that did clear. Finally, move the cursor to cell R79C7 and enter the net amount of any bank-initiated charges or credits for the period.

Position the cursor to display the entire reconciliation box on the screen. Type F4 or ! to recalculate the worksheet. Cells R83C7 and R84C7 will display the total amount of any outstanding items, and cell R87C7 will show the computed bank balance. Compare this amount with the balance on your bank statement. If the two numbers agree, fine. If they don't, review the worksheet, making sure that all check amounts have been input correctly, that all outstanding items (and only outstanding items) are properly coded, and that the bank charges have been computed properly. If no errors are found, check again, then consider whether there may be an error in the bank statement. If you find an error, enter the adjusting amount in cell R85C7 and call the bank to have an official correction made.

After the checkbook and the bank balance are reconciled, save the sheet by typing **TSB:CHECKBK** (CR). Use data codes in the name as necessary and change the file name as you desire. Then print the model by typing **PP**. You can use the completed worksheet to update the model for the following month, which should be partially completed by this time. Post the ending book balance from the old model to cell R16C8 in the new one and record any checks outstanding at the end of the prior period in the PREVIOUSLY OUTSTANDING area of the current model. The cycle is now complete, and you're ready for the next end of month, the next statement, and so on.

Modifications

The Checkbook Balancer model can be easily expanded to accommodate more checks and deposits or previously outstanding items by inserting rows as needed and copying the relevant formulas into the new rows.

This model and the Cash Disbursements Spreadsheet can work well together. Take the time to review that model, then consider expanding the check register by adding the spreader to it. Alternatively, you could use Multiplan's **X**ternal **C**opy command to copy the necessary check data from the checkbook model to the disbursements model. Either procedure will create the Multiplan equivalent of a one-write cash management system, with the added advantage of simplifying your month-end reconciliations.

Tracking Cash Disbursements

Many small companies do not have enough accounting activity to justify the time and expense required to maintain a complete general ledger system. They do, however, need financial records. It is particularly important that these businesses monitor their expenditures because reliable budgets are almost impossible to develop and maintain without accurate expense information.

Spreading the checkbook is a technique used by many businesses to provide expense information quickly and easily. The term "spreading the checkbook" is derived from the use of accountants' spreadsheet paper to do the job. With this method, each check written in a period of time is assigned to one of several "accounts." The accounts summarize the disbursements in that period for different types of expense activity (for example, salaries, rent, or supplies).

Each spreadsheet column represents one account. Check amounts are posted in the appropriate column. When all the checks are posted, each column is totaled to arrive at the balance for each account. The spreadsheet is essentially a simple general ledger.

One of the primary assumptions of *Multiplan Models for Business* is that what can be done with a manual spreadsheet can be done better with Multiplan. Let's see what Multiplan can do with a checkbook-spreading model.

Principles

Spreading the checkbook with traditional tools (pencil, paper, and calculator) is a fairly simple job. Each check is listed at the left on the spreadsheet paper. The check is then assigned to an account, and the check amount is written in the appropriate column.

```
          1        2        3         4         5         6         7
 1 ======================================================================
 2 CASH DISBURSEMENTS SPREADSHEET            Copyright (C) QUE Corp. 1983
 3 ======================================================================
 4
 5          For CHECK DATA, (G)oto (N)ame `CHECKDATA'
 6          For SPREADING TABLE, (G)oto (N)ame `TABLE'
 7          For INSTRUCTIONS, (G)oto (N)ame `INSTRUCTIONS'
 8
 9 ======================================================================
10 CHECK DATA (Continues to row 42)                               Sheet 1.1
11 ======================================================================
12 Disbursements for Month of: August 1984
13
14          Check                                         Check
15 Date     Number             Description                Amount     Code
16 ----     -------  ------------------------------  --------  --------
17 8-1      1001     Typing Service                   $100.00         7
18 8-2      1002     ASC Salary                      $3500.00         1
19 8-2      1003     Landlord                         $545.00         3
20 8-3      1004     Phone Company                    $244.00         4
21 8-4      1005     Office Supply Co.                $567.00         5
22 8-6      1006     WSC Salary                      $4478.00         1
23 8-6      1007     Landlord                          $35.00         3
24 8-6      1008     Typing Service                   $188.00         7
25 8-11     1009     Federal Government              $2555.00         2
26 8-13     1010     Office Supply Co.                 $89.00         5
27 8-15     1011     A Magazine Subscription           $33.00         9
28 8-15  ①  1012     US Postal Service                 $12.00         8
29 8-16     1013     Insurance Co.                    $183.00         6
30 8-16     1014     IRS                              $122.00        13
31 8-16     1015     Insurance Co.                   $2258.00         6
32 8-16     1016     State Government                 $447.00         2
33 8-20     1017     Trade Show Company               $111.00         9
34 8-22     1018     Overnight Delivery Co.           $367.00         8
35 8-25     1019     Office Supply Co.                 $55.00         5
36 8-25     1020     Long Distance Service Co.        $779.00         4
37 8-25     1021     Leasing Company                  $544.00        11
38 8-25     1022     Accountant                       $155.00        10
39 8-27     1023     DEC - Salary Adjustment          $100.00         1
40
41                                                     --------
42                                                ② $17467.00
43                                                     ========
44
45
46
47
48
49 ======================================================================
50 INSTRUCTIONS                                                   Sheet 3.1
51 ======================================================================
52
53                     1) Enter CHECK DATA
54                     2) Recalculate by typing: F4 or !
55                     3) Review SPREADING TABLE
56                     4) SAVE by typing: TSB:CDSPREAD (CR)
57                     5) PRINT by typing: PP
```

```
         8         9         10        11        12        13        14
 1 ========================================================================
 2 CASH DISBURSEMENTS SPREADSHEET            Copyright (C) QUE Corp. 1983
 3 ========================================================================
 4
 5           For CHECK DATA, (G)oto (N)ame `CHECKDATA'
 6           For SPREADING TABLE, (G)oto (N)ame `TABLE'
 7           For INSTRUCTIONS, (G)oto (N)ame `INSTRUCTIONS'
 8
 9 ========================================================================
10 SPREADING TABLE (Continues to row 42)                         Sheet 2.1
11 ========================================================================
12
13     1         2         3         4         5         6         7
14            Payroll    Office                                  Office
15  Salaries   Taxes      Rent     Phone   Supplies Insurance  Services
16  --------  --------  --------  --------  --------  --------  --------
17                                                               $100.00
18  $3500.00
19                       $545.00
20                                 $244.00
21                                           $567.00
22  $4478.00
23                        $35.00
24                                                               $188.00
25            $2555.00
26                                            $89.00
27
28                                  (6)
29                                                     $183.00
30
31                                                    $2258.00
32             $447.00
33
34
35                                            $55.00
36                                 $779.00
37
38
39   $100.00
40
41  --------  --------  --------  --------  --------  --------  --------
42  $8078.00  $3002.00   $580.00  $1023.00   $711.00  $2441.00   $288.00
43  ========  ========  ========  ========  ========  ========  ========
44
45                                  (3)
```

```
        15        16        17        18        19        20        21
 1 =======================================================================
 2 CASH DISBURSEMENTS SPREADSHEET            Copyright (C) QUE Corp. 1983
 3 =======================================================================
 4
 5           For CHECK DATA, (G)oto (N)ame `CHECKDATA'
 6           For SPREADING TABLE, (G)oto (N)ame `TABLE'
 7           For INSTRUCTIONS, (G)oto (N)ame `INSTRUCTIONS'
 8
 9 =======================================================================
10 SPREADING TABLE (Continues to row 42)                        Sheet 2.2
11 =======================================================================
12
13     8         9        10        11        12        13
14          Dues and    Pro.   Equipment                           Total
15  Postage Subscript. Services  Rental   Interest    Other       Spread
16 -------- --------  --------  --------  --------  --------     --------
17                                                                $100.00
18                                                               $3500.00
19                                                                $545.00
20                                                                $244.00
21                                                                $567.00
22                                                               $4478.00
23                                                                 $35.00
24                                                                $188.00
25                                                               $2555.00
26                                                                 $89.00
27            $33.00                                               $33.00
28   $12.00                                                        $12.00
29                                                                $183.00
30                                                   $122.00      $122.00
31                                                               $2258.00
32                                                                $447.00
33           $111.00                                              $111.00
34  $367.00                                                       $367.00
35                                                                 $55.00
36                                                                $779.00
37                               $544.00                          $544.00
38                     $155.00                                    $155.00
39                                                                $100.00
40                                                                  $0.00
41 --------  --------  --------  --------  --------  --------    --------
42  $379.00   $144.00   $155.00   $544.00     $0.00   $122.00   $17467.00
43 ========  ========  ========  ========  ========  ========    ========
44
45
```

CASH DISBURSEMENTS SPREADSHEET

NUMBER	LOCATION(S)	FORMULA
1	R18:39C2	R[-1]C+1
2	R42C6	SUM(AMOUNT)
3	R42C8:20	SUM(R[-25]C:R[-1]C)
4	R42C21	SUM(TOTALS)
5	R17:41C21	SUM(RC[-13]:RC[-1])
6	R17:41C8:20	IF(CODE=ACCOUNT,AMOUNT,"")

The problem comes at the end, when the columns must be totaled. If a number of checks have been processed, computing the total in each column is sure to be a time-consuming task. At best, the addition will have to be performed only once. If there is any discrepancy between the original total of the checks and the sum of the totals of the spreading columns, however, the entire process must be repeated, taking far more time than such a simple operation deserves.

Using Multiplan to spread the checkbook eliminates all of this addition and ensures that every column has been properly totaled.

The Model

The model has two sections: CHECK DATA and SPREADING TABLE. Unlike most of the models in this book, the sections in this model are arranged from side to side, rather than from top to bottom. The CHECK DATA section begins at cell R10C1. Columns 1, 2, 3, 4, 5, and 6 record the date, number, description, and amount of each check. This part of the model should be used the same way you use your check register or check stubs.

CDSPREAD: Locations of Named Cells and Ranges

Description	Location	Name
CHECK DATA	R11C1	CHECKDATA
SPREADING TABLE	R11C9	TABLE
Account Categories	R13C8:20	ACCOUNT
Check Amounts	R17:41C6	AMOUNT
Account Codes	R17:41C7	CODES
Total Disbursement by Check	R17:41C21	TOTALS
INSTRUCTIONS	R51C1	INSTRUCTIONS

In the SPREADING TABLE section, which begins at cell R10C8 and continues at cell R10C15, columns 8 through 20 contain the "accounts" established to summarize the period's activity. Column 21 totals the amount spread in each row in columns 8 through 20.

Column 7, labled Code, is one of the time savers in this model. Study the example. You will notice that each check has been assigned a code that matches the number of one of the 13 spreading account columns. The amount of the check appears in the column that matches the code. These codes serve as automatic spreaders, eliminating the need to scroll left and right with the cursor to spread the checks. Checks are spread through the use of conditional statements in each cell in the posting range. For example, cell R18C8 is defined as

R18C8 $ = IF(R18C7=R13C8,R18C6,"")

or

R18C8 $ = IF(CODE=ACCOUNT,AMOUNT,"")

Similarly, the following formula can be found in cell R25C10:

R25C10 $ = IF(R25C7=R13C10,R25C6,"")

or

R25C10 $ = IF(CODE=ACCOUNT,AMOUNT,"")

This formula means: If the code in cell R25C7, CODE, is the same as column 10's account number, found in cell R13C10. ACCOUNT, then post the value of the check found in cell R25C6, AMOUNT, into cell R25C10; otherwise, set cell R25C10 to blank (denoted by the double quotation marks). This technique saves much time during posting.

The cells in row 42 total the amounts posted in each spreading column. Figures in these cells are determined through simple addition. The formula in cell R42C9 is an example

R42C9 $ = SUM(R[-25]C:R[-1]C)

You will notice that cell R41C6 in the example contains a dashed line. The inclusion of this line in the summing range allows the model to be expanded without modifications to the formulas in row 42. To add one more check to the model, place the cursor at cell R41C1 and type

IR(the number of rows to add) **(CR)**

After the row is inserted, look at the cells in what is now row 43. You will see that the formulas in those cells have been altered to include the new row 42. For example, cell R43C6 is now defined as

R43C6 $ = SUM(R[-26]C:R[-1]C)

Similarly, if you have used the range name reference for R17:42C6, then the formula

R43C6 $ = SUM(AMOUNT)

need not be changed to account for the additional insertion of a row. Be careful to copy the spreading formulas contained in columns 8 through 20 into the new row or rows, so that the checks in each new row will be properly spread across the accounts.

The model is now ready for you to enter new check data. This technique can save much time, especially in models you expand frequently.

Finally, look at column 21. The cells in this column total the amounts posted in columns 8 through 20, using formulas similar to the one in cell R30C21

R30C21 $ = SUM(RC[-13]:RC[-1])

The totals in column 21 serve as error checks. Compare the amounts in column 21 with those in column 6. You will see that the two columns are identical, indicating that the checks in column 6 have been spread completely. This error-checking feature is particularly valuable when checks are posted manually.

Using the Model

At the beginning of a new period, call up a blank copy of the model from disk. Each day as you write checks, enter the requested data (date, check number, description, and amount) in columns 1 through 6. Be sure to save the model under a descriptive file name at the end of the day by typing **TSB:**(filename) (CR).

At the end of the month, load the model again and move the cursor to cell R17C7. Move down the worksheet, coding each check in the appropriate category. When this task has been completed, type F4 or ! to recalculate the model. Each check amount should be posted to the cell you have indicated, and all totals should be computed automatically.

Sometimes a check must be posted to more than one column. For example, loan repayments usually include principal and interest, and the two amounts must be separated for accounting purposes. When you come to a check like this in your posting process, do not enter a code for the check in column 7. Instead, move the cursor across the sheet to the appropriate columns and type in the correct amounts. When the sheet is recalculated, column 21 will total the amounts posted to the various columns. Be sure to check the total in column 21 against the check amount total in column 6. If the totals do not agree, review your entries to find the error. After you check for errors, save the worksheet and print it by typing **PP**.

After the model has been saved, move the cursor to the cell, or cells, to be corrected and enter the new information. After the changes are made, recalculate, save, and print the sheet again.

Modifications

The simplest modification you can make to this model is to add more rows and columns to the spreadsheet. Depending on the memory capacity of your computer, you may be able to build a sheet that spreads 100 checks across 50 columns. This modification requires the use of the **I**nsert **C**opy commands.

Modifying the model to accommodate more categories requires adding one or more columns that recognize ever-increasing category identification numbers. By using Multiplan's **I**nsert **C**olumn command, you can insert a new category column. The formula in the Total Spread column must then be changed so that it includes the new columnar category entered.

Several profit centers can be linked to a master sheet. As an example, if you have three profit centers, use three different sheets to track them. Using the **X**ternal **C**opy command, the totals in row 42 (assuming row 42 is the totals-by-category row in each model) can be linked to a master sheet that is the summary for the three profit centers. Each time the master sheet is loaded, if the links have been established correctly, it will be updated with the disbursements entered on each profit center's sheet.

You may also want to combine this model with one of the other models in this book, such as the Checkbook Balancer, or with one of your own models.

Managing Cash Flow

If you are like most business people, managing cash flow is one of the most important financial planning activities you perform. This is especially true for managers in small businesses, where growth can strain cash balances to the limit. Even the treasurers of Fortune 500 companies, however, must keep tight control over cash. Every business person would like to know weeks or months in advance when cash crunches will occur, or when cash will be available for discretionary expenditures.

This model is designed to help the business, professional, or personal Multiplan user manage cash. By tracking cash balances on a day-to-day basis, the model may help you avoid nerve-shattering cash lows, and may even help you put excess funds to work earning interest.

Principles

Cash flow activities can be divided into two broad categories: disbursements and receipts. The task of cash flow management is to match these outflows and inflows as closely as possible so that a given cash balance is maintained. Managing cash flows also requires the ability to predict periods of unacceptably low and high cash balances so that corrective action can be taken. The problem with cash flow planning is that it requires predicting the future—something people still don't have the knack of, after centuries of trying. The trick of cash flow planning, then, is to estimate accurately the timing of future receipts and disbursements.

Cash receipts are usually generated by sales, although receipts may also be either refunds for merchandise exchanged or inflows of borrowed money. Receipts are difficult to time precisely, because the payment decision comes from someone else. Estimating exactly when an overdue invoice will be paid is probably the toughest part of

```
         1          2          3          4          5          6          7          8
 1 ===========================================================================================
 2 CASH FLOW MANAGER                                       Copyright (C) QUE Corp. 1983
 3 ===========================================================================================
 4
 5                    For DAILY ACTIVITY (G)oto (N)ame 'ACTIVITY'
 6                    For INSTRUCTIONS (G)oto (N)ame 'INSTRUCTIONS'
 7
 8 ===========================================================================================
 9 DAILY ACTIVITY                                                                Sheet 1.1
10 ===========================================================================================
11 Month of: April 1984
12
13                        Receipts                          Disbursements
14                   -------------------------     -------------------------
15       Date      Description         Amount     Description          Amount    Balance
16      ------  ----------------- --------     ----------------- --------   --------
17              Opening Balance   $3156.00                                       $3156.00 ②
18        4-1                                  Rent                  $312.00   $2844.00
19                                             Equipment Lease       $309.00   $2535.00
20         -2                                                                  $2535.00
21                                                                             $2535.00
22         -3   Payment, Job 1004 $1255.00                                     $3790.00
23                                                                             $3790.00
24         -4                                                                  $3790.00
25                                                                             $3790.00
26         -5                                  Payroll              $1000.00   $2790.00
27                                                                             $2790.00
28         -6                                                                  $2790.00
29                                                                             $2790.00
30         -7   Payment, Job 1003 $3575.00                                     $6365.00
31                                                                             $6365.00
32         -8                                                                  $6365.00
33                                                                             $6365.00
34         -9                                  Invoice 35-234       $2389.00   $3976.00
35                                                                             $3976.00
36        -10                                                                  $3976.00
37                                                                             $3976.00
38   ①    -11   Payment, Job 1010 $2499.00                                     $6475.00  ③
39                                                                             $6475.00
40        -12                                                                  $6475.00
41                                                                             $6475.00
42        -13                                  Payroll              $1000.00   $5475.00
43                                             Health Insurance      $250.00   $5225.00
44        -14                                                                  $5225.00
45                                                                             $5225.00
46        -15                                                                  $5225.00
47                                                                             $5225.00
48        -16                                  Telephone             $450.00   $4775.00
49                                                                             $4775.00
50        -17                                                                  $4775.00
51                                                                             $4775.00
52        -18                                                                  $4775.00
53                                                                             $4775.00
54        -19                                                                  $4775.00
55                                                                             $4775.00
56        -20                                  Payroll              $1000.00   $3775.00
57                                                                             $3775.00
```

```
           1          2          3          4          5          6          7          8
58       ┌-21 Payment, Job 1017 $3577.00                                          $7352.00
59       │                                                                        $7352.00
60       │ -22                            Pay Invoice 1005   $2987.20 $4364.80
61       │                                                                        $4364.80
62       │ -23                                                                    $4364.80
63       │                                                                        $4364.80
64       │ -24                                                                    $4364.80
65       │                                                                        $4364.80
66       │ -25 Payment, Job 1019 $2400.00                                         $6764.80
67       │                                                                        $6764.80
68   ①   │ -26                                                                    $6764.80  ③
69       │                                                                        $6764.80
70       │ -27                            Payroll             $1000.00 $5764.80
71       │                                                                        $5764.80
72       │ -28                            Debt Service        $2500.00 $3264.80
73       │                                                                        $3264.80
74       │ -29                                                                    $3264.80
75       │                                                                        $3264.80
76       │ -30                                                                    $3264.80
77       │                                                                        $3264.80
78       │ -31                                                                    $3264.80
79       └                                                                        $3264.80
80 ---------------------------------------------------------------------------------
81  NEXT     Various Jobs     $6500.00 Machine Purchase  $7500.00 $2264.80  ④
82  MONTH                                                          $2264.80
83                                                                          ⑤
84
85 ===================================================================================
86 INSTRUCTIONS                                                            Sheet 2.1
87 ===================================================================================
88
89                        1) Enter DAILY ACTIVITY
90                        2) RECALCULATE by typing: F4 or !
91                        3) SAVE by typing: TSB:CASHFLOW (CR)
92                        4) PRINT by typing: PP
```

MANAGING CASH FLOW

NUMBER	LOCATION(S)	FORMULA
		(EVEN NUMBERED ROWS)
1	R22:78C1	R[-2]C-1
2	R17C8	RC[-4]
3	R18:79C8	R[-1]C+RECEIPTS-DISBURSEMENTS
4	R81C8	R[-2]C+RECEIPTS-DISBURSEMENTS
5	R82:84C8	R[-1]C+RECEIPTS-DISBURSEMENTS

planning cash flows. Most business people, however, can estimate to within a week or two when their customers will pay. Such an estimate will be sufficient for this model. Predicting when borrowed cash will be repaid is generally easier because borrowing is usually a discretionary activity.

Cash disbursements are typically easier to plan. Regular disbursements, such as rent and payroll payments, occur at the same time every month (or week, as the case may be). These payments can easily be assigned a payment date. Payments for merchandise or other goods purchased on credit can also be planned fairly accurately. These bills usually carry terms (for example, Net 30 Days) that provide a range of acceptable payment dates. Purely discretionary disbursements, such as dividend payments, offer more flexibility because they have no due date.

One type of disbursement—emergency expenditures—is not easy to forecast. When an important machine breaks down, there is no time to be concerned with the cash flow implications of the repair. The machine must be fixed. In fact, the possibility of emergency expenditures is one of the strongest arguments in favor of cash flow planning. A company with a planned cash reserve is more likely to weather such a crisis.

After all disbursements and receipts have been assigned a planned activity date, you have the beginnings of a cash flow model. All that remains is to arrange the various activities in chronological order and to add or subtract them from the previous balance. None of these procedures requires the power of Multiplan.

One factor has not been fully considered, however. Because each planned activity date is a prediction, it involves some uncertainty. If even a few dates are wrong, the model's results can be seriously flawed. Multiplan has the power to help you manage that uncertainty, through the use of "what if" analysis.

A Note on "What If" Analysis

"What if" analysis is useful for factoring away uncertainty in models that make predictions. In this kind of analysis, different versions of a model are developed, each based on a different revised set of assumptions. A worst-case scenario would include the most pessimistic assumptions, and a best-case version would illustrate the most optimistic outcome. Between these two cases lies one that illustrates the most likely outcome. Each case can be thought of as the answer to a different "what if" question, such as: What if bill XYZ isn't paid as rapidly as planned? What if an emergency expenditure is required? Analyzing the problem with "what if" analysis lets you see how changes in your assumptions affect the expected outcome. Even though "what if" analysis does not eliminate the risk of erroneous estimates, it does help you evaluate the consequences of errors and decide if the risk can be absorbed.

The obvious problem with "what if" analysis is that it takes a great deal of time to develop successive versions of a model when traditional computing tools like paper, pencils, and calculators are used. Multiplan, however, can compute each version of a model in a matter of seconds, letting you develop as many "what if" cases as you wish.

The Model

This model has only one section, DAILY ACTIVITY, which begins at row 9. Side-to-side scrolling is not necessary to view your results because the model is exactly one 80-column CRT screen wide.

CASHFLOW: Locations of Named Cells and Ranges

Description	**Location**	**Name**
DAILY ACTIVITY	R10C1	ACTIVITY
Receipts	R18:82C4	RECEIPTS
Disbursements	R18:82C7	DISBURSEMENTS
INSTRUCTIONS	R87C1	INSTRUCTIONS

The model has been given the **C**ontinuous default format. This allows the labels in columns 2, 3, 5, and 6 to be displayed wider than the default cell width. This technique saves time in displaying labels of your choice, but also consumes memory at a faster rate than non-continuous formats.

The far left column, labeled Date, contains the days of the month for the month selected, in this case April. Cell R18C1 contains the first day of the month, entered as a label,

R18C1 FR = "4-1

Cell R20C1 contains the second day of the month, entered as a number

R20C1 = -2

Each date cell below row 20 in column 1 is defined by subtracting one from the immediately preceding date. For example, cell R26C1 is defined as

R26C1 = +R[-2]C-1

Moving from left to right, notice that columns 2, 3, and 4 are labeled Receipts, with the subheadings Description and Amount. These three columns are used to enter actual and estimated cash inflows. Similarly, columns 5, 6, and 7, labeled Disbursements, are used for cash outflows. The final column, 8, shows the balance after each day, which is calculated as the previous balance, plus receipts, less disbursements. Cell R18C8 is therefore defined as

R18C8 $ = R17C8+R18C4-R18C7

or

R18C8 $ = R[-1]C+RECEIPTS-DISBURSEMENTS

This relationship is repeated in each cell in column 8.

Using the Model

Move the cursor to cell R11C2 and input the name of the month to be planned. Next, move to R18C1 and change the label in that cell to the first day of the month in MM-DD format.

Cell R17C4 shows the beginning cash balance for the period. This amount should equal your reconciled closing checkbook balance for the previous month. Every balance in the model builds on this amount; therefore, it is very important that the amount be correct.

After recalculating the sheet by typing F4 or ! you will be ready to begin. If no entries have been posted, your opening balance should appear in every cell from R17C8 to R79C8. The proper dates should also appear in column 1. Move the cursor to an entry cell in column 5. Enter a description, then move the cursor to column 7, same row, and enter an amount. Type F4 or ! to recalculate the sheet. Notice that every cell in column 8 below the row you just defined equals the beginning balance less the application you posted. All entries are posted to the model this way.

Once you feel ready to solo, begin entering your own data into the model. Start with your regular disbursements, such as rent and payroll. Next, enter any payments on account you know will come due in the current month. Finally, post your estimated receipts. Be certain that every entry is posted to the proper date.

Move the cursor up and down along column 8. Does your cash balance become negative at any point? Does it soar above a level of reasonable reserves? If so, then you are ready to do some "what if" analysis. If your payment on invoice XYZ is delayed 10 days, what happens to your cash balance? If you hold payment on bill ABC for 15 days, will you avoid a cash crunch? Can you make a discretionary expenditure that you've been wanting to make? Be sure to consider what will happen if a major receipt is delayed for a few days. Would such a delay be a problem?

Juggle your estimates until you are satisfied that the best balance has been reached. Then save the model by typing **TSB:CASHFLOW** (CR) and print it by typing **PP**. You now have a cash budget for the month.

You can also use this model to track your actual cash inflows and outflows. As each day ends, call up the model. If the activity for the day was according to plan, no changes are required. If any disbursements or receipts were made that were not in accordance with the budget, adjust the day's activity to reflect those changes so that your running balance will be correct. Finally, consider whether any changes must be made to the forecast for the rest of the month. If so, revise your budget accordingly.

Modifications

This model has two rows for each day of the month so that two receipts and two disbursements can be posted each day. If you need more space, add a row and replicate the formula for the previous cell into that row and down the rest of the worksheet. For example, the commands to insert a row between the current rows 27 and 28 (to create more entry space for the date 4-5) would be

Insert **R**ow (TAB) **28** (CR)
Copy **F**rom **R27C8**(TAB) **R28C8** (CR)

Larger companies can use this model for cash flow management on a wider scale. Rather than showing day-by-day activity, the model can display a weekly or monthly budget. The scale in column 1, currently showing days, can be set to months. Instead of indicating each transaction separately, one entry can summarize all results from operations for the period. Other entries can then represent capital or various discretionary expenditures.

This model can also be used by individuals for home budgeting. In fact, nearly anyone can implement this model to keep track of income and expenses. When used with the Checkbook Balancer, the Cash Projection model, and the Cash Disbursements model, an overall cash management system allows easy control of both personal and business income and disbursements.

Projecting Cash Flow

For many businesses, cash flow is as important as profitability. This is especially true of start-up companies, rapidly growing firms, and companies that have seasonal sales. Often a new or fast-growing company has a product that sells, but has a difficult time meeting expenses between the time the product is made and the time the actual payment from the sale is received. Companies with seasonal sales must build inventories during the off-season in order to have sufficient products to sell during the peak period. Off-season production means that materials must be purchased, workers paid, and other expenses met several months before any sales revenue is received. These obligations are often covered by a line of bank credit that is used several months each year and paid off during the rest of the year.

This model requires a full 64K of RAM to operate. If you have a Texas Instruments 99/4A, Apple II with Softcard, Commodore 64, or another system with less than 64K of user-available memory, you will have to condense the model to make it fit. One solution is to omit the Table of Contents and the Instructions sections from the model itself and refer to them in the book when necessary.

Principles

With Multiplan, a business manager can project future cash flows using assumed sales, collections, and disbursements to indicate how much financing will be needed and when. This forecast can be valuable when a company is uncertain of its ability to meet its needs with its current short-term credit, or where conditions of a line of credit are difficult to meet. For example, a company may have a $50,000 line of credit that must be fully paid off for 120 days each year. Will this amount meet peak borrowing needs? Will the company be able to keep a zero balance for four months? These questions can be answered with a cash projection model.

A cash projection model can also be used to analyze and manage a cash account. With today's high interest rates, most companies should limit their debt financing and invest their excess cash in interest-bearing securities. Knowing what the future pattern of borrowing and excess cash will be can facilitate this kind of management. Often a firm that experiences seasonal cash lows also experiences seasonal cash gluts.

This Multiplan model is designed to project cash flows for a business with seasonal sales. Projections for one year are made based on sales, collections, inventory build-up, disbursements for expenses, and loan repayments. A minimum cash balance is assumed. If this balance cannot be met in a given month, then the difference between the cash minimum and the available cash is borrowed on a line of credit.

This Multiplan model accounts for all the fundamental financial relationships that characterize the financial planning process. Three of these relationships are particularly important:

1. The lag between raw material purchases and the sale of the finished product
2. The lag between raw material purchases and payment for these materials
3. The lag between the sale of the finished product and the collection of receipts for that sale

The time between the initial purchases of raw materials and the collection of cash for the sale of finished products varies widely from company to company. For firms that buy on credit but sell for cash, this interval may be 30 days or less. For firms that buy for cash but sell on credit, the interval can be as long as 180 days or more. For example, if an item purchased C.O.D. is not sold for 90 days, it produces no income for those 90 days. If another 90 days is required to collect the cash from that sale, a full 180 days has elapsed between cash outflow and cash inflow.

Accounts receivable and accounts payable terms vary widely from industry to industry and from company to company. Careful planning and negotiation can sometimes stretch the accounts payable beyond 60 days, whereas other purchases can be made only on a cash basis. By negotiating favorable accounts receivable terms, collections can be speeded.

The Model

The Cash Projections Model is really two models: an assumptions model, DATAPROJ, and the analysis of cash flow, CASHPROJ. What would otherwise be a very large model is broken into two smaller models; yet Multiplan's model-linking feature maintains the intricate relationships needed for comprehensive cash flow planning.

DATAPROJ: Locations of Named Cells and Ranges

Description	Location	Name
SALES DATA	R11C1	SALESDATA
Gross Sales	R18C5:18	SALES
Accounts Receivable Collections	R25C7:18	ARCOLLECT
Cash Sales	R28C7:18	CASH*
Accounts Receivable Balance	R30C6:18	AR*
PURCHASES	R34C1	PURCHASES
Gross Margin Percentage	R35C6:18	GM
Cost of Goods Sold	R36C6:18	CGS
Inventory Purchases	R42C6:18	INVPURCHASES
Total Purchases on Credit	R45C5:18	CREDIT
Inventory Balance	R47C6:18	INVENTORY*
Payment for Purchases	R53C7:18	PAYMENT*
Accounts Payable Balance	R55C6:18	AP*
DEBT	R59C1	DEBT
Long-Term Debt Payment Schedule	R62C7:18	LTDPAYMENT*
Long-Term Debt Interest Portion	R63C6:18	LTDINTEREST
Principal Portion on Long-Term Debt	R64C6:18	LTDPRINCIPAL
INSTRUCTIONS	R71C1	INSTRUCTIONS

* The asterisk denotes that this named range will be linked to CASHPROJ.

This model uses a large number of named and relative references. Although you can use the absolute equivalents of these references when you build the model, relative and named references are far easier to use in the **C**opy command. By using the cursor (see Notes on Conventions) to point to the areas we identify, you can grasp the relationships more easily.

The DATAPROJ Model

The first model, DATAPROJ, tracks sales data, purchases, and long- and short-term debt.

The SALES DATA section, which begins at R10C1, summarizes data by first combining the gross sales from five different profit centers. Then it amortizes the accounts receivable collections expected from each prior month and adds these figures to the actual cash receipts from the current month in order to arrive at total cash receipts.

Notice that although the model is designed to track collections for a single calendar year, November and December from the previous year are included. These months are included because the accounts receivable balances in January and February depend on the sales that occur in the months of November and December.

The gross sales from each profit center are entered in rows 12 through 16, columns 5 through 18. Gross sales for all profit centers are totaled monthly in row 18, for example,

R18C5 I = SUM(R[-6]C:R[-1]C)

A portion of each month's sales will be for cash and another portion will be made on credit. The portion made for cash or credit varies widely among businesses. The percentages of cash sales, 30-day collections, and 60-day collections are entered in rows 21 to 23.

The cells in row 21, starting at cell R21C5 and continuing through R21C18, show the projected percentage of each month's sales. The percentage of each month's sales expected to be collected in 30 days is similarly placed in row 22. The percentage of sales projected for collection in 60 days is computed by the model by subtracting the cash and 30-day percentages from 1 (100%). For example, the formula in cell R23C7 is

R23C7 % = 1-R[-2]C-R[-1]C

In our example, we have used 10% as the percentage of cash sales, with 20% collectible in 30 days and 70% collectible in 60 days (the month after the next). These cells are formatted with Multiplan's % format. Remember that a percentage must be entered in Multiplan as its decimal equivalent, so 10% is entered as .1. Multiplan will automatically display this number as a percent. The command

Format**C**ells**R21C7:R23C18**(TAB) (TAB)**%**(CR)

formats the cells in this range to display as percentages.

Notice also that the cells in rows 21 and 22 in columns 6 through 18 are defined by referring to the cells immediately to their left. For example, cell R22C7 is defined as

R22C7 % = RC[-1]

This technique causes every month to assume the percentages for cash sales and accounts receivable collections that are entered in the first month. This feature speeds the process of building the model. You can change the assumed percentages in any month simply by entering the new percentage in the proper cell.

Row 25, total collections on sales, projects the total cash receipts for the month. The amount that will be collected in any month includes all cash sales in the current month plus receivables from prior months that are collected. Figures for receivables must be based on the estimated receivables percentage from those prior months. The formula in cell R25C7, ARCOLLECT, does just this.

R25C7 I = (R[-7]C[-2]*R[-2]C[-2])	} 60-Day Collection of November's Sales
+(R[-7]C[-1]*R[-3]C[-1])	} 30-Day Collection of December's Sales
+(R[-7]C*R[-4]C)	} Cash Percentage of January's Sales

```
        1        2        3        4        5        6        7        8        9       10
 1 ===============================================================================
 2 CASH PROJECTIONS SALES AND PURCHASES            Copyright QUE Corp. 1983
 3 ===============================================================================
 4
 5                For Sales Data, (G)oto (N)ame 'SALESDATA'
 6                For Purchases, (G)oto (N)ame 'PURCHASES'
 7                For Debt, (G)oto (N)ame 'DEBT'
 8                For Instructions, (G)oto (N)ame 'INSTRUCTIONS'
 9 =======================================================================================
10 SALES DATA             Sheet 1.1     Nov      Dec      Jan      Feb      Mar      Apr
11 =============================== ======= ======= ======= ======= ======= =======
12 Profit Center 1                   20,321  40,212  37,893  42,566  46,505  56,995
13 Profit Center 2                   17,800  16,099  27,637  32,908  45,314  56,105
14 Profit Center 3                   12,513   4,533  10,211  14,835  20,634  38,110
15 Profit Center 4                   30,367  31,833  27,344  30,689  37,377  47,375
16 Profit Center 5                   18,999  17,323  16,915  19,002  30,170  41,415
17                                   ------  ------  ------  ------  ------  ------
18 Total Sales                      100,000 110,000 120,000 140,000 180,000 240,000  (1)
19                                   ======  ======  ======  ======  ======  ======
20                                                                                   (2)
21 Percentage      Cash Sales           10%     10%     10%     10%     10%     10%
22 Collections     30 days              20%     20%     20%     20%     20%     20%  (3)
23                 60 days              70%     70%     70%     70%     70%     70%  (4)
24
25 Total Collections on Sales                       104,000 115,000 130,000 158,000  (5)
26 Other Cash Receipts                                    0       0       0       0
27                                                  ------  ------  ------  ------
28 Total Cash Receipts                              104,000 115,000 130,000 158,000  (6)
29
30 Accounts Receivable Balance               50,000 |66,000  91,000 141,000 223,000
31                                                                 (7)
32 =======================================================================================
33 PURCHASES                         Sheet 2.1     Dec      Jan      Feb      Mar      Apr
34 ======================================== ======= ======= ======= ======= =======
35 Average Gross Margin Percentage:             30%     30%     30%     30%     30%  (8)
36 Cost of Goods Sold:                       77,000  84,000  98,000 126,000 168,000  (9)
37
38 Inventory       30 Days in Advance           50%     50%     50%     50%     50%  (11)
39 Purchasing      60 Days in Advance           50%     50%     50%     50%     50%  (12)
40                 90 Days in Advance            0%      0%      0%      0%      0%  (13)
41
```

```
     1         2         3         4         5         6       7       8       9      10
42 Purchases on    Inventory                       91,000 112,000 147,000 168,700 150,150 (14)
43 Credit          Other                            5,000   5,000   5,000   5,000   5,000
44                                                -------  ------- ------- ------- -------
45 Total Purchases on Credit              95,000   96,000 117,000 152,000 173,700 155,150 (15)
46
47 Inventory Balance                      26,000   40,000  68,000 117,000 159,700 141,850 (16)
48
49 Payment           Cash                    40%      40%     40%     40%     40%     40% (17)
50 Schedule          30 Days                 40%      40%     40%     40%     40%     40% (18)
51                   60 Days                 20%      20%     20%     20%     20%     20% (19)
52
53 Payment for Purchases                               104,200 126,800 153,680 161,940 (20)
54
55 Accounts Payable Balance                       100,000 112,800 138,000 158,020 151,230 (21)
56
57 ==================================================================================
58 DEBT                                Sheet 3.1      Dec     Jan     Feb     Mar     Apr
59 ================================================ ======= ======= ======= ======= =======
60 Long-Term Debt Interest Rate                        18%     18%     18%     18%     18% (22)
61
62 Long-Term Debt Payment Schedule                  2,500   2,500   2,500   2,500   2,500 (23)
63   Interest Portion                               1,500   1,485   1,470   1,454   1,439 (24)
64   Principal Portion                              1,000   1,015   1,030   1,046   1,061 (25)
65
66 Long-Term Debt Balance                100,000   99,000  97,985  96,955  95,909  94,848 (26)
67
68
69 ========================================================================
70 INSTRUCTIONS                                                   Sheet 4.1
71 ========================================================================
72
73         1) Enter assumptions into Sales Data, and Purchases Sections
74         2) Recalculate by typing: F4 or !
75         3) SAVE by typing: TSB:WORKING (CR)
76         4) Print by typing: PP
77         5) To continue, type: TLB:CASHPROJ, which is linked
78            to this model and will use its data when loading.
```

	11	12	13	14	15	16	17	18		19	20
1											
2											
3											
4											
5											
6											
7											
8											
9	========	========	========	========	========	========	========	========			
10	May	Jun	Jul	Aug	Sep	Oct	Nov	Dec			
11	=======	=======	=======	=======	=======	=======	=======	=======			
12	57,044	48,703	35,633	31,469	30,477	30,477	30,477	31,469			
13	55,781	45,314	41,276	19,877	16,386	16,386	16,386	19,877			
14	40,176	23,335	18,488	18,302	21,577	21,577	21,577	18,302			
15	47,375	37,377	21,470	22,800	18,101	18,101	18,101	22,800			
16	41,624	32,271	37,133	28,552	23,459	23,459	23,459	28,552			
17	------	------	------	------	------	------	------	------			
18	242,000	187,000	154,000	121,000	110,000	110,000	110,000	121,000	(1)		
19	======	======	======	======	======	======	======	======			
20											
21	10%	10%	10%	10%	10%	10%	10%	10%	(2)		
22	20%	20%	20%	20%	20%	20%	20%	20%	(3)		
23	70%	70%	70%	70%	70%	70%	70%	70%	(4)		
24											
25	198,200	235,100	222,200	173,800	143,000	117,700	110,000	111,100	(5)		
26	0	0	0	0	0	0	0	0			
27	------	------	------	------	------	------	------	------			
28	198,200	235,100	222,200	173,800	143,000	117,700	110,000	111,100	(6)		
29											
30	266,800	218,700	150,500	97,700	64,700	57,000	57,000	66,900			
31				(7)							
32	========	========	========	========	========	========	========	========			
33	May	Jun	Jul	Aug	Sep	Oct	Nov	Dec			
34	=======	=======	=======	=======	=======	=======	=======	=======	(8)		
35	30%	30%	30%	30%	30%	30%	30%	30%			
36	169,400	130,900	107,800	84,700	77,000	77,000	77,000	84,700		84,700	84,700
37										(10)	
38	50%	50%	50%	50%	50%	50%	50%	50%	(11)		
39	50%	50%	50%	50%	50%	50%	50%	50%	(12)		
40	0%	0%	0%	0%	0%	0%	0%	0%	(13)		
41											

	11	12	13	14	15	16	17	18	19	20
42	119,350	96,250	80,850	77,000	77,000	80,850	84,700	84,700	(14)	
43	5,000	5,000	5,000	5,000	5,000	5,000	5,000	5,000		
44	-------	-------	-------	-------	-------	-------	-------	-------		
45	124,350	101,250	85,850	82,000	82,000	85,850	89,700	89,700	(15)	
46										
47	91,800	57,150	30,200	22,500	22,500	26,350	34,050	34,050	(16)	
48										
49	40%	40%	40%	40%	40%	40%	40%	40%	(17)	
50	40%	40%	40%	40%	40%	40%	40%	40%	(18)	
51	20%	20%	20%	20%	20%	20%	20%	20%	(19)	
52										
53	146,540	121,270	99,710	87,390	82,770	83,540	86,620	88,930	(20)	
54										
55	129,040	109,020	95,160	89,770	89,000	91,310	94,390	95,160	(21)	
56										
57	=======	=======	=======	=======	=======	=======	=======	=======		
58	May	Jun	Jul	Aug	Sep	Oct	Nov	Dec		
59	=======	=======	=======	=======	=======	=======	=======	=======		
60	18%	18%	18%	18%	18%	18%	18%	18%	(22)	
61										
62	2,500	2,500	2,500	2,500	2,500	2,500	2,500	2,500	(23)	
63	1,423	1,407	1,390	1,374	1,357	1,339	1,322	1,304	(24)	
64	1,077	1,093	1,110	1,126	1,143	1,161	1,178	1,196	(25)	
65										
66	93,770	92,677	91,567	90,441	89,297	88,137	86,959	85,763	(26)	
67										
68										
69										
70										
71										
72										
73										
74										
75										
76										
77										
78										

CASH PROJECTIONS SALES AND PURCHASES (DATAPROJ)

NUMBER	LOCATION(S)	FORMULA
1	R18C5:18	SUM(R[-6]C:R[-1]C)
2	R21C6:18	RC[-1]
3	R22C6:18	RC[-1]
4	R23C5:18	1-R[-2]C-R[-1]C
5	R25C8:18	(R[-7]C[-2]*R[-2]C[-2])+ (R[-7]C[-1]*R[-3]C[-1])+R[-7]C*R[-4]C)
6	R28C7:18	R[-3]C+R[-1]C
7	R30C7:18	RC[-1]+SALES-CASH
8	R35C7:18	RC[-1]
9	R36C6:18	(1-GM)*SALES
10	R36C19:20	RC[-1]
11	R38C7:18	RC[-1]
12	R39C7:18	RC[-1]
13	R40C6:18	1-R[-2]C-R[-1]C
14	R42C6:18	R[-4]C*R[-6]C[+1]+R[-3]C*R[-6]C[+2]+ R[-2]C+R[-6]C[+3]
15	R45C6:18	R[-3]C+R[-2]C
16	R47C6:18	RC[-1]+INVPURCHASES-CGS
17	R49C6:18	RC[-1]
18	R50C6:18	RC[-1]
19	R51C6:18	1-R[-2]C-R[-1]C
20	R53C7:18	R[-4]C*R[-8]C+R[-3]C*R[-8]C[-1]+ R[-2]C*R[-8]C[-2]
21	R55C7:18	RC[-1]+CREDIT-PAYMENT
22	R60C7:18	RC[-1]
23	R62C7:18	RC[-1]
24	R63C6:18	R[-3]C/12*R[+3]C[-1]
25	R64C6:18	R[-2]C-R[-1]C
26	R66C6:18	RC[-1]-R[-2]C

Other cash receipts (row 26) are added to total collections on sales (row 25) to derive total cash receipts (row 28). An example of this addition is R28C7, CASH,

R28C7 I =+R[-3]C+R[-2]C

Row 30, accounts receivable balance, adds the prior month's accounts receivable balance to this month's sales, then subtracts from that sum the total collections for the current month. The formula in cell R30C7, AR, is an example.

R30C7 I = RC[-1]+SALES-CASH

or

R30C7 I = RC[-1]+R[-12]C-R[-5]C

The second section of the model, PURCHASES, begins on row 33. This section tracks gross margin and shows inventory purchasing plans, including the purchases, the planned payment schedule for those purchases, and the accounts payable balance.

The cost of goods sold (row 36) is figured by taking the gross sales for the current month and multiplying this amount by the result of 100% minus the average gross margin percentage as found in row 35. Note that row 35 is formatted for percent. The formula in cell R36C6, CGS, is typical of formulas in this row.

R36C7 I = (1-GM)*SALES

or

R36C6 I = (1-R[-1]C)*R[-18]C

The cells in the range R38:40C6:18 help make the model more realistic by considering the lag between the purchase of raw materials and the actual sale of the finished product. Most products require that cash be invested in raw materials months before finished goods are produced.

Cells R38C6 and R39C6 are used to enter the percentage of inventory purchases that will be made 30 days (row 38) and 60 days (row 39) prior to the sale of the finished product. The values placed in these cells are then carried forward monthly by cells R38:39C7:18 using the formula

R38:39C8:18 % = +RC[-1]

The percentage for purchases 90 days in advance is the amount not purchased 30 or 60 days in advance. The formula in cell R40C6,

R40C6 % = 1-R[-2]C-R[-1]C

subtracts R38C6 and R39C6 from 1 (100%) to arrive at this percentage.

Row 42 converts the percentages in rows 38, 39, and 40 into projected inventory purchasing requirements. January's inventory purchases on credit number is computed by multiplying the 30-days percentage in cell R38C7 times February's cost of goods sold, plus the 60-days percentage in cell R39C7 times March's cost of goods sold, plus the 90-days percentage in cell R40C7 times April's cost of goods sold. The formula in cell R42C6 is an example of the formulas in row 42.

R42C7 I = +R[-4]C*R[-6]C[+1])+(R[-3]C*R[-6]C[+2])+(R[-2]
C*R[-6]C[+3]]

The formula literally reads

R42C7 I =
(30 Days in Advance Percentage*Feb. Cost of Goods Sold)
+(60 Days in Advance Percentage*March Cost of Goods Sold)
+(90 Days in Advance Percentage*April Cost of Goods Sold)

The cost of goods sold row has been extended in R36C19:21 so that the advance purchasing information may be carried forward for the entire calendar year you are tracking. These cells extend the December cost of goods sold figure by the reference

R36C19 I = +RC[-1]

You can alter this number by typing a new value in cell R36C19 or R36C20.

Row 45, total purchases on credit, adds inventory purchases on credit and other purchases on credit. Other purchases may include supplies and other noninventory items bought on credit.

The inventory balance, in row 47, adds the previous month's inventory balance and inventory purchases for the current month and subtracts from that total the current month's cost of goods sold. The remainder reflects the current month's dollar value of inventory.

Cell R47C5 is an input cell for November's inventory balance; R47C6 contains the formula that will be used for January through December.

R47C6 I = +RC[-1]+INVPURCHASES-CGS

or

R47C6 I = +RC[-1]+R[-5]C-R[-11]C

The cells in the range R49C6 to R51C18 consider the lag between the purchase of inventory and other assets on credit and the payment for those assets. Some assets must be purchased for cash or on terms that allow 10 days to pay; other accounts payable carry terms of 30 or 60 days.

Cells R49C5 and R50C5 are used to enter the percentage of December's purchases that will be bought with cash (R49C5) and on terms of 30 days (R50C5). These percentages are carried forward monthly in rows 49 and 50 by the formula

R49:50C7:18 % = +RC[-1]

The cells in row 51 find the percentage of purchases that will be paid in 60 days by adding cash and 30-day payment percentages and subtracting that total from 100% with the formula

R51C6 % = 1-R[-2]C-R[-1]C

Row 53, payment for purchases, multiplies in a fashion identical to that used in inventory purchases on credit. Cell R53C7, PAYMENT, contains a formula identical to R42C7:

R53C7 % = R[-4]C*R[-8]C+R[-3]C*R[-8]C[-1]+R[-2]
C*R[-8]C[-2]

The formula in R53C7 works the same way as the formula in R42C7, except that it tracks the payment of the materials, rather than projected needs, in successive months.

The formula in cell R55C7

R55C7 I = +RC[-1]+CREDIT-PAYMENT

or

R55C7 I = +RC[-1]+R[-10]C-R[-2]C

adds the previous month's accounts payable balance to the current month's total purchases on credit and subtracts the current month's payments for purchases from that total.

The third section of the model, DEBT, tracks the long-term debt payment schedule and projects the long-term debt balance.

Row 60 contains the long-term debt interest rate. The rate is entered into R60C6 and copied from January through December with the formula

R60C7:18 % = +RC[-1]

The long-term debt payment schedule is located in row 62. In the model we assume that the payment schedule calls for a monthly payment of $2500. This amount is entered into R62C6, LTDPAYMENT, and is carried forward from R62C7 through R62C18 by the formula

R62C7:18 I = +RC[-1]

Row 63 contains the interest portion of the repayment of the long-term debt. The formula in R63C6, LTDINTEREST, is representative of row 63. This formula divides the annual interest rate, R60C6, by 12 to derive a monthly rate. Then the formula multiplies that interest rate by the previous month's long-term debt balance, R66C5.

R63C6 I = +R[-3]C/12*R[+3]C[-1]

To find the principal portion of the long-term debt payment, subtract the interest, R63C6, from the payment, R62C6. Cell R64C6 does this

R64C6 = +R[-2]C-R[-1]C

The long-term debt balance for November is located in Cell R66C5. This amount is entered from the keyboard. Successive months' long-term debt balance figures are derived by the formulas in R66C6:18

R66C6:18 = +RC[-1]-R[-2]C

The formulas subtract the current month's principal payment from the previous month's long-term debt balance.

Linking DATAPROJ with CASHPROJ

Much of the data computed in our first model, DATAPROJ, is used by the CASHPROJ model to develop the cash flow forecast. All the ranges in DATAPROJ that are linked to CASHPROJ have been named. These are indicated by an asterisk in the table of names and ranges for DATAPROJ. The models are linked by using the command **X**ternal **C**opy, as explained in the following section.

The CASHPROJ Model

The CASHPROJ model shows a twelve-month cash requirement forecast for a mythical company. It has four sections: ASSUMPTIONS, CASH RECEIPTS SUMMARY, ANALYSIS OF CASH REQUIREMENTS, and BALANCES IN KEY ACCOUNTS.

CASHPROJ: Locations of Named Cells and Ranges

Description	**Location**	**Names**
ASSUMPTIONS	R11C1	ASSUMPTIONS
Line-of-Credit Interest Rate	R13C7:18	LOCRATE
Minimum Acceptable Cash Balance	R15C7:18	MINCASH
CASH RECEIPTS SUMMARY	R22C1	CASHRECEIPTS
ANALYSIS OF CASH REQUIREMENTS	R38C1	ANALYSIS
Amount below Minimum Acceptable Balance	R43C7:18	DEFICIT
BALANCES IN KEY ACCOUNTS	R53C1	BALANCE
INSTRUCTIONS	R68C1	INSTRUCTIONS

Line-of-credit interest rate is located in cell R13C7, LOCRATE, and is continued from R13C8 through R13C18 by the formula

R13C8:18 = +RC[-1]

```
          1         2         3         4         5         6         7         8         9
 1 ====================================================================== ===================
 2 CASH PROJECTION                          Copyright (C) QUE Corp. 1983
 3 ====================================================================== ===================
 4          For ASSUMPTIONS, (G)oto (N)ame  `ASSUMPTIONS'
 5          For CASH RECEIPTS SUMMARY, (G)oto (N)ame `CASHRECEIPTS'
 6          For ANALYSIS OF CASH REQUIREMENTS, (G)oto (N)ame `ANALYSIS'
 7          For BALANCES IN KEY ACCOUNTS, (G)oto (N)ame `BALANCE'
 8          For INSTRUCTIONS, (G)oto (N)ame `INSTRUCTIONS'
 9 ====================================================================== ===================
10 ASSUMPTIONS                                          Sheet 1.1      Jan       Feb       Mar
11 ===========================================================      =======   =======   =======
12
13 Line-of-Credit Interest Rate                                         14%       14%       14%
14
15 Minimum Acceptable Cash Balance                          $      20,000    20,000    20,000  (2)
16
17
18
19
20
21 CASH RECEIPTS SUMMARY                                Sheet 2.1      Jan       Feb       Mar
22 ===========================================================      =======   =======   =======
23
24 Total Cash Collections                                         104,000   115,000   130,000  (3)
25                                                                =======   =======   =======
26 Cash Disbursements
27  Payment for Purchases on Credit                               104,200   126,800   153,680  (4)
28  Operating Expenses                                             12,250    12,250    12,250
29  Long Term Debt Service                                          2,500     2,500     2,500  (5)
30  Interest Payment on Line of Credit                                  0       116       427  (6)
31  Income Taxes                                                   10,000         0         0
32  Other                                                               0         0         0
33                                                                -------   -------   -------
34 Total Cash Disbursements                                       128,950   141,666   168,857  (7)
35                                                                =======   =======   =======
36
```

```
        1         2         3         4         5         6         7         8         9

37 ANALYSIS OF CASH REQUIREMENTS                          Sheet 3.1       Jan       Feb       Mar
38 ==============================================================   =======   =======   =======
39 Net Cash Generated This Period                                   -24,950   -26,666   -38,857  (8)
40 Beginning Cash Balance                                            35,000    20,000    20,000  (9)
41
42 Cash Balance before Borrowings                                    10,050    -6,666   -18,857  (10)
43 Amount below Minimum Acceptable Balance                           -9,950   -26,666   -38,857  (11)
44
45 Current-Period Short-Term Borrowings                               9,950    26,666    38,857  (12)
46 Total Short-Term Borrowings                                        9,950    36,616    75,473  (13)
47                                                                  -------   -------   -------
48 Ending Cash Balance                                               20,000    20,000    20,000  (15)
49                                                                  =======   =======   =======
50
51
52 BALANCES IN KEY ACCOUNTS                               Sheet 4.1       Jan       Feb       Mar
53 ==============================================================   =======   =======   =======
54 Assets
55  Cash                                                      35000   20,000    20,000    20,000  (16)
56  Accounts Receivable                                       50000   66,000    91,000   141,000  (17)
57  Inventory                                                 40000   68,000   117,000   159,700  (18)
58 Liabilities
59  Accounts Payable                                         100000  112,800   138,000   158,020  (19)
60  Line of Credit                                                0    9,950    36,616    75,473  (20)
61
62 Net Working Capital                                               31,250    53,384    87,207  (21)
63
64
65
66 ======================================================================
67 INSTRUCTIONS
68 ======================================================================
69
70                    1) Enter DATA into DATAPROJ model
71                    2) SAVE DATAPROJ by typing: TSB:DATAPROJ (CR)
72                    3) Enter ASSUMPTIONS
73                    4) Recalculate by typing: F4 or !
74                    5) PRINT by typing: PP
75                    6) SAVE by typing: TSB:CASHPROJ
```

	10	11	12	13	14	15	16	17	18	
1	========	========	========	========	========	========	========	========		
2										
3	========	========	========	========	========	========	========	========		
4										
5										
6										
7										
8										
9	========	========	========	========	========	========	========	========		
10	Apr	May	Jun	Jul	Aug	Sep	Oct	Nov	Dec	
11	=======	=======	=======	=======	=======	=======	=======	=======	=======	
12										
13	14%	14%	14%	14%	14%	14%	14%	14%	14%	(1)
14										
15	20,000	20,000	20,000	20,000	20,000	20,000	20,000	20,000	20,000	(2)
16										
17										
18										
19										
20										
21	Apr	May	Jun	Jul	Aug	Sep	Oct	Nov	Dec	
22	=======	=======	=======	=======	=======	=======	=======	=======	=======	
23										
24	158,000	198,200	235,100	222,200	173,800	143,000	117,700	110,000	111,100	(3)
25	=======	=======	=======	=======	=======	=======	=======	=======	=======	
26										
27	161,940	146,540	121,270	99,710	87,390	82,770	83,540	86,620	88,930	(4)
28	12,250	12,250	12,250	12,250	12,250	12,250	12,250	12,250	12,250	
29	2,500	2,500	2,500	2,500	2,500	2,500	2,500	2,500	2,500	(5)
30	881	1,226	809	0	0	0	0	0	0	(6)
31	10,000	0	0	10,000	0	0	100,000	0	0	
32	0	0	0	0	0	0	0	0	0	
33	-------	-------	-------	-------	-------	-------	-------	-------	-------	
34	187,571	162,516	136,829	124,460	102,140	97,520	198,290	101,370	103,680	(7)
35	=======	=======	=======	=======	=======	=======	=======	=======	=======	
36										

	10	11	12	13	14	15	16	17	18	
37	Apr	May	Jun	Jul	Aug	Sep	Oct	Nov	Dec	
38	=======	=======	=======	=======	=======	=======	=======	=======	=======	
39	-29,571	35,684	98,271	97,740	71,660	45,480	-80,590	8,630	7,420	(8)
40	20,000	20,000	20,000	48,912	146,652	218,312	263,792	183,202	191,832	(9)
42	-9,571	55,684	118,271	146,652	218,312	263,792	183,202	191,832	191,832	(10)
43	-29,571	35,684	98,271	126,652	198,312	243,792	163,202	171,832	171,832	(11)
45	29,571	-35,684	-69,359	0	0	0	0	0	0	(12)
46	105,044	69,359	0	0	0	0	0	0	0	(14)
47	-------	-------	-------	-------	-------	-------	-------	-------	-------	
48	20,000	20,000	48,912	146,652	218,312	263,792	183,202	191,832	191,832	(15)
49	=======	=======	=======	=======	=======	=======	=======	=======	=======	
52	Apr	May	Jun	Jul	Aug	Sep	Oct	Nov	Dec	
53	=======	=======	=======	=======	=======	=======	=======	=======	=======	
55	20,000	20,000	48,912	146,652	218,312	263,792	183,202	191,832	191,832	(16)
56	223,000	266,800	218,700	150,500	97,700	64,700	57,000	57,000	66,900	(17)
57	141,850	91,800	57,150	30,200	22,500	22,500	26,350	34,050	34,050	(18)
59	151,230	129,040	109,020	95,160	89,770	89,000	91,310	94,390	95,160	(19)
60	105,044	69,359	0	0	0	0	0	0	0	(20)
62	128,576	180,201	215,742	232,192	248,742	261,992	175,242	188,492	197,622	(21)

CASH PROJECTION - CASHPROJ

NUMBER	LOCATION(S)	FORMULA
1	R13C8:18	RC[-1]
2	R15C8:18	RC[-1]
3	R24C7:18	LINKED TO DATAPROJ CASH
4	R27C7:18	LINKED TO DATAPROJ PAYMENT
5	R29C7:18	LINKED TO DATAPROJ LTDPAYMENT
6	R30C7:18	LOCRATE/12*R[+30]C[-1]
7	R34C7:18	SUM(R[-7]C:R[-1]C)
8	R39C7:18	COLLECTIONS-DISBURSEMENTS
9	R40C7:18	R[+15]C[-1]
10	R42C7:18	R[-3]C+R[-2]C
11	R43C7:18	R[-1]C-MINCASH
12	R45C7:18	IF(DEFICIT<0,ABS(DEFICIT),IF(AND(DEFICIT>=0, R[+1]C[-1]<0),IF(R[+1]C[-1]>ABS(DEFICIT), -DEFICIT,-R[+1]C[-1],0))
13	R46C7	R[-1]C+R[+14]C[-1]
14	R46C8:18	R[-1]C+RC[-1]
15	R48C8:18	R[-6]C+R[-3]C
16	R55C7:18	R[-7]C
17	R56C6:18	LINKED TO DATAPROJ AR
18	R57C6:18	LINKED TO DATAPROJ INVENTORY
19	R59C6:18	LINKED TO DATAPROJ AP
20	R60C6:18	R[-14]C
21	R62C7:18	R[-7]C+R[-6]C+R[-5]C-R[-3]C-R[-2]C

The minimum acceptable cash balance figure is input in cell R15C7, MINCASH, and spread from R15C8 through R15C18 by the same relative formula as above.

The CASH RECEIPTS SUMMARY begins at row 21. This section summarizes the cash receipts and disbursements for each month. Total cash collections (row 24) is the first account that must be linked with the DATAPROJ model. To establish this link over the range R24C7:18, move the cursor to R24C7 and type the following (assuming that you have used the range names listed in Table DATAPROJ):

Xternal**C**opy**B:DATAPROJ**(TAB)**CASH**(TAB) (TAB)**Y**es(CR)

The example above assumes that the DATAPROJ model is located on Drive B:. CP/M, PC DOS, and MS-DOS versions of Multiplan use this drive name designation. Apple II users will want to change the B:DATAPROJ to DATAPROJ,D2.

Row 27, payment for purchases on credit, is linked with the DATAPROJ range named PAYMENT. To establish this link, move the cursor to R27C7 and use the linking example above, but substitute the name PAYMENT for CASH.

Operating expense (row 28) shows your estimation of total operating expenses by month. Input these operating expense estimates in cells R28C7 through R28C18.

Row 29, long-term debt service, is linked with the LTDPAYMENT range from the DATAPROJ model. To link these ranges, simply move the cursor to R29C7 and substitute LTDPAYMENT for CASH in the example above.

Interest payment on line of credit (row 30) is derived by dividing the line-of-credit interest rate (row 13) by 12 to obtain a monthly rate and multiplying this figure by the line-of-credit balance from row 60. For example, cell R30C7 contains the formula

```
R30C7 I = +LOCRATE/12*R[+30]C[-1]
```

Income tax disbursements (row 31) are entered to reflect quarterly income tax payments. Other disbursements are entered into row 32.

Total cash disbursements totals the cash disbursements with the formula

```
R34C7 I = SUM(R[-7]C:R[-1]C)
```

The formula is then copied from R34C8 through R34C18.

The ANALYSIS OF CASH DISBURSEMENTS starts at row 37. This section analyzes the company's cash flow each month and determines the amount of financing, if any, that is required to meet the company's obligations. Net cash generated this period (row 39) subtracts the cash collected this period from the cash disbursements with the formula

```
R39C7 I = COLLECTIONS-DISBURSEMENTS
```

or

```
R39C7 I = +R[-15]C-R[-5]C
```

The beginning cash balance (row 40) is computed by referring to the cash balance for the prior period in row 55. The formula in cell R40C7 is

```
R40C7 I = +R[+15]C[-1]
```

All the entries in row 40 use this formula.

The cash balance before borrowings (row 42) is equal to the beginning cash balance minus the net cash generated this period. Cell R42C7 contains the formula

```
R42C7 I = +R[-3]C+R[-2]C
```

The amount below the minimum acceptable balance (row 43) must be, therefore, the cash balance before borrowings minus the minimum acceptable cash balance (row 15). This number is the current cash surplus or deficit. The formula in R43C7 is typical of those in this row.

```
R43C7 I = R[-1]C-MINCASH
```

Current period short-term borrowings (row 45) uses If-Then logic to test three conditions:

1. Is the cash balance before borrowings below the minimum acceptable balance? If it is, the amount of borrowings must be the amount below the minimum acceptable balance.
2. If the cash balance before borrowings is greater than the minimum acceptable balance (that is, a cash surplus has been created) and the total short-term borrowings for the previous month are greater than zero (meaning that there are previous short-term borrowings), then you want to repay the prior short-term borrowings.
3. If the total short-term borrowings are greater than the cash surplus, repay an amount equal to the cash surplus. If the total short-term borrowings are less than the cash surplus, repay the entire total short-term borrowings.

The formula in cell R45C7 is typical of the formulas in this row

```
R45C7 I = IF(DEFICIT<0,ABS(DEFICIT),IF(AND(DEFICIT>=0,
          R[+1]C[-1]>0,IF(R[+1]C[-1]>ABS(DEFICIT]),
          -DEFICIT,-R[+1]C[-1]),0))
```

or

R45C7 I = IF(R[-2]C<0,ABS(R[-2]C),IF(AND(R[-2]C>=0,R[+1]C[-1]>0),IF(R[+1]C[-1]>ABS(R[-2]C[-1]),-R[-2]C,-R[+1]C[-1]),0))

Total short-term borrowings begins in R46C7 with the formula

R46C7 I = +R[-1]C+R[+14]C[-1]

This adds the current-period short-term borrowings to the prior month's line-of-credit balance. Subsequent cells in this row, R42C8:18, add last month's total short-term borrowings to current-period (this month's) short-term borrowings with the formula

R46C8:18 I = +R[-1]C+RC[-1]

The ending cash balance (row 48) is the cash balance before borrowings added to current short-term borrowings. Cell R48C7 is typical of the cells in this range.

R48C7 I = +R[-6]C+R[-3]C

BALANCES IN KEY ACCOUNTS begins in row 52. Cash, accounts receivable, and inventory for December are entered in R55:57C6.

The December cash balance must be entered in cell R55C6. The cash balance for January through December is derived from row 48, ending cash balance. For example, cell R55C7 contains the formula

R55C7 I = +R[-7]C

Accounts receivable, in row 56, is linked to the DATAPROJ model's range named AR. To define this cell, simply substitute AR for CASH in the linking example we have used before. Similarly, inventory (row 57) is linked to DATAPROJ's INVENTORY range. Accounts payable (row 59) links with AP in DATAPROJ.

The line-of-credit balance in row 60 is equal to total short-term borrowings (row 46). Net working capital (row 62) is equal to the sum of cash and accounts receivable and inventory minus accounts payable and line of credit. The formula

R62C7:18 I = +R[-7]C+R[-6]C+R[-5]C-R[-3]C-R[-2]C

produces net working capital on the basis of the accounts summarized in this section.

Using the Model

Because of its complexity, this model is more difficult to use than some of the others in this book. The first step in using the model is to collect the data about sales, purchases, interest rates, and so forth, that must be entered in the DATAPROJ model. When the data is ready, enter it into the appropriate cells. You will also need to enter some information in the CASH RECEIPTS SUMMARY and CASH DISBURSEMENTS SUMMARY sections of the CASHPROJ model. After the data has been entered in either model, type F4 or ! to recalculate the model. You can save each model by typing **TSB:** (either DATAPROJ or CASHPROJ) and print each by typing **PP**.

You can also make extensive use of "what if" analysis in this model. Adjust your sales figures, interest rates, minimum cash balance, or any other data, and track the changes through to the BALANCES IN KEY ACCOUNTS section.

Modifications

This model can be modified to fit your business in many ways. Taking the time to customize a cash projection model for your firm can provide you with an extremely valuable financial management tool. Here are some suggestions for modification.

Accounts receivable collection varies significantly from company to company. Some firms do most of their business on a cash basis, whereas others may wait as long as 100 days to receive payment. You can use the Accounts Receivable Collections Tracker in Chapter 5 to help you determine your own business collection pattern, then substitute your figures for those used in this model.

The Cash Projections model includes only summary data for sales and purchases. You may need a model that shows detailed information for each product you sell. Such a model can be built by adding extra rows to the basic layout to include unit sales, price per unit, unit purchases, cost per unit, and net inventory change for each product. An alternative would be to use a separate spreadsheet to compute totals for this data on all products and then use those totals in the model.

Of course, your firm's list of cash disbursements will vary from the one in this model. Any cash outflows you expect in the projection period should be listed under CASH DISBURSEMENTS SUMMARY.

3

Debt Management

Amortizing a Loan

Spreadsheet software is often used to compute loan amortization tables. (Amortization is the process of paying off a loan by installment payments.) Unfortunately, amortizing some loans requires a table that exceeds the memory capacity of most spreadsheets, including Multiplan's. The usual solution to this problem is to build a mortgage model that computes one portion of the table at a time—for example, 60 months—and then use the model repeatedly until the mortgage is completely amortized.

Although most financial spreadsheet software cannot repeat the same operation automatically, Multiplan can. The BASIC programming language, which allows the user to build FOR-NEXT loops to repeat processes, and Multiplan, which is published by the leading publisher of the BASIC programming language, can make several passes through a model at a time. To keep Multiplan from constantly recalculating (because of its topological recalculation feature) a trick is used. The same trick allows amortizations that would otherwise be too long, and therefore too memory consuming, for most microcomputers.

Principles

To build a loan amortization table, you will need three pieces of information: the principal amount borrowed, the annual interest rate charged, and the term of the loan. Using this information, you can compute the monthly payment with the formula

$$(i/(1-((1+i)^{(-n)})))*P$$

Where: i = the monthly interest rate
n = the term of the loan in months
p = the principal borrowed

```
        1        2         3          4          5         6         7
 1 ======================================================================
 2 LOAN AMORTIZATION CALCULATOR                Copyright (C) QUE Corp. 1983
 3 ======================================================================
 4
 5           For ASSUMPTIONS (G)oto (N)ame `ASSUMPTIONS'
 6           For AMORTIZATION TABLE, (G)oto (N)ame `TABLE'
 7           For INSTRUCTIONS, (G)oto (N)ame `INSTRUCTIONS'
 8
 9 ======================================================================
10 ASSUMPTIONS                                                 Sheet 1.1
11 ======================================================================
12
13
14           Annual Interest Rate:                                 18%
15           Principal Amount:                          $  100,000
16           Term in Months:                                     240
17           Monthly Payment:                       (1) $1,543.31
18
19
20
21 ======================================================================
22 AMORTIZATION TABLE (Continues to row 87)                    Sheet 2.1
23 ======================================================================
24                      Beginning                       Remaining    Next
25                      Principal  Interest  Principal  Principal  Period &
26                Month  Balance     Paid      Paid      Balance    Amount
27                ----- ---------  --------- ---------  ---------  ---------
28            (2)  1 100,000.00(4)1,500.00  (7)43.31  99,956.69        61 (12)
29                 2  99,956.69  1,499.35    43.96   99,912.73 95,832.80 (13)
30                 3  99,912.73  1,498.69    44.62   99,868.11
31                 4  99,868.11  1,498.02    45.29   99,822.82
32                 5  99,822.82  1,497.34    45.97   99,776.85
33                 6  99,776.85  1,496.65    46.66   99,730.19
34                 7  99,730.19  1,495.95    47.36   99,682.83
35                 8  99,682.83  1,495.24    48.07   99,634.76
36                 9  99,634.76  1,494.52    48.79   99,585.97
37                10  99,585.97  1,493.79    49.52   99,536.45
38                11  99,536.45  1,493.05    50.26   99,486.18
39                12  99,486.18  1,492.29    51.02   99,435.17
40                13  99,435.17  1,491.53    51.78   99,383.38
41            (3) 14  99,383.38(5)1,490.75(6)(8)52.56  99,330.82(9)
42                15  99,330.82  1,489.96    53.35   99,277.47
43                16  99,277.47  1,489.16    54.15   99,223.32
44                17  99,223.32  1,488.35    54.96   99,168.36
45                18  99,168.36  1,487.53    55.79   99,112.57
46                19  99,112.57  1,486.69    56.62   99,055.95
47                20  99,055.95  1,485.84    57.47   98,998.48
48                21  98,998.48  1,484.98    58.33   98,940.14
49                22  98,940.14  1,484.10    59.21   98,880.94
50                23  98,880.94  1,483.21    60.10   98,820.84
51                24  98,820.84  1,482.31    61.00   98,759.84
52                25  98,759.84  1,481.40    61.91   98,697.92
53                26  98,697.92  1,480.47    62.84   98,635.08
54                27  98,635.08  1,479.53    63.79   98,571.30
55                28  98,571.30  1,478.57    64.74   98,506.55
56                29  98,506.55  1,477.60    65.71   98,440.84
```

	1	2	3	4	5	6	7
57		30	98,440.84	1,476.61	66.70	98,374.14	
58		31	98,374.14	1,475.61	67.70	98,306.44	
59		32	98,306.44	1,474.60	68.71	98,237.73	
60		33	98,237.73	1,473.57	69.75	98,167.98	
61		34	98,167.98	1,472.52	70.79	98,097.19	
62		35	98,097.19	1,471.46	71.85	98,025.34	
63		36	98,025.34	1,470.38	72.93	97,952.41	
64		37	97,952.41	1,469.29	74.03	97,878.38	
65		38	97,878.38	1,468.18	75.14	97,803.24	
66		39	97,803.24	1,467.05	76.26	97,726.98	
67		40	97,726.98	1,465.90	77.41	97,649.57	
68		41	97,649.57	1,464.74	78.57	97,571.01	
69		42	97,571.01	1,463.57	79.75	97,491.26	
70		43	97,491.26	1,462.37	80.94	97,410.32	
71		44	97,410.32	1,461.15	82.16	97,328.16	
72		45	97,328.16	1,459.92	83.39	97,244.77	
73		(3) 46	97,244.77 (5)	1,458.67 (6)	(8) 84.64	97,160.13 (9)	
74		47	97,160.13	1,457.40	85.91	97,074.22	
75		48	97,074.22	1,456.11	87.20	96,987.02	
76		49	96,987.02	1,454.81	88.51	96,898.52	
77		50	96,898.52	1,453.48	89.83	96,808.68	
78		51	96,808.68	1,452.13	91.18	96,717.50	
79		52	96,717.50	1,450.76	92.55	96,624.95	
80		53	96,624.95	1,449.37	93.94	96,531.02	
81		54	96,531.02	1,447.97	95.35	96,435.67	
82		55	96,435.67	1,446.54	96.78	96,338.89	
83		56	96,338.89	1,445.08	98.23	96,240.67	
84		57	96,240.67	1,443.61	99.70	96,140.96	
85		58	96,140.96	1,442.11	101.20	96,039.77	
86		59	96,039.77	1,440.60	102.72	95,937.05	
87		60	95,937.05	1,439.06	104.26	95,832.80 (10)	
88						TRUE (11)	
89							

```
 90 ===========================================================
 91 INSTRUCTIONS                                       Sheet 3.1
 92 ===========================================================
 93           1) Enter ASSUMPTIONS
 94           2) Recalculate by typing: F4 or !
 95           3) PRINT by typing: POR9C1:R87C6 (CR) P
 96           4) If loan term exceeds 60 periods:
 97              a) Recalculate again by typing: F4 or !
 98              b) PRINT by typing: POR28C1:R87C6 (CR) P
 99              c) Repeat a) and b) until finished
100           5) To clear model, enter 0 in R15C6
```

AMORTIZING A LOAN (MORTGAGE)

NUMBER	LOCATION(S)	FORMULA
1	R17C6	(RATE/12)/(1-((1+RATE/12))^(-TERM)))*AMOUNT
2	R28C2	RC[+5]
3	R29:87C2	R[-1]C+1
4	R28C3	IF(R[+1]C[+4]=0,AMOUNT,R[+1]C[+4])
5	R29:87C3	R[-1]C[+3]
6	R28:87C4	RC[-1]*RATE/12
7	R28C5	IF(RC[-2]>0.005,PAYMENT-RC[-1],0)
8	R29:87C5	IF(RC[-2]<0.005,0,PAYMENT-RC[-1])
9	R28:86C6	RC[-3]-RC[-1]
10	R87C6	IF(AMOUNT=0,0,RC[-3]-RC[-1])
11	R88C6	TRUE() *NOTE THIS IS THE COMPLETION TEST
12	R28C7	IF(TEST<0.005,1,R87C2+1)
13	R29C7	IF(TEST<0.005,AMOUNT,TEST)

Simple relationships govern the computation of month-by-month amortization. The interest paid in any given month is computed by multiplying the monthly interest rate by the outstanding principal balance. The amount of principal paid in a month is determined by subtracting the interest payment from the total monthly payment. The principal balance at the end of the month is derived by subtracting the principal payment for the month from the beginning principal balance.

The model shows how these relationships work. In the example, the principal amount borrowed is $100,000. The annual interest rate is 18%, and the term is 240 months. The monthly payment, computed using the formula above, is $1,543.31. The interest payment for the first month is

$100,000 X (.18/12) = $1,500

The amount of principal repaid the first month is therefore

$1,543.31 - $1,500.00 = $43.31

This payment reduces the outstanding principal balance to $99,956.69. For the following month, the interest payment will be

$99,956.69 X (.18/12) = $1,499.35

The principal repayment in that month has increased by $.65 to $43.96. The same pattern of decreasing interest payments and increasing principal payments continues until the loan is completely repaid after 240 months.

The Model

The Loan Amortization Calculator has two sections: ASSUMPTIONS and the AMORTIZATION TABLE.

MORTGAGE: Locations of Named Cells and Ranges

Description	**Location**	**Name**
ASSUMPTIONS	R11C1	ASSUMPTIONS
Interest Rate	R14C6	RATE
Principal Amount	R15C6	AMOUNT
Term in Months	R16C6	TERM
Monthly Payment	R17C6	PAYMENT
AMORTIZATION TABLE	R23C1	TABLE
COMPLETION TEST	R88C6	TEST
INSTRUCTIONS	R92C1	INSTRUCTIONS

The ASSUMPTIONS section begins at row 10. Cells R14C6 (which is formatted to display a percentage), R15C6, and R16C6 are used to input the annual interest rate; the principal borrowed; and the term, in months, of the loan. Cell R17C6 uses this information to compute the monthly loan payment. The formula in this cell is

```
R17C6 F2 = (R14C6/12)/(1-((1+(R14C6/12))^
            (-R16C6)))*R15C6
```

or

```
R17C6 F2 = (RATE/12)/(1-((1+(RATE/12))^
            (-TERM)))*AMOUNT
```

The Amortization Table begins in cell R28C7. This cell checks cell R87C6 to see if the model is in the middle of a sequence of calculations. It uses the If-Then-Else logic of

R28C7 = IF(R88C6<0.005,1,R87C2+1)

or

R28C7 = IF(TEST<0.005,1,R87C2+1)

If there is no remaining Principal Balance in cell R87C2, the loan has been fully amortized and the number 1 is placed in cell R28C7. If Cell R87C2 has a balance (a number greater than .005), cell R28C7 adds 1 to the last month number and places it in cell R28C2. The formula in R28C2

R28C2 I = R28C7

or

R28C2 I = +RC[+5]

refers to R28C7, the cell that determines the month number of the amortization. The formula in cell R29C2 represents the next number in whichever 60-month cycle the model is currently amortizing. The formula

R29C2 I = R28C2+1

or

R29C2 I = +R[-1]C+1

adds 1 to the previous number. If you use Multiplan's **C**opy command, the cell can be **C**opied **D**own 58 rows in just 5 keystrokes.

Cell R29C7 performs a similar check. If the Principal Remaining in cell R88C6, TEST, is 0, the formula returns the Beginning Balance from cell R15C6, AMOUNT. If the Principal Remaining is greater than 0, cell R29C7 returns the last calculated Principal Remaining. The formula in R29C7 is

R29C7 F2 = IF(R88C6<0.005,R15C6,R88C6)

or

R29C7 F2 = IF(TEST<0.005,AMOUNT,TEST)

Beginning Principal Balance for each amortizing period is calculated in cell R28C3, which contains the formula

R28C3 F2 = IF(R[+1]C[+4]=0,AMOUNT,R[+1]C[+4])

Cell R28C3 checks R29C7. If the Remaining Principal Balance is 0, cell R29C7 returns the Beginning Principal. If cell R29C7 is greater than 0, the last Remaining Principal Balance in R29C7 is returned.

The formula in R28C4,

R28C4 F2 = +RC[-1]*R[-14]C[+2]/12

shows Interest Paid for each monthly period. This value is determined by taking the Annual Interest Rate, multiplying by the Beginning Principal Balance for the monthly period, and dividing the result by 12 (the interest rate is based on 12 months).

Principal Paid, shown in cell R28C5, is the amount of the payment less the Interest Paid for each monthly period. The formula in cell R28C5 is

R28C5 F2 = IF(RC[-2]>0.005PAYMENT-RC[-1],0)

In the amortization process, the Beginning Principal Balance can become so small that the model shows a negative Principal Paid amount (obviously incorrect). The formula checks each month's Beginning Principal Balance. If this value is greater than .005, the Beginning Principal Balance minus the interest paid that month is returned. If the Principal is fully repaid, cell RC[-2] will be less than .005, and a 0 is returned. The formula can then be **C**opied **D**own 59 rows, again saving hundreds of keystrokes

The Remaining Principal Balance is the Beginning Principal Balance minus Interest Paid. The formula

R28C6 F2 = +RC[-3]-RC[-1]

calculates this, and it too can be **C**opied **D**own 58 rows. However, the last formula in column 6, R87C6, checks to see if the Principal Amount is 0, so that the model can be reset to begin a different amortization.

R87C6 F2 = IF(AMOUNT=0,0,RC[-3]-RC[-1])

If the value in R15C6 is 0, a 0 is returned; otherwise, the model performs the normal "Beginning Principal Balance minus Interest Paid" Calculation. Cell R87C6 is named TEST, and the name is used in formulas in cells R28C7 and R29C7.

For the remaining months, the Beginning Principal Balance is equal to the Remaining Principal Balance for the month before. The formula in R29C3

R29C3 F2 = +R[-1]C[+3]

which determines this balance, can be **C**opied **D**own 58 rows.

Using the Model

To use the model, enter the loan data shown in the example in cells R14C6, R15C6, and R16C6. You can enter the monthly payment in cell R17C6 or let the model make that computation for you. Be sure to set Multiplan to manual recalculation by typing **O**ptions **N**o.

Type F4 or ! to recalculate the model. It will take a few seconds for the whole table to finish calculating. Scroll the cursor around the table, looking at the flow of the amortization through the cells. (You may want to split the screen to view the top and the bottom of the model at the same time.)

Notice that cell R87C6 contains the value 95832.80. This is the principal balance remaining at the end of 60 months. Before you do anything else, print a copy of this portion of the amortization, using the command **POR9C1:R88C6**(CR)**P**.

To activate the loop, type F4 or ! If all is well, cell R28C2 will show the number 61, and cell R28C3 will assume the value that just appeared in cell R87C6. The model will then automatically flow through another 60 months. Row 87 will display the 120th amortization period, and cell R87C6 will contain an ending balance of 85651.40.

Print the model again, this time beginning at row 28 with the subcommand **P**rint **O**ptions **R28C1:R88C1**(CR)**P**.

The second 60 months of the table will be printed. If you have not taken out the paper from the first output, your printout will appear as one long table.

To complete the amortization process, repeat the last steps two more times, as this example has a term of 240 months. Once the loan is completely amortized, type F4 or ! to start the amortization over from the beginning.

To clear the model, enter 0 in cell R15C6 and type F4 or ! twice. At the end of that process, the model will be filled with zeros, and you will be ready to begin a new problem.

Modifications

You can use this model even if your computer has less than 64K of RAM memory. By shortening the length of each pass through the table from 60 periods to 30 or 20 periods, you can make the model work on almost any machine. However, more passes will be needed to solve a problem completely.

This model illustrates one way to approach a problem creatively while using Multiplan fully. By altering the model to meet your own needs, you will find other ways to use this looping technique in your models.

Prepaying a Loan

If you decide to pay off a loan early, how do you determine what amount to pay? A simple mathematical technique can answer this question. Known as the Rule of 78s, it has been incorporated into this Multiplan model.

Principles

Many loans are paid off according to a schedule of uniform monthly payments, each consisting of an interest portion and a principal portion. The interest payment is based on the amount of principal owed and the interest rate on the loan. As the payments progress and the amount of principal owed declines, the interest charges are reduced. This reduction changes the composition of the loan payments. At first, each payment consists of a high interest component and a low principal component because interest is being computed based on the full principal amount. Toward the end of the term of the loan, the composition of the loan payment changes to a low interest component and a high principal component.

For example, consider a $1,500 loan with an annual add-on interest rate of 12.75% and 24 monthly payments of $71.58. The first payment includes the interest owed on $1,500 for one month. This amount is calculated as one-twelfth (or one month's worth) of 12.75% of $1,500, or $15.94. The rest of the payment, $55.54, is applied to paying off the principal. Since this loan carries add-on interest, the interest component for the next monthly payment is also computed from the principal of $1,500.00. Each monthly payment of $71.58 consists of a $15.94 interest payment and a $55.54 principal payment.

When you pay off a loan early, you receive an interest rebate from the bank. The amount of the rebate depends on the amount of

```
      1        2        3        4        5        6        7        8
 1 ========================================================================
 2 LOAN PAYOFF CALCULATOR                            Copyright (C) QUE Corp. 1983
 3 ========================================================================
 4
 5          For ASSUMPTIONS (G)oto (N)ame 'ASSUMPTIONS'
 6          For SOLUTIONS (G)oto (N)ame 'SOLUTIONS'
 7          For INSTRUCTIONS (G)oto (N)ame 'INSTRUCTIONS'
 8
 9 ========================================================================
10 ASSUMPTIONS                                                    Sheet 1.1
11 ========================================================================
12
13
14          Principal Amount:                        $1500.00
15          Annual Interest Rate:                      12.67%
16          Term in Months:                                24
17          Last Payment Made Was Number:                  19
18          Monthly Payment:                           $71.58
19
20
21 ========================================================================
22 SOLUTIONS                                                      Sheet 2.1
23 ========================================================================
24
25          Total Interest Paid at Full Term:         $380.10 ①
26
27          Total of Remaining Payments:              $357.90 ②
28          Interest Rebate Due:                       $19.01 ③
29                                                     ------
30          Payment Required to Retire Loan:          $338.90 ④
31                                                     ======
32
33
34
35
36
37
38
39
40 ========================================================================
41 INSTRUCTIONS                                                   Sheet 3.1
42 ========================================================================
43
44
45                   1) Enter ASSUMPTIONS
46                   2) RECALCULATE by typing: F4 or !
47                   3) SAVE by typing: TSB:RULE78S (CR)
48                   4) PRINT by typing: PP
```

PREPAYING A LOAN (RULE OF 78'S)

NUMBER	LOCATION(S)	FORMULA
1	R25C6	(PAYMENT*TERM)-PRINCIPAL
2	R27C6	(TERM-LASTPAY)*PAYMENT
3	R28C6	((TERM-LASTPAY+1)*(TERM-LASTPAY))/ ((TERM^2)+TERM)*TOTALINT
4	R30C6	REMAININGPAY-REBATE

interest in the remaining monthly payments. However, it is not easy to determine what part is interest and what part is principal. To solve this problem, use the Rule of 78s formula for calculating the interest rebate due if the loan is retired. This amount can then be subtracted from the total of the remaining payments to yield the payment needed to retire the loan early. The Rule of 78s formula for interest rebate is

$$\frac{(n - k + 1)(n - k)}{n^2 + n} \times \text{total interest cost of loan}$$

where n equals the number of payments in full term and k equals the number of payment periods that will have expired when the loan is paid off.

The first step in using this formula is to compute the total interest cost of the loan. To do this, multiply the principal borrowed by the number of original payment periods and again by the interest rate (divided by 12) to determine the total interest that would be paid for the full term of the loan. For example, in the loan described above, the total interest paid over the term of the loan is $1,500 multiplied by 24 months multiplied by 12.67 divided by 12, or $380.10.

The next step is to plug this interest cost as well as the other variables into the Rule of 78s equation. Let's assume that 19 payments have been made and that the borrower wants to go ahead and pay off the rest of the loan. Because there is a 24-month payment schedule, "n" in the formula is 24; "k" in the formula is 19 because 19 payments have been made. Plugging in these numbers gives us the equation

$$\frac{(24 - 19 + 1)(24 - 19)}{24^2 + 24} \times 380.10$$

The solution to this equation is $19.01, which represents the interest rebate due on the loan. This amount must now be subtracted from the amount we would pay if we were to continue making monthly payments, which is calculated as (24 - 19) x $71.58, or $357.90. Subtracting $19.01 from $357.90 yields $338.90 as the amount needed to pay off the loan after 19 monthly payments.

The Model

The Loan Payoff Calculator has two sections: ASSUMPTIONS and SOLUTIONS. The ASSUMPTIONS section, which begins at row 10, contains information about the loan being evaluated: the principal amount, annual interest rate, term in months, the number of the last payment made, and the monthly payment amount.

RULE78S: Locations of Named Cells and Ranges

Description	**Location**	**Name**
ASSUMPTIONS	R11C1	ASSUMPTIONS
Principal Amount	R14C6	PRINCIPAL
Annual Interest Rate	R15C6	INTEREST
Term in Months	R16C6	TERM
Last Payment Made Was Number	R17C6	LASTPAY
Monthly Payment	R18C6	PAYMENT
SOLUTIONS	R23C1	SOLUTIONS
Total Interest Paid at Full Term	R25C6	TOTALINT
Total of Remaining Payments	R27C6	REMAININGPAY
Interest Rebate Due	R28C6	REBATE
INSTRUCTIONS	R42C1	INSTRUCTIONS

The SOLUTIONS section begins at row 22. Cell R25C6, TOTALINT, contains the calculation for the total amount of interest paid if all payments are made. This amount is computed by multiplying the monthly payment by the term in months and then subtracting the principal.

R25C6 $ = (R14C6*R15C6/12*R16C6)

or

R25C6 $ = (PRINCIPAL*INTEREST/12*TERM)

Next, cell R27C6, REMAININGPAY, computes the amount due on the loan by multiplying the number of remaining payments by the monthly payment amount, using the formula

R27C6 $ = (R16C6-R17C6)*R18C6

or

R27C6 $ = (TERM-LASTPAY)*PAYMENT

Cell R28C6, REMAININGPAY, uses the Rule of 78s equation to compute the interest component for future payments:

R28C6 $ = ((R16C6-R17C6+1)*(R16C6-R17C6))/((R16C6^2)+R16C6)*R25C6

or

R28C6 $ = ((TERM-LASTPAY+1)*(TERM-LASTPAY))/((TERM^2)+TERM)*TOTALINT

Finally, cell R30C6 displays the amount needed to pay off the loan, which is computed by subtracting the result in cell R28C6, REBATE, from the value in cell R27C6, REMAININGPAY, using the formula

R30C6 $ = R27C6-R28C6

or

R30C6 $ = REMAININGPAY-REBATE

Using the Model

To use this model, enter the ASSUMPTIONS data and type F4 or ! to recalculate. The amount required to pay off the loan will appear in cell R30C6. You can save a completed calculation by typing **TSB:RULE78S** (CR) and print the model by typing **PP**.

Note that banks in some states use formulas other than the Rule of 78s to compute loan rebates. Be sure to check with your banker to see if this formula applies in your state.

Modifications

Designed to work with any loan that has a uniform series of payments, this model can be modified to reflect payments made on a quarterly or annual basis. For a quarterly repayment plan, substitute the quarterly payment amount for the monthly payment amount, then state the term of the loan as well as the number of payments made in quarters. For example, if a loan has a five- year term of which two years have elapsed, then the term of the loan is 20 quarters, and the last payment will be number 8 (2 years times 4 quarters per year).

Tracking a Line of Credit

Does your company have a line of credit with a bank? If so, you may have found that following the activity in that line of credit is not an easy task. This Multiplan model can help you track line-of-credit activity and calculate a total interest expense for each month.

Principles

Knowing how much you use your line of credit and what it costs your company is essential to good financial management. Many short-term credit arrangements require that the borrowing company pay off its loans completely in a specified period of time. Meeting this condition may be difficult for a rapidly growing company. An expanding company must also know when its current line of credit has become inadequate and more funds must be negotiated.

The interest you pay for your line of credit depends on both the amount you borrow and the interest rate on your loan. The amount of your loan can change frequently, depending on the cash inflows and outflows of your operations. Typically, the interest rate on a line of credit is tied to the bank's prime rate; therefore, the rate will vary as the prime goes up or down.

Tracking the activity in your line of credit requires daily monitoring of the interest rate being charged and the amount of the loan outstanding. If you use the line of credit frequently, this monitoring can become a complex task.

The Model

This model is designed to keep a daily record of the outstanding balance of funds borrowed from a line of credit and the interest rate

```
        1        2        3        4        5        6        7        8
 1 ========================================================================
 2 LINE-OF-CREDIT TRACKER                     Copyright (C) QUE Corp. 1983
 3 ========================================================================
 4
 5          For DAILY ACTIVITY (G)oto (N)ame 'ACTIVITY'
 6          For TOTALS AND AVERAGES (G)oto (N)ame 'TOTALSANDAVERAGES'
 7          For INSTRUCTIONS, (G)oto (N)ame 'INSTRUCTIONS'
 8
 9 ========================================================================
10 DAILY ACTIVITY (Continues to R47C1)                             Sheet 1.1
11 ========================================================================
12
13                   Previous                      Annual             Total
14                     Day's      New            Interest Interest   Credit
15          Date     Balance   Credit Repayment    Rate   Expense   Balance
16          ----    --------  ------- --------  --------  --------  -------
17          9-1     $3500.00                      15.50%     $1.49  $3501.49
18           -2     $3501.49                      15.50%     $1.49  $3502.97
19           -3     $3502.97          $3502.97    15.50%     $0.00     $0.00
20           -4        $0.00                      15.50%     $0.00     $0.00
21           -5        $0.00 $1500.00             15.50%     $0.64  $1500.64
22           -6     $1500.64                      15.50%     $0.64  $1501.28
23           -7     $1501.28                      15.50%     $0.64  $1501.92
24           -8     $1501.92                      15.50%     $0.64  $1502.55
25           -9     $1502.55                      15.50%     $0.64  $1503.19
26           -10    $1503.19                      15.50%     $0.64  $1503.83
27           -11    $1503.83                      15.50%  ③ $0.64  $1504.47
28           -12    $1504.47                      15.50%     $0.64  $1505.11
29           -13    $1505.11                      15.50%     $0.64  $1505.75
30           -14    $1505.75                      15.50%     $0.64  $1506.39 ⑥
31           -15 ②  $1506.39          $1506.39    15.50%     $0.00     $0.00
32      ①    -16       $0.00                      15.50%     $0.00  ⑤  $0.00
33           -17       $0.00                      15.50%     $0.00     $0.00
34           -18       $0.00 $2200.00             15.50%     $0.93  $2200.93
35           -19    $2200.93                      15.50%     $0.93  $2201.87
36           -20    $2201.87                      15.50%     $0.94  $2202.80
37           -21    $2202.80                      15.50%     $0.94  $2203.74
38           -22    $2203.74                      15.50%     $0.94  $2204.67
39           -23    $2204.67                      16.50%     $1.00  $2205.67
40           -24    $2205.67                      16.50%     $1.00  $2206.67
41           -25    $2206.67                      16.50%     $1.00  $2207.67
42           -26    $2207.67                      16.50%     $1.00  $2208.66
43           -27    $2208.66                      16.50%  ④ $1.00  $2209.66
44           -28    $2209.66                      16.50%     $1.00  $2210.66
45           -29    $2210.66                      16.50%     $1.00  $2211.66
46           -30    $2211.66                      16.50%     $1.00  $2212.66
47           -31    $2212.66                      16.50%     $1.00  $2213.66
48
49
```

```
      1         2         3         4         5         6         7         8
50 ========================================================================
51 TOTALS AND AVERAGES                                             Sheet 2.1
52 ========================================================================
53
54          Total Interest Expense:                        $23.02 (7)
55
56          Average Daily Outstanding Credit Balance:    $1707.76 (8)
57
58
59
60
61
62
63
64 ========================================================================
65 INSTRUCTIONS                                                    Sheet 3.1
66 ========================================================================
67
68
69                   1) Enter DAILY ACTIVITY data
70                   2) RECALCULATE by typing: F4 or !
71                   3) SAVE by typing: TSB:LOCTRACK (CR)
72                   4) PRINT by typing: PP
```

LINE-OF-CREDIT TRACKER (LOCKTRACK)

NUMBER	LOCATION(S)	FORMULA
1	R19:47C2	R[-1]C-1
2	R18:47C3	R[-1]C[+5]
3	R18:38C6	R[-1]C
4	R40:47C6	R[-1]C
5	R17:47C7	(RATE/365)*(PREVBAL+NEWCREDIT-REPAY)
6	R17:47C8	PREVBAL+NEWCREDIT-REPAY+EXPENSE
7	R54C7	SUM(EXPENSE)
8	R56C7	SUM(CRBALANCE)/ABS(LASTDAY)

applied to that balance. Each day, new extensions or repayments of credit can be added to or subtracted from the outstanding balance to yield a new balance. Daily interest charges are also added to the balance. To compute daily interest charges, each day's interest rate is multiplied by the outstanding balance. At the end of the month, the daily interest charges are added to yield the total interest expense for the month. The daily outstanding credit balances are also added and then divided by the number of days in the month to yield the average daily credit balance.

LOCTRACK: Locations of Named Cells and Ranges

Description	**Location**	**Name**
DAILY ACTIVITY	R11C1	ACTIVITY
Previous Day's Balance	R17:47C3	PREVBAL
New Credit Today	R17:47C4	NEWCREDIT
Repayment	R17:47C5	REPAY
Annual Interest Rate	R17:47C6	RATE
Interest Expense	R17:47C7	EXPENSE
Total Credit Balance	R17:47C8	CRBALANCE
(The last day of the month tracked)	R47C2	LASTDAY
TOTALS AND AVERAGES	R52C1	TOTALSANDAVERAGES
INSTRUCTIONS	R66C1	INSTRUCTIONS

The model has two sections: DAILY ACTIVITY and TOTALS AND AVERAGES. The DAILY ACTIVITY section begins at row 10. Column 2 contains the dates for the current month. The first date, in cell R17C2, is entered as a label.

R17C2 = "9-1"

The second date, in cell R18C2, is entered as the number -2. Multiplan computes the other dates by subtracting 1 from the date above. For example, cell R19C2 contains the formula

R19C2 I = +R[-1]C-1

This formula is replicated to cells R20C2 through R47C2 for a 31-day month.

The cells in column 3 contain the balance outstanding at the beginning of each day in the current month. Cell R17C3, PREVBAL, shows the current month's opening credit balance.

Columns 4 and 5 are used to post any new borrowing or repayments that occur during the month.

Column 6 shows the annual interest rate on the line of credit for each day in the current month. Cell R17C6 contains the rate that is in effect on the first of the month. Notice that cell R18C6 is defined as equal to R17C6.

R18C6 % = +R[-1]C

All the cells in column 6 are similarly defined. The model assumes that the interest rate in effect on the first of the month will remain in effect until you change the figure manually. As the month progresses and interest rates change, you can alter the rate in effect by entering a new number in the appropriate cell in column 6. The new rate will be carried forward to the end of the period or until changed again.

Multiplan computes the daily interest expense in column 7. First, the annual interest rate is divided by 365 to obtain a daily rate. Then the daily rate is multiplied by the previous day's balance (column 4) plus any new extensions, less repayments. For example, the daily interest expense for September 1, displayed in cell R17C7 is calculated by the formula

R17C7 F2 = (R17C6/365)*(R17C3+R17C4-R17C5)

or

EXPENSE F2= (RATE/365)*(PREVBAL+
NEWCREDIT-REPAY)

Column 8 displays the daily outstanding credit balance. This balance is computed by adding the new extensions of credit to the previous day's balance, subtracting repayments, and adding the day's interest charge. As an example, consider the formula for total outstanding credit on September 1, in cell R17C8, CRBALANCE,

R17C8 $ = R17C3+R17C4-R17C5+R17C7

or

CRBALANCE $ = PREVBAL+NEWCREDIT-REPAY+EXPENSE

This balance appears again in column 3 as the following day's "Previous Day's Balance." Each cell in column 3 refers to a cell in column 8 on the immediately preceding row. For example, the previous day's balance in cell R25C3 contains the reference

R25C3 $ = R24C8

or

R25C3 $ = +R[-1]C[+5]

The TOTALS AND AVERAGES section of the model begins at row 51. The total interest expense for the month, in cell R54C7, is calculated by adding the daily interest charges. The formula in this cell is

R54C7 $ = SUM(R17C7:R47C7)

or

R54C7 $ = SUM(EXPENSE)

The average daily outstanding credit, displayed in cell R56C7, is computed by adding the daily balances in column 8 and dividing the total by the number of days in the month. This number is calculated by taking the absolute value of the last date in column 2. The formula to compute the average credit outstanding is

R56C7 F2 = SUM(R17C8:R47C8)/ABS(R47C2)

or

R56C7 F2 = SUM(CRBALANCE)/ABS(LASTDAY)

Using the Model

Begin each month by entering the outstanding balance and the interest rate for the first day of the month into cells R17C3, PREVBAL, and R17C6, RATE. As the month progresses, post additional borrowings or repayments to the appropriate cells in columns 4 and 5. Be sure to track the rate of interest being charged by your bank and post any changes to the model as they occur. At the end of each day, type F4 or ! to recalculate. You can save the model by typing **TSB:LOCTRACK** (CR). At the end of the month, print the model by typing **PP**.

You should recognize that the average daily outstanding credit balance will not be accurate until the entire month's activity has been posted. Because some months have fewer than 31 days, you will need to modify the model at the beginning of these months by using Multiplan's **DR** command to eliminate one or more rows. When you make this change, be sure you do not delete row 47. Instead, delete a row or rows further up in the model to prevent #VALUE! error messages in cell R56C7.

Modifications

You may want to consider a few modifications when you build a model to track your firm's line-of-credit activity. If you add a column for the daily prime rate, then you can enter a formula that will compute the interest rate based on the prime rate for you, instead of having to figure the rate manually. For example, your interest rate might be 1 point below the prime if the prime is greater than or equal to 15%, and 14% if the prime is less than or equal to 15%. These conditions can be built into a formula using Multiplan's IF function.

With sufficient computer memory and disk space, you can also build several months' credit tracking on several spreadsheets, and compute both monthly and quarterly averages on the outstanding principal.

If you have lines of credit with different lenders, you can build a model for each source of funds and then combine the averages of these models into one summary model.

4

Fixed Asset Management

Calculating ACRS Depreciation

Calculating ACRS Depreciation

The Economic Recovery Tax Act of 1981, passed by Congress on August 4, 1981, overhauled the federal income tax system by cutting tax rates, increasing certain deduction amounts, and changing regulations in many areas. One of these changes was the introduction of a new set of depreciation rules called the accelerated cost recovery system (ACRS). ACRS differs from past tax depreciation methods in significant ways. Let's take a look at ACRS and at a Multiplan model that calculates ACRS depreciation schedules.

Principles

Before ACRS, assets were depreciated using the straight-line, the declining-balance, or the sum-of-the-years'-digits method. All three methods involved assigning a "useful life" to an asset and then computing depreciation expense in relation to the age of the asset. For example, with the straight-line method, a $10,000 asset with a useful life of 10 years would be depreciated at the rate of $1,000 per year, computed as 1/10 times $10,000 (the asset value).

ACRS abandons the concept of useful life. Instead, it assigns assets to one of five recovery-life categories: 3-year property, 5-year property, 10-year property, 15-year utility property, and 15-year real property. The 3-year class includes automobiles, light trucks, and equipment used in research and development. Most other machinery and equipment fall into the 5-year category. The 10-year property and 15-year utility classes cover public utility property and certain types of real estate, such as theme parks. The 15-year real property category covers all other real estate.

In each range, ACRS specifies the amount of depreciation that may be taken in a year. The tables below show the annual percentages for all five classes of assets. These tables are reproduced in two tables—a Lookup table and an Index table—in this Multiplan model.

ACRS DEPRECIATION TABLES

Property:	**Percentage**
3-year:	
Year 1	25
Year 2	38
Year 3	37
5-year:	
Year 1	15
Year 2	22
Year 3	21
Year 4	21
Year 5	21
10-year:	
Year 1	8
Year 2	14
Year 3	12
Year 4	10
Year 5	10
Year 6	10
Year 7	9
Year 8	9
Year 9	9
Year 10	9
15-year Public Utility Property	
Year 1	5
Year 2	10
Year 3	9
Year 4	8
Year 5	7
Year 6	7
Year 7	6
Year 8	6
Year 9	6
Year 10	6

Year 11	6
Year 12	6
Year 13	6
Year 14	6
Year 15	6

ACRS COST RECOVERY TABLE FOR REAL ESTATE

If the Recovery Year is:	The percentage is determined by the month in the first year the asset was placed in service:											
	1	2	3	4	5	6	7	8	9	10	11	12
1	12	11	10	9	8	7	6	5	4	3	2	1
2	10	10	11	11	11	11	11	11	11	11	11	12
3	9	9	9	9	10	10	10	10	10	10	10	10
4	8	8	8	8	8	8	9	9	9	9	9	9
5	7	7	7	7	7	7	8	8	8	8	8	8
6	6	6	6	6	7	7	7	7	7	7	7	7
7	6	6	6	6	6	6	6	6	6	6	6	6
8	6	6	6	6	6	6	5	6	6	6	6	6
9	6	6	6	6	5	6	5	5	5	6	6	6
10	5	6	5	6	5	5	5	5	5	5	6	5
11	5	5	5	5	5	5	5	5	5	5	5	5
12	5	5	5	5	5	5	5	5	5	5	5	5
13	5	5	5	5	5	5	5	5	5	5	5	5
14	5	5	5	5	5	5	5	5	5	5	5	5
15	5	5	5	5	5	5	5	5	5	5	5	5
16	0	0	1	1	2	2	3	3	4	4	4	5

Basis is another important tax concept. The basis of an asset is the original cost of the asset less depreciation expense (and, in some cases, less a portion of the investment tax credit). When the asset is purchased, its basis equals its purchase price. After two years, the basis is reduced by two years' depreciation.

Depreciation is not the only expense that affects the basis of an asset. The 1981 Act also allows a business to consider as an expense a portion of its capital investment in the year the expenditure is made. This expense is limited to $5,000 in 1982 and 1983, $7,500 in 1984 and 1985, and $10,000 after 1985. This rule benefits small businesses that make limited capital investments every year.

For example, if a company purchases less than $5,000 of assets in 1982, it can fully treat as an expense those assets the same year, lowering income tax by as much as $2,500. Companies that purchase more assets can also benefit under this rule, although the relative benefit declines as the level of investment rises.

The final element in the tax treatment of assets is the INVESTMENT TAX CREDIT (ITC), which was exacted by Congress in the 1960s to encourage businesses to invest in capital goods. The 1981 Act liberalized the ITC rules. Under the new provisions, 3-year assets earn a 6% ITC, and all other assets earn a 10% credit. Unlike depreciation (obtained by deducting tax expense from income to arrive at taxable income), the ITC is a credit that is subtracted directly from the tax owed. For example, if a company invests $25,000 in 5-year class assets in a year, it can claim an ITC of $2,500, which will offset an equal amount of taxes otherwise owed.

In 1983 a new rule regarding ITC went into effect. This rule requires companies to choose between taking the full ITC on some assets and reducing the basis of those assets or taking a lesser ITC and not affecting the asset's basis. The specific rule is as follows: if the company chooses to take the full ITC available on a 3- or 5-year asset, then 50% of the ITC must be deducted to arrive at the asset's basis before depreciation is computed. If, on the other hand, the company wishes to preserve the basis of the asset, then the ITC percentage must be reduced by 2%, or from 10% to 8% on 5-year assets and from 6% to 4% on 3-year assets.

For an example of this rule, suppose that your company bought a 5-year asset for $1,000. For simplicity, suppose that all of the company's $5,000 special depreciation had been used up. Your company has two choices: to take a 10% ITC of $100, and reduce the basis of the asset by $50 before computing depreciation; or to take an 8% ITC of $80, leaving the basis of the asset at $1,000. Since the asset's basis would be reduced if the full ITC were taken, the depreciation deduction in each year would also be lower. On the other hand, taking a reduced ITC would allow larger annual depreciation deductions for each period.

Choosing ITC over basis can be a complex issue, and you should seek help from a tax professional before you choose one alternative over the other.

The Model

The ACRS Depreciation Calculator has two sections: ASSUMPTIONS and DEPRECIATION TABLE. The ASSUMPTIONS section begins at cell R10C1. Cell R12C7 contains the description of the asset being depreciated. Cell R13C7 displays the cost (beginning basis) of the asset. The ACRS life of the asset appears in cell R14C7, and cells R15C7 and R16C7 indicate the year and month that the asset is placed in service. Cell R17C7 answers the question: "Is the Asset Real Property?" A 1 is used to signal yes; 2 means no. If the full investment tax credit is desired, a 1 is placed into R18C7; otherwise, you should enter a 2 here. The amount of available first-year expense is entered in cell R19C7. If you have not purchased assets in the current year, this number should be 5000; otherwise, enter the amount, if any, that has not been used on other assets.

ACRS: Locations of Named Cells and Ranges

Description	Location	Name
ASSUMPTIONS	R11C1	ASSUMPTIONS
Net Purchase Cost of Asset	R13C7	COST
ACRS Life of Asset	R14C7	LIFE
Year Placed in Service	R15C7	YEAR
Month Placed in Service	R16C7	MONTH
Real Property (Yes/No)	R17C7	REAL
Full ITC (Yes/No)	R18C7	FULLITC
First-Year Expense Available (Yes/No)	R19C7	FSTYEAREXP
DEPRECIATION TABLE	R23C1	TABLE
Period	R27:42C3	PERIOD
Depreciation Expense	R27:42C6	EXPENSE
Real Estate Index Table	R27:42C10:21	RETABLE
INSTRUCTIONS	R47C1	INSTRUCTIONS

The DEPRECIATION TABLE begins at cell R22C1 and continues through row 42. Columns 2 and 3 define the depreciable life of the

```
        1         2         3         4         5         6         7
 1 =======================================================================
 2 ACRS DEPRECIATION CALCULATOR               Copyright (C) QUE Corp. 1983
 3 =======================================================================
 4
 5          For ASSUMPTIONS, (G)oto (N)ame 'ASSUMPTIONS'
 6          For DEPRECIATION TABLE, (G)oto (N)ame 'TABLE'
 7          For INDEX TABLE, (G)oto (N)ame 'INDEX'
 8          For INSTRUCTIONS, (G)oto (N)ame 'INSTRUCTIONS'
 9 =======================================================================
10 ASSUMPTIONS                                                   Sheet 1.1
11 =======================================================================
12          Description of Asset:                                 Computer
13          Net Purchase Cost of Asset:                           $8900.00
14          ACRS Life of Asset:                                          5
15          Year Placed in Service                                    1982
16          Month Placed in Service:                                     1
17          Is This Asset Real Property? (1=Yes,2=No)                    2
18          Take Full ITC? (1=Yes,2=No)                                  1
19          First-Year Expense Available (If Any):                $5000.00
20
21 =======================================================================
22 DEPRECIATION TABLE (Continues to row 42)                      Sheet 2.1
23 =======================================================================
24                                First-Year      Depreciation Remaining
25             Year     Period     Expense   ITC     Expense      Basis
26             ----     ------    ---------- ---  ------------ --------
27             1982①       1     $5000.00  $390.00     $555.75  $3149.25⑦
28             1983        2        ④        ⑤         $815.10  $2334.15
29             1984        3                           $778.05  $1556.10
30             1985        4                           $778.05   $778.05
31             1986        5                           $778.05     $0.00
32             1987        6                             $0.00     $0.00
33             1988        7                             $0.00     $0.00
34             1989 ②      8 ③                           $0.00 ⑥   $0.00 ⑧
35             1990        9                             $0.00     $0.00
36             1991       10                             $0.00     $0.00
37             1992       11                             $0.00     $0.00
38             1993       12                             $0.00     $0.00
39             1994       13                             $0.00     $0.00
40             1995       14                             $0.00     $0.00
41             1996       15                             $0.00     $0.00
42             1997       16                             $0.00     $0.00
43
44
45 =======================================================================
46 INSTRUCTIONS                                                  Sheet 3.1
47 =======================================================================
48
49                      1) Enter ASSUMPTIONS
50                      2) Recalculate by typing: F4 or !
51                      3) Review results
52                      4) SAVE by typing: TSB:ACRS (CR)
53                      5) PRINT by typing: PP
```

8 9 10 11 12 13 14

Year	Percent
1	15%
2	22%
3	21%
4	21%
5	21%
6	0%
7	0%
8	0%
9	0%
10	0%
11	0%
12	0%
13	0%
14	0%
15	0%
16	0%

(9) (10)

	1	2	3	4	5
1	12%	11%	10%	9%	8%
2	10%	10%	11%	11%	11%
3	9%	9%	9%	9%	10%
4	8%	8%	8%	8%	8%
5	7%	7%	7%	7%	7%
6	6%	6%	6%	6%	6%
7	6%	6%	6%	6%	6%
8	6%	6%	6%	6%	6%
9	6%	6%	6%	6%	5%
10	5%	6%	5%	6%	5%
11	5%	5%	5%	5%	5%
12	5%	5%	5%	5%	5%
13	5%	5%	5%	5%	5%
14	5%	5%	5%	5%	5%
15	5%	5%	5%	5%	5%
16	0%	0%	1%	1%	2%

	15	16	17	18	19	20	21
1							
2							
3							
4							
5							
6							
7							
8							
9							
10							
11							
12							
13							
14							
15							
16							
17							
18							
19							
20							
21							
22							
23							
24							
25							
26	6	7	8	9	10	11	12
27	7%	6%	5%	4%	3%	2%	1%
28	11%	11%	11%	11%	11%	11%	12%
29	10%	10%	10%	10%	10%	10%	10%
30	8%	9%	9%	9%	9%	9%	9%
31	7%	8%	8%	8%	8%	8%	8%
32	7%	7%	7%	7%	7%	7%	7%
33	6%	6%	6%	6%	6%	6%	6%
34	6%	5%	6%	6%	6%	6%	6%
35	6%	5%	5%	5%	6%	6%	6%
36	5%	5%	5%	5%	5%	6%	5%
37	5%	5%	5%	5%	5%	5%	5%
38	5%	5%	5%	5%	5%	5%	5%
39	5%	5%	5%	5%	5%	5%	5%
40	5%	5%	5%	5%	5%	5%	5%
41	5%	5%	5%	5%	5%	5%	5%
42	2%	3%	3%	4%	4%	4%	5%
43							
44							
45							
46							
47							
48							
49							
50							
51							
52							
53							

```
ACRS DEPRECIATION CALCULATOR
CALCULATING FIXED ASSET MANAGEMENT
1         R27C2          YEAR
2         R28:42C2       1+R[-1]C
3         R28:42C3       1+R[-1]C
4         R27C4          IF(FSTYEAREXP>COST,COST,FSTYEAREXP)
5         R27C5          IF(REAL=1,0,IF(FULLITC=1,IF(LIFE>3,(COST-
                         R27C4)*0.1,(COST-R27C4)*0.06),IF(LIFE>3,(COST-
                         R27C4)*0.08,(COST-R27C4)*0.04)))
6         R27:42C6       (COST-R27C4-IF(FULLITC=1,(R27C5*0.5),0))*(IF(REAL=1,
                         INDEX(RETABLE,PERIOD,MONTH),LOOKUP(PERIOD,
                         R8C9:R23C10)))
7         R27C7          COST-RC[-3]-IF(FULLITC=1,(RC[-2]*0.5),0)-RC[-1]
8         R28:42C7       R[-1]C-EXPENSE
9         R9:23C9        1+R[-1]C
10        R9:23C10       SEE TEXT
```

asset. Cell R27C2 repeats the year from cell R15C7, YEAR. Cell R28C2 is then calculated in relation to cell R27C2

R28C2 = R27C2+1

or

R28C2 = R[-1]C+1

Cell R27C3, PERIOD, which contains the number *1*, is used to define cell R28C3

R28C3 = R27C3+1

or

R28C3 = R[-1]C+1

In cell R27C4 the model computes the amount of first year expense to be taken on this asset by referring to cells R13C7, COST, and R19C7, FSTYEAREXP. The formula used is

R27C4 $ = IF(R19C7>R13C7,R13C7,R19C7)

or

R27C4 $ = IF(FSTYEAREXP>COST,COST,FSTYEAREXP)

If the full $5,000 allowance is available and the cost of the asset is $4,500, the model will post 4500 to cell R27C4. If the cost of the asset is $6,000, then 5000 will appear in R27C4.

Cell R27C5 computes the Investment Tax Credit to be taken against the asset. The formula in this cell is

```
R27C5 $ = IF(REAL=1,0,IF(FULLITC=1,IF(LIFE>3,
          (COST-R27C4)*0.1,(COST-R27C4)*0.06),IF(LIFE>
          3,(COST-R27C4)*0.08,(COST-R27C4)*0.04)))
```

Column 6 computes the ACRS depreciation for each year in the asset's recovery life, using the basis of the asset *after* any first-year expense has been taken. In the example, the asset's basis after first-year expense equals $3,705—a figure reached by the following calculations: $8,900 (the asset's cost) minus $5,000 (first-year depreciation) minus 50% of the ITC of $390 ($195). This is an interim figure that does not appear on the table. Using the ACRS table for 5-year assets, you can see that 15% of the cost of the asset should be recovered in the first year. In our example, cell R27C6, EXPENSE, displays $555.75, which is obtained by multiplying .15 by $3,705. The formula in this cell is

```
R27C6 = (COST-R27C4-(IF(FULLITC=1,R27C5*0.5),0))*(IF
  (REAL=1,INDEX(RETABLE,PERIOD,MONT H),LOOKUP
  (PERIOD,R8C9:R23C10)))
```

Fortunately, this formula can be entered once into cell R27C6 and **C**opied **D**own 15 rows. Do not try to use relative references to define this cell because Multiplan cannot tolerate the large number of characters in the formula that relative references would render.

The formula means: take the cost, minus the first year expense, minus either half of the ITC or zero, times either the indexed real estate depreciation factor (if the question in R17C6 is marked 1), or the looked-up depreciation factor located at R8C9:R23C10 (if the asset is not real property, as indicated in R17C6).

The LOOKUP table that begins at R8C9 holds the ACRS depreciation tables that are used by the model to calculate the values in column 6. Because of Multiplan's IF function, this one table can hold the depreciation rate data for all ACRS asset classifications except for the 15-year real estate assets. The formulas for each of the cells in column 10 are reproduced below.

R8C10 % = IF(LIFE=3,0.25,IF(LIFE=5,0.15,IF
(LIFE=10,0.08,0.05)))
R9C10 % = IF(LIFE=3,0.38,IF(LIFE=5,0.22,IF(LIFE=10,0.14,0.1)))
R10C10 % = IF(LIFE=3,0.37,IF(LIFE=5,0.21,IF
(LIFE=10,0.12,0.09)))
R11C10 % = IF(LIFE=3,0,IF(LIFE=5,0.21,IF(LIFE=10,0.1,0.08)))
R12C10 % = IF(LIFE=3,0,IF(LIFE=5,0.21,IF(LIFE=10,0.1,0.07)))
R13C10 % = IF(LIFE=3,0,IF(LIFE=5,0,IF(LIFE=10,0.1,0.07)))
R14C10 % = IF(LIFE=3,0,IF(LIFE=5,0,IF(LIFE=10,0.09,0.06)))
R15C10 % = IF(LIFE=3,0,IF(LIFE=5,0,IF(LIFE=10,0.09,0.06)))
R16C10 % = IF(LIFE=3,0,IF(LIFE=5,0,IF(LIFE=10,0.09,0.06)))
R17C10 % = IF(LIFE=3,0,IF(LIFE=5,0,IF(LIFE=10,0.09,0.06)))
R18C10 % = IF(LIFE=3,0,IF(LIFE=5,0,IF(LIFE=10,0,0.06)))
R19C10 % = IF(LIFE=3,0,IF(LIFE=5,0,IF(LIFE=10,0,0.06)))
R20C10 % = IF(LIFE=3,0,IF(LIFE=5,0,IF(LIFE=10,0,0.06)))
R21C10 % = IF(LIFE=3,0,IF(LIFE=5,0,IF(LIFE=10,0,0.06)))
R22C10 % = IF(LIFE=3,0,IF(LIFE=5,0,IF(LIFE=10,0,0.06)))
R23C10 % = IF(LIFE=3,0,IF(LIFE=5,0,IF(LIFE=10,0,0.06)))

The way that the formulas work can be explained by examining R8C10. The formula in this cell first checks the LIFE (the ACRS life of the asset). If the life is 5 years, then the factor is 0.15, or 15%. If the life of the asset is 3 years, then the factor is .25, or 25%. If the life of the asset is 10 years, then the factor is .08, or 8%; for other assets the factor *must* be .05, or 5%.

The conditional statements in the lookup table make the depreciation table adaptable to a variety of situations. Because most microcomputers have memory limitations, a trick like this can be worth its weight in RAM.

Multiplan is the only spreadsheet that includes index tables. Let's take a look at the construction of the table. Notice that row 26 and column 9 both contain a list of numbers. Row 26 contains the numbers 1 through 12, which correspond to the month the asset was purchased (MONTH). Column 9 is numbered 1 to 16, corresponding to the year of the asset life for which depreciation is being computed (PERIOD).

The portion of the equation in R27C6 that performs the indexing is

INDEX(RETABLE,PERIOD,MONTH)

The remaining basis, to be used as the beginning basis for next year, is located in column 7. The first year expense, R27C7, also subtracts investment tax credit, if you desire to take it, with the formula

R27C7 = COST-RC[-3]-IF(FULLITC=1,(RC[-2]*0.5),0)-RC[-1]

This formula subtracts the first-year expense; the ITC, if there is any and it is taken; and the ACRS depreciation expense from the net purchase cost of the asset. Successive years use the formula

R28:42C7 = +R[-1]C-EXPENSE

This formula subtracts the current year's expense from the remaining basis for the year before.

The index table, to be used for real estate, is located at R27C9 through R42C21. Across the top of the table at R26C9:21 and along the left side of the table from R27C9 to R42C9 are year numbers. Real estate depreciation factors are indexed by these keys. The top row of years contains the year of the depreciation, and the row of years along the left side of the table indicates the number of years chosen for the basis of the depreciation.

The 15-year-long table for non-real estate depreciation is located at R8C9 and continues through to R23C10.

Using the Model

To use this model, supply the requested information in column 7, rows 12 through 19, and recalculate by typing F4 or ! Multiplan will do the rest. You can save the completed table by typing **TSB:ACRS** (CR) and print it by typing **PP**.

Be sure to consult your accountant or other tax professional if you are unsure about the recovery life of a particular asset, its true cost, or the amount of first-year expense that is still available to you. If the law is not changed, the ACRS rate tables in the model are good for all assets purchased before January 1, 1985.

Modifications

This model can be very useful, particularly if your work involves frequent analyses of fixed assets. Because the model is compact, it can be used also as part of other templates; or the ACRS calculation of several items or profit centers can be linked to form a comprehensive ACRS depreciation calculator.

5

Working Capital Management

Tracking Accounts Receivable Collections

Calculating Economic Order Quantity

Tracking Accounts Receivable Collections

Because monitoring cash flow is so important to a small business, a simple way of analyzing the monthly accounts receivable collection cycle can be a useful tool. Managers can use this analysis to develop a "feel" for when payments will arrive, which will help in planning cash disbursements and maintaining the required cash balances. One possible result is a reduction in collection time for outstanding bills. Although performing an accounts receivable collections analysis manually is time-consuming and tedious, Multiplan can make this a quick and easy task.

Principles

Each day of credit that you extend to your customers is equivalent to loaning them the cash generated by one day's sales. If your business has annual sales of $1 million, its average daily sales are nearly $2,800. By allowing your customers to wait 30 days before paying, you have "loaned" them the use of 30 days' worth of sales, or over $80,000. If your actual collection cycle increases to 45 days, the loan jumps to nearly $125,000. To look at it yet another way, cutting 10 days from your collection cycle would free close to $30,000—cash that is now being loaned, interest free, to your customers.

Of course, there are also costs associated with *not* offering reasonable credit terms. Some customers may insist on a certain level of credit and shift their business to other vendors if their requirements are not met. Extending credit also makes order-taking more convenient.

The collection cycle begins at the point of sale. Most companies generate both cash and credit sales, although the percentage of each varies widely from business to business. Cash sales have no collection cycle to speak of; the sale is made, and the cash is collected at the same time. Credit sales have a collection cycle that is determined, at least nominally, by the seller. Payment terms specify a time factor (10 days, 30 days, etc.) and sometimes a discount for early payment. The problem occurs when the seller's terms are not honored by customers. The purpose of managing accounts receivable collections is to eliminate, as much as possible, any discrepancy between the terms stated on the invoice—your credit policy—and the actual time the customers take to pay.

Sophisticated accounts receivable systems eliminate the discrepancy by tracking an invoice from the point of sale to the point of collection. However, much of the same information can be acquired by using a model that maintains records on an aggregate basis. The model must provide two pieces of information: data about the percentage of a given period's sales collected for each period that follows, and the pattern of collections during each month. The percentage of sales collected is a direct result of a company's credit policy. Companies that extend net-30-days terms should have a fairly high collection percentage the following month. A business that offers only net-10-days terms should collect most of its bills within one month. The model illustrates a company that offers 30-days credit to its customers.

The collections pattern for a month is determined by computing the percentage of the month's total collections that are received each day. This computation indicates the flow of payments that can be expected in a given month.

The Model

This model contains two sections: SALES DATA and COLLECTIONS DATA.

ARCOLLEC: Locations of Named Cells and Ranges

Description	Location	Name
SALES DATA	R11C1	SALESDATA
Total Sales Last Month	R17C4	LMTOTALSALES
Total Sales Month before Last	R18C4	TMATOTALSALES
Returns Last Month	R17C5	LMRETURNS
Returns Month before Last	R18C5	TMARETURNS
Cash Sales Last Month	R17C6	LMCASHSALES
Cash Sales Month before Last	R18C6	TMACASHSALES
Net Credit Sales Last Month	R17C7	LMCREDITSALES
Net Credit Sales Month before Last	R18C7	TMACREDITSALES
COLLECTIONS DATA	R23C1	COLLECTIONS
Last Month Amount Collected	R30:60C3	LASTMONTH
Month before last Amount Collected	R30:60C4	TWOMONTHSAGO
All Previous Months Amount Collected	R30:60C5	ALLPRIOR
Total Collections Amount by Day	R30:60C6	AMOUNT
Total Collections Percent	R30:60C7	PERCENT
Total Collections Last Month	R62C3	LMTOTAL
Total Collections Month before Last	R62C4	TMATOTAL
Gross Amount Collected	R62C6	TOTALAMOUNT
INSTRUCTIONS	R72C1	INSTRUCTIONS

The SALES DATA section, named SALESDATA and beginning at row 10, summarizes all sales and calculates credit sales for the two months that immediately precede the month being monitored. Cells R17C4, LMTOTALSALES, and R18C4, TMATOTALSALES, display gross sales for both months. Cells R17C5, LMRETURNS, and R18C5, TMARETURNS, contain the dollar amount of any returns, discounts, or allowances made during the two-month period. The amount of cash sales for the period is entered in cells R17C6, LMCASHSALES, and R18C6, TMACASHSALES. Finally, cells R17C7, LMCREDITSALES, and R18C7, TMACREDITSALES, com-

```
         1         2         3         4         5         6         7         8
 1 ==========================================================================
 2 ACCOUNTS RECEIVABLE COLLECTIONS TRACKER                (C) QUE Corp 1983
 3 ==========================================================================
 4
 5                   For SALES DATA (G)oto (N)ame 'SALESDATA'
 6                   For COLLECTIONS (G)oto (N)ame 'COLLECTIONS'
 7                   For INSTRUCTIONS (G)oto (N)ame 'INSTRUCTIONS'
 8
 9 ==========================================================================
10 SALES DATA                                                      Sheet 1.1
11 ==========================================================================
12 Report for Month of: August 1983
13                                                         Net
14                             Total               Cash   Credit
15                             Sales   Returns    Sales    Sales
16                           -------   -------  -------  -------
17 Last Month:             $ 100,000     1,000    5,000   94,000 (1)
18 Month before Last:      $  96,000     4,000    4,000   88,000 (2)
19
20
21 ==========================================================================
22 COLLECTIONS DATA (Continues to row 66)                          Sheet 2.1
23 ==========================================================================
24                      Amount Collected          Total Collections
25                  -------------------------  --------------------------
26                             Month      All
27                     Last   before Previous                  Cumulative
28              Date  Month     Last   Months   Amount  Percent   Percent
29              ---- -------- -------- -------- -------- -------  -------
30                -1 1,000.00   250.00     0.00 1,250.00      2%       2% (7)
31                -2 2,000.00   400.00     0.00 2,400.00      3%       5%
32                -3     0.00   350.00     0.00   350.00      0%       5%
33                -4 1,675.00   350.00     0.00 2,025.00      3%       8%
34                -5 2,608.00   200.00     0.00 2,808.00      4%      11%
35                -6 1,665.00     0.00   255.00 1,920.00      2%      14%
36                -7   966.00   180.00   378.00 1,524.00      2%      16%
37                -8 1,788.00   430.00 1,000.00 3,218.00 (4)  4%      20%
38                -9 1,009.00   505.00 1,000.00 2,514.00      3%      23%
39               -10     0.00     0.00     0.00     0.00      0% (5)  23%
40         (3)   -11 2,445.00   550.00   244.00 3,239.00      4%      27%
41               -12   768.00   348.00   477.00 1,593.00      2%      30% (6)
42               -13 2,278.00     0.00     0.00 2,278.00      3%      32%
43               -14   120.00   543.00     0.00   663.00      1%      33%
44               -15 2,455.00   612.00   244.00 3,311.00      4%      38%
```

	1	2	3	4	5	6	7	8
45		-16	4,167.00	213.00	0.00	4,380.00	6%	43%
46		-17	0.00	355.00	0.00	355.00	0%	44%
47		-18	5,346.00	288.00	117.00	5,751.00	7%	51%
48		-19	4,678.00	666.00	0.00	5,344.00	7%	58%
49		-20	4,212.00	0.00	0.00	4,212.00 ④	5%	63%
50	③	-21	4,867.00	476.00	0.00	5,343.00	7%	70%
51		-22	2,213.00	356.00	0.00	2,569.00	3%	74%
52		-23	2,440.00	305.00	0.00	2,745.00	4% ⑤	77%
53		-24	0.00	678.00	0.00	678.00	1%	78%
54		-25	795.00	380.00	0.00	1,175.00	2%	80%
55		-26	3,356.00	587.00	0.00	3,943.00	5%	85% ⑥
56		-27	2,667.00	0.00	0.00	2,667.00	3%	88%
57		-28	378.00	950.00	400.00	1,728.00	2%	90%
58		-29	1,478.00	704.00	0.00	2,182.00	3%	93%
59		-30	4,590.00	345.00	0.00	4,935.00	6%	100%
60		-31	0.00	307.00	0.00	307.00	0%	100%
61			--------	--------	--------	--------	------	------
62	Total Collections		61,964	11,328	4,115	77,407	100%	
63			========	========	========	========	======	
64			⑧	⑨	⑩	⑪	⑫	
65	Percent of Sales		66%	13%				
66			======	======				
67			⑬	⑭				
68								
69								

```
70 ========================================================================
71 INSTRUCTIONS                                                   Sheet 3.1
72 ========================================================================
73
74                    1) Enter SALES DATA
75                    2) Daily, enter COLLECTIONS DATA
76                    3) RECALCULATE by typing: F4 or !
77                    4) SAVE by typing: TSB:ARCOLLEC (CR)
78                    5) PRINT by typing: PP
```

TRACKING ACCOUNTS RECEIVABLE COLLECTIONS (ARCOLLEC)

NUMBER	LOCATION(S)	FORMULA
1	R17C7	LMTOTALSALES-LMRETURNS-LMCASHSALES
2	R18C7	TMATOTALSALES-TMARETURNS-TMACASHSALES
3	R32:60C2	R[-1]C-1
4	R30:60C6	LASTMONTH+TWOMONTHSAGO+ALLPRIOR
5	R30:60C7	AMOUNT/TOTALAMOUNT
6	R31:60C8	PERCENT+R[-1]C
7	R30C8	PERCENT
8	R62C3	SUM(LASTMONTH)
9	R62C4	SUM(TWOMONTHSAGO)
10	R62C5	SUM(ALLPRIOR)
11	R62C6	SUM(AMOUNT)
12	R62C7	SUM(PERCENT)
13	R65C3	LMTOTAL/LMCREDITSALES
14	R65C4	TMATOTAL/TMACREDITSALES

pute net credit sales by subtracting cash sales and adjustments from total sales. As an example, the formula for cell R17C7, LMCREDITSALES, is

R17C7 I = R17C4-R17C5-R17C6

or

LMCREDITSALES I = LMTOTALSALES-LMRETURNS-
LMCASHSALES

The COLLECTIONS DATA section, beginning at row 22, lists the dates for the current month in column 2. Notice that the automatic dating function, developed in the Checkbook Balancer model, is used again here. Columns 3, 4, and 5 list the dollar amount of collections received each day. The total day's collections are split into three groups for posting to the three columns. Collections against invoices written last month are posted to column 3, and payments received for bills written the month before that are posted to column 4. All other collections are assigned to column 5.

For example, on the 8th day of the month, shown in row 37, a total of $3,218 was collected, as shown in cell R37C6 by the formula

R37C6 F2 = R37C3+R37C4+R37C5

or

R37C6 F2 = LASTMONTH+TWOMONTHSAGO+ALLPRIOR

Of the amount collected, the $1,788 related to last month's sales has been posted to cell R37C3. Collections against two-month-old invoices, $430, have been posted to cell R37C4. The remaining $1,000, posted to cell R37C5, includes several payments made on even older bills.

Row 62 contains totals for each of the data columns. Cell R62C3, LMTOTAL, for example, contains the formula

R62C3 F2 = SUM(R30C3:R61C3)

or

R62C3 F2 = SUM(LASTMONTH)

The same relative formula is used in cells R62C4, TMATOTAL, R62C5, R62C6, and R62C7.

The model returns its first important information in cells R65C3 and R65C4. These cells compute the ratio of the total collected in the current month against prior months' sales to the sales amounts themselves. For example, in cell R65C3

R65C3 % = R62C3/R17C7

or

R65C3 % = LMTOTAL/LMCREDITSALES

Looking at the numbers in the example, we can see that the total credit sales for the prior month were $94,000 (cell R17C7, LMCREDITSALES). In addition, cell R62C3, LMTOTAL shows that $61,964 was collected against that amount in the current month. When the amount collected is divided as indicated in the formula in R65C3, the result is 66%.

Move back up the model to cell R30C7, which contains the formula

R30C7 % = R30C6/R62C6

or

PERCENT % = AMOUNT/TOTALAMOUNT

The cells in column 7 return the second important type of information produced by this model: the percentage of the total month's collections received each day.

Column 8 takes this analysis one step further by computing the cumulative percentage collected on a day-by-day basis. Each cell in this column adds the cells above it to the cell immediately to its left in column 7. For example, cell R38C8 is defined as

R38C8 % = R37C8+R[-1]C

or

R38C8 % = PERCENT+R[-1]C

Using the Model

At the beginning of every month, set up the model by entering your SALESDATA for the preceding two months. Then post your daily collections to the appropriate cells in the model. By typing F4 or ! you can recalculate the model at any time. Notice, however, that the collection percentage information in columns 7 and 8 and in row 65 will not be correct until the entire month's collections are posted. At the end of the month, you can print the SALES DATA and COLLECTION DATA sections by typing **PP**. You can save the model by typing **TSB:ARCOLLEC** (CR).

Interpreting the information provided by this model is fairly simple. When you look at the results in the example, you will see, in row 65, that about 66% of last month's sales and 13% of the previous month's sales were collected in the current month. Assuming that our example company is offering 30-days credit, the collection cycle seems to be fairly close to target. If we extrapolate from the data for this month, we notice that in two months' time, 79% of a month's sales have been collected—not bad at all, but still improvable.

Column 7 shows a surge of activity between the 16th and the 22nd of the month. Column 8 indicates that 74% of the total month's collections have already been received by the 22nd, which is just about two-thirds of the way through the month. This slight skewing of the collections flow might have an impact on purchasing or payment decisions.

Modifications

This model can be easily expanded in a number of ways. You may want to add a column to track collections against an additional month. To make that change, insert a column at the current column 5 and copy the formulas from columns 3 or 4. This expansion could be particularly useful if you offer unusually long credit terms.

The model can also be condensed for use by companies with shorter collection cycles. If you offer net-10-days terms, each column can represent a two-week period of sales. Because collections would be tracked across a 10-day span, you could delete several rows.

You may use this model to test the effectiveness of different credit policies. For example, suppose that you are currently extending 30-days credit, but your average collection period is 45 days. You wonder whether a 2% discount for early payment would help speed collections. As an experiment, offer the terms for a one-month period, and use the worksheet to track the payments as they come in across the next few months. When completed, the collections worksheet will allow you to compare the results of your experiment to your regular collection pattern.

Calculating Economic Order Quantity

Are you effectively managing your inventory costs? If you stock goods for production or resale, you know the costs associated with carrying inventory. They include the interest cost of financing the inventory until it is resold, as well as the cost of shrinkage, which arises from the inevitable damage, loss, and pilferage that occur over time. The longer you hold your inventory, the greater the interest and shrinkage costs.

The cost of carrying inventory must also be balanced against the cost of ordering it. The ordering cost is usually harder to determine because it is based on the personnel time used to place, track, and receive an order. The more often you order, the higher your ordering costs will be. Yet, at the same time, if you order frequently, you can reduce your inventory carrying costs by keeping less inventory in stock.

There is a way to balance the carrying and ordering costs for inventory. Using a mathematical formula, you can determine the economic order quantity (EOQ), or number of units you should purchase each time you place an order. By ordering the EOQ, you can minimize the total cost of inventory, which is the sum of the ordering and carrying costs.

The Model

This model has two sections: ASSUMPTIONS and SOLUTIONS. To calculate an EOQ, you must first enter several facts about your inventory in the ASSUMPTIONS section of the model, which begins at row 10.

EOQ: Locations of Named Cells and Ranges

Description	**Location**	**Name**
ASSUMPTIONS	R11C1	ASSUMPTIONS
Number of Units Sold per Week	R13C6	AVGSOLDWEEKLY
Purchase Price per Unit	R14C6	UNITPRICE
Ordering Cost	R15C6	ORDERINGCOST
Order Lead Time in Weeks	R16C6	LEADTIME
Annual Interest Rate	R17C6	INTERESTRATE
Annual Shrinkage Allowance	R18C6	SHRINKAGE
SOLUTIONS	R23C1	SOLUTIONS
Carrying Cost per Unit	R25C6	CARRYINGCOST
Number of Units to Order	R26C6	TOORDER
INSTRUCTIONS	R35C1	INSTRUCTIONS

The estimated number of units sold during a given period is entered in cell R13C6, AVGSOLDWEEKLY. (One week is the period used in this model.) If you purchase inventory for production rather than resale, enter the number of units used in production. Enter your per-unit purchase price in cell R14C6, UNITPRICE. Cell R15C6, ORDERINGCOST, contains the cost of placing an order, which is assumed to be the same for each order.

The order lead time, entered in cell R16C6, LEADTIME, can help you set a safety stock level. If you know that an order takes two weeks to arrive, then you need at least two weeks of inventory on hand. You will probably want even more on hand in case an order is delayed, but knowing the lead time can help you establish a minimum. The safety stock level is not related to the EOQ.

Cell R17C6, INTERESTRATE, contains the interest rate for financing the inventory purchase; and cell R18C6, SHRINKAGE, contains the percentage of your inventory that is lost to shrinkage annually.

After all assumptions are entered, Multiplan computes the carrying cost, the EOQ, the required frequency of ordering, and the minimum safety stock level in the SOLUTIONS area, which begins at row 22. Carrying cost is computed in cell R25C6, CARRYINGCOST, by

```
      1          2          3          4          5          6          7          8
 1 ==========================================================================
 2 EOQ INVENTORY ORDERING CALCULATOR           Copyright (C) QUE Corp. 1983
 3 ==========================================================================
 4
 5          For ASSUMPTIONS (G)oto (N)ame `ASSUMPTIONS'
 6          For SOLUTIONS (G)oto (N)ame `SOLUTIONS'
 7          For INSTRUCTIONS (G)oto (N)ame `INSTRUCTIONS'
 8
 9 ==========================================================================
10 ASSUMPTIONS                                                     Sheet 1.1
11 ==========================================================================
12
13          Number of Units Sold per Week:                  400
14          Purchase Price per Unit:                     $20.00
15          Ordering Cost:                                $9.00
16          Order Lead Time in Weeks:                         3  weeks
17          Annual Interest Rate:                           14%
18          Annual Shinkage Allowance:                       3%
19
20
21 ==========================================================================
22 SOLUTIONS                                                       Sheet 2.1
23 ==========================================================================
24
25          Carrying Cost per Unit:                  (1) $0.07
26          Number of Units to Order:                (2)   332  Units
27          Orders Placed Every:                     (3)     6  Days
28          Minimum Safety Stock:                    (4)  1200  Units
29
30
31
32
33 ==========================================================================
34 INSTRUCTIONS                                                    Sheet 3.1
35 ==========================================================================
36
37                      1) Enter ASSUMPTIONS
38                      2) Recalculate by typing: F4 or !
39                      3) SAVE by typing: TSB:EOQ (CR)
40                      4) PRINT by typing: PP
```

CALCULATING ECONOMIC ORDER QUANTITY (EOQ)

NUMBER	LOCATION(S)	FORMULA
1	R25C6	((INTERESTRATE+SHRINKAGE)/52)*UNITPRICE
2	R26C6	SQRT((2*ORDERINGCOST*AVGSOLDWEEKLY)/CARRINGCOST)
3	R27C6	(TOORDER/AVGSOLDWEEKLY)*7
4	R28C6	AVGSOLDWEEKLY*LEADTIME

converting the interest and shrinkage rates to weekly percentages and then multiplying the result by the per-unit inventory cost. The formula for this computation is

R25C6 $ = ((R17C6+R18C6)/52)*R14C6

or

R25C6 $ = ((INTERESTRATE+SHRINKAGE)/52)*UNITPRICE

The result, $.07 in our example, indicates that the carrying cost for each unit of inventory is seven cents per week. The carrying cost and the demand (or unit sales) are always computed for the same period.

The number of units to order, the EOQ, is displayed in cell R26C6. It is computed by the formula

R26C6 I = SQRT((2*R15C6*R13C6)/R24C6)

or

R26C6 I = SQRT((2*ORDERINGCOST*AVGSOLDWEEKLY)
/CARRYINGCOST)

Cell R27C6 displays order frequency, which is determined by dividing the number of units ordered (the EOQ) by the weekly demand, then multiplying by seven to express the frequency in days rather than weeks. Notice that this formula does not allow for safety stock; the number of units ordered is exactly equal to the demand expected during the time between orders. It is assumed that a safety stock level has already been established. Order frequency is computed by the formula

R27C6 I = (R26C6/R13C6)*7

or

R27C6 I = (TOORDER/AVGSOLDWEEKLY)*7

Minimum safety stock can now be computed by multiplying weekly demand by the order lead time, using the formula

R28C6 I = R13C6*R16C6

or

R28C6 I = AVGSOLDWEEKLY*LEADTIME

Using the Model

After you have built the basic model described above, you must gather the required data—unit sales, purchase prices, ordering costs, and order lead time—to perform the EOQ calculation. Although most of this information should be easily obtained, the ordering cost figure may be tough to pin down. When you determine this number, remember to include the time of the person who prepares the order, the cost of any supplies used, the cost of postage or telephone, and any other costs that are relevant to your business.

Once the data is gathered, insert the figures in the proper places in the model and type F4 or ! to recalculate. You can save the completed model by typing **TSB:EOQ** (CR) and print the ASSUMPTIONS and SOLUTIONS sections by typing **PP**.

This model, or any EOQ model, is restricted to computing an EOQ for one item at a time because the cost per item is one of the inputs in the computations. A different EOQ model must be developed for each type of item stocked. Some items may be ordered from the same supplier; if their demand is similar, it makes sense to order them all on the same P.O. In such a case, you will not be able to optimize the EOQ for each item, but by experimenting with your Multiplan models, you can find a workable compromise.

Modifications

You may want to modify the model by changing the inventory analysis period from weeks to months or days. Assuming that you want to use months, you would first change the demand assumption (Number of Units Sold) to indicate the number of units sold or used in production for one month. Lead time would also be expressed in months. If lead time is less than one month, you can use a fractional number such as .5 to express it. To compute carrying cost per unit, convert the interest and shrinkage rates to monthly rather than weekly percentages, then divide by 100 and then by 12. None of the other formulas will need adjustment when you modify the model in this manner.

6
Financial Statements

Producing a Comprehensive Financial Statement

Performing Ratio Analysis

Using Interactive Financial Statements

Producing a Comprehensive Financial Statement

Every business produces financial statements at one time or another. For some businesses, this process is reserved for tax time and the infrequent visit to the bank. For others, it is a monthly, or even weekly, procedure. Whatever your situation, this Five-in-One Financial Statement model can make the job easier.

Principles

The most commonly used financial statements and supporting schedules are the Income Statement and its subsidiaries, the Statement of Operating Expenses, the Statement of Cost of Goods Sold, the Balance Sheet, the Statement of Stockholders' Equity, and the Statement of Changes in Financial Position (SCFP). Every business uses the Balance Sheet and the Income Statement. Many businesses also use the other four statements to report the results of operations. This model includes all of these statements, except the Statement of Changes because its form and content vary too widely from company to company to be useful in a model like this one. If you use the SCFP, you can add it to your version of the model. Let's take a brief look at the other statements.

The Income Statement shows the results of a firm's operations over a period, usually a year, and includes information about sales, cost of goods sold, operating expenses, and interest and tax expenses. The bottom line of the Income Statement is usually labeled net income, which represents the profit earned by the firm during the period covered by the statement.

The Statement of Operating Expenses details the operating expenses line from the income statement. Operating expenses include management salaries, office rent, postage, and telephone expenses, which can be presented in decreasing numerical order, in alphabetical order according to the label assigned to each expense, or in logical groupings (salary-related, office-related, fixed asset-related, etc.). This schedule can help a manager control expenses.

The Statement of Cost of Goods Sold shows the computation of the cost of the products sold by the company in the period. The business in the model illustration is engaged in a simple manufacturing process. If the product sold is purchased for resale, a different set of calculations would be used.

The cost of goods sold has three components: materials cost, labor cost, and overhead. Materials cost is computed by adding inventory purchases in the current period to the inventory balance at the end of the last period. After adjustments for returned goods and any other items are made, the amount remaining, called total goods available for sale, represents the total of all the goods the firm had to sell during that period.

The materials cost of the goods sold in the period is equal to the total goods available for sale minus the inventory remaining at the end of the month. Think of it this way: if you started the month with 6 widgets, bought 5 more during the month, and had only 4 left at the end of the month, you must have sold 7 widgets. If widgets cost you $2,000 apiece, then the cost of material for the period was $14,000. Cost of goods sold equals the materials cost plus any labor and factory costs that went into manufacturing the finished product.

The Statement of Stockholders' Equity shows the changes in equity for the current period. The major activities on this schedule are dividend payments, accumulation of retained earnings, and the sales and purchase of stock by the company.

Finally, the Balance Sheet is a "snapshot" of a company's financial position as of the last date in the reporting period. The Balance Sheet is divided into assets and liabilities (which must always be equal in total). Assets and liabilities are usually subdivided into current and noncurrent (or long-term) portions. The Balance Sheet shows what a company owns (cash, inventory, and equipment) and what it owes (accounts payable and debt). It also shows the firm's retained earnings, which are the accumulated past profits of the business.

The Model

The Five-in-One model uses the financial relationships shown on the chart to build statements. They appear in the spreadsheet at the following locations:

Statement of Operating Expenses	Row 11
Statement of Cost of Goods Sold	Row 42
Statement of Income	Row 68
Statement of Retained Earnings	Row 102
Balance Sheet - Assets	Row 123
Balance Sheet - Liabilities	Row 163

Columns 1 through 3 contain the statement labels. The labels in the example are fairly common, but you may need to change them to fit your situation.

Columns 6 and 7 contain the actual numbers. Column 7 shows the balances for the current year (called 19XY in the example), and column 6 contains the preceding year's balances (19XX).

FINSTATE: Locations of Named Cells and Ranges

Description	Location	Name
STATEMENT OF OPERATING EXPENSES	R12C1	OPERATINGEXPENSES
STATEMENT OF COST OF GOODS SOLD	R43C1	COGS
STATEMENT OF INCOME	R69C1	INCOME
STATEMENT OF RETAINED EARNINGS	R103C1	EARNINGS
BALANCE SHEET - ASSETS	R124C1	ASSETS
Current Assets (Year 19XX)	R136:142C6	CURASSETSY1

```
       1         2       3       4             5                6                 7
 1 ===========================================================================
 2 FIVE-IN-ONE FINANCIAL STATEMENTS                        (C) QUE Corp. 1983
 3 ===========================================================================
 4     For INSTRUCTIONS (G)oto (N)ame 'INSTRUCTIONS'
 5     For STATEMENT OF OPERATING EXPENSES (G)oto (N)ame 'OPERATINGEXPENSES'
 6     For COST OF GOODS SOLD STATEMENT (G)oto (N)ame 'COGS'
 7     For INCOME STATEMENT (G)oto (N)ame 'INCOME'
 8     For STATEMENT OF RETAINED EARNINGS (G)oto (N)ame 'EARNINGS'
 9     For BALANCE SHEETS (G)oto (N)ame 'ASSETS' or 'LIABILITIES'
10 ===========================================================================
11 STATEMENT OF OPERATING EXPENSES (Continues to row 38)            Sheet 1.1
12 ===========================================================================
13                                  ANY COMPANY
14                         Statement of Operating Expenses
15                   For the Years ending Any Day, 19XX and 19XY
16
17                                                        19XX           19XY
18                                                      --------       --------
19
20 Salaries and Wages                                 $90,000.00    $101,000.00
21 Employee Benefits                                    3,000.00       3,500.00
22 Health Insurance                                     4,950.00       5,010.00
23 Payroll Taxes                                        7,500.00       8,350.00
24 Office Rent                                         18,420.00      20,450.00
25 Supplies                                             4,000.00       3,500.00
26 Postage                                              1,200.00       1,350.00
27 Telephone                                            1,200.00       1,350.00
28 Insurance                                           10,500.00      12,800.00
29 Dues and Subscriptions                                 750.00         988.00
30 Advertising and Promotion                            1,200.00       1,170.00
31 Travel and Entertainment                            30,000.00      57,000.00
32 Professional Fees                                   15,230.00      17,890.00
33 Depreciation                                         7,500.00       8,300.00
34 Equipment Rental                                    43,800.00      25,370.00 (53)
35 Maintenance                                          9,000.00       9,000.00
36 Other                                                3,899.00       4,700.00
37                                                      4,000.00       1,200.00
38 Total Operating Expenses                         -----------    -----------
39                                              (1) $254,949.00    $281,578.00 (2)
40                                                  ===========    ===========
```

PRODUCING A COMPREHENSIVE FINANCIAL STATEMENT (FINSTATE)

NUMBER	LOCATION(S)	FORMULA
1	R38C6	SUM(R20C6:R36C6)
2	R38C7	SUM(R20C7:R36C7)

```
      1         2      3      4          5               6                  7
41 ========================================================================
42 STATEMENT OF COST OF GOODS SOLD (Continues to row 65)         Sheet 2.1
43 ========================================================================
44                                    ANY COMPANY
45                           Statement of Cost of Goods Sold
46                       For the Years Ended Any Day,19XX and 19XY
47
48                                                      19XX           19XY
49                                                    --------       --------
50 Direct Materials
51  Beginning Inventory                             $327,000.00    $354,000.00 (54)
52  Plus: Purchases                                  375,000.00     431,520.00
53  Less: Returns and Allowances                       3,400.00      10,250.00
54                                                  -----------    -----------
55 Total Materials Available                     (3) 698,600.00     775,270.00 (4)
56
57 Ending Inventory                                  354,000.00     327,000.00
58                                                  -----------    -----------
59 Direct Materials Expense                      (5) 344,600.00     448,270.00 (6)
60
61 Direct Labor                                      234,500.00     272,000.00
62
63 Factory Overhead                                   50,000.00      63,750.00
64                                                  -----------    -----------
65 Total Cost of Goods Sold                      (7)$629,100.00    $784,020.00 (8)
66                                                  ===========    ===========
```

PRODUCING A COMPREHENSIVE FINANCIAL STATEMENT (FINSTATE)

NUMBER	LOCATION(S)	FORMULA
3	R55C6	R51C6+R52C6-R53C6
4	R55C7	R51C7+R52C7-R53C7
5	R59C6	R55C6-R57C6
6	R59C7	R55C7-R57C7
7	R65C6	R59C6+R61C6+R63C6
8	R65C7	R59C7+R61C7+R63C7

```
          1          2     3     4          5            6                7
 67 =========================================================================
 68 STATEMENT OF INCOME (Continues to row 98)                        Sheet 3.1
 69 =========================================================================
 70                                     ANY COMPANY
 71                                 Statement of Income
 72                    For the Years Ended Any Day, 19XX and 19XY
 73
 74
 75                                                        19XX           19XY
 76                                                      --------       --------
 77
 78 Gross Sales                                    $1,045,000.00  $1,256,300.00
 79
 80  Less: Returns and Allowances                       1,000.00           0.00
 81                                                   -----------    -----------
 82 Net Sales                                   (9) 1,044,000.00   1,256,300.00(10)
 83
 84 Cost of Goods Sold                         (11)   629,100.00     784,020.00(12)
 85                                                   -----------    -----------
 86 Gross Margin                               (13)   414,900.00     472,280.00(14)
 87
 88 Operating Expenses                         (15)   254,949.00     281,578.00(16)
 89
 90 Interest Expense                                   11,296.00       6,476.00
 91
 92 Other Income/Expense                               13,450.00      37,540.00
 93                                                   -----------    -----------
 94 Profit before Taxes                        (17)   135,205.00     146,686.00(18)
 95
 96 Income Taxes                                       50,898.00      61,000.00
 97                                                   -----------    -----------
 98 Net Income                                 (19)   $84,307.00     $85,686.00(20)
 99                                                   ===========    ===========
100
```

PRODUCING A COMPREHENSIVE FINANCIAL STATEMENT (FINSTATE)

NUMBER	LOCATION(S)	FORMULA
9	R82C6	R78C6-R80C6
10	R82C7	R78C7-R80C7
11	R84C6	R65C6
12	R84C7	R65C7
13	R86C6	R82C6-R84C6
14	R86C7	R82C7-R84C7
15	R88C6	R38C6
16	R88C7	R38C7
17	R94C6	R86C6-R88C6-R90C6-R92C6
18	R94C7	R86C7-R88C7-R90C7-R92C7
19	R98C6	R94C6-R96C6
20	R98C7	R94C7-R96C7

```
             1          2       3       4             5               6                 7

101 =========================================================================================
102 STATEMENT OF RETAINED EARNINGS (Continues to row 119)                         Sheet 4.1
103 =========================================================================================
104                                          ANY COMPANY
105                                   Statement of Retained Earnings
106                             For the Years Ended Any Day, 19XX and 19XY
107
108                                              Common                          Retained
109                                              Stock                           Earnings
110                                           ----------                         --------
111 Balance at Any Day, 19XW                 $100,000.00                      $132,954.00
112
113 Net Income for 19XX                                                  (23)  $84,307.00
114                                           ----------                       ----------
115 Balance at Any Day,19XX                  $100,000.00 (21)            (24) $217,261.00
116
117 Net Income for 19XY                                                  (25)  $85,686.00
118                                           ----------                       ----------
119 Balance at Any Day, 19XY                 $100,000.00 (22)            (26) $302,947.00
120                                           ==========                       ==========
121
```

PRODUCING A COMPREHENSIVE FINANCIAL STATEMENT (FINSTATE)

NUMBER	LOCATION(S)	FORMULA
21	R115C5	R111C5+R113C5
22	R119C5	R115C5+R117C5
23	R113C7	R98C6
24	R115C7	R111C7+R113C7
25	R117C7	R98C7
26	R119C7	R115C7+R117C7

```
        1          2       3      4            5              6                 7
122 ================================================================================
123 BALANCE SHEET - ASSETS (Continues to row 159)                       Sheet 5.1
124 ================================================================================
125                                 ANY COMPANY
126                                Balance Sheet
127                         At Any Day, 19XX and 19XY
128
129                                    Assets
130
131                                                          Any Day
132                                                  -----------------
133                                                    19XX          19XY
134                                                  -------       -------
135 Current Assets
136 Cash                                             $27,500.00    $62,567.00
137 Accounts Receivable
138  Less Doubtful Accounts of $23,000.00 in (27)
139   19XX and $19,400.00 in 19XY (28)               105,555.00     99,177.00
140 Inventory                                   (29) 354,000.00    327,000.00 (30)
141  Prepaid Expenses                                  7,800.00      3,000.00
142  Other                                             5,900.00          0.00
143                                                 -----------   -----------
144 Total Current Assets                        (31) $500,755.00   $491,744.00 (32)
145
146 Plant, Property, and Equipment
147 Leasehold Improvements                           $35,670.00    $35,670.00
148 Furniture and Fixtures                           $47,900.00    $53,600.00
149  Equipment                                      $155,920.00   $155,920.00
150                                                 -----------   -----------
151 Total Plant, Property, and Equipment        (33) $239,490.00   $245,190.00 (34)
152
153 Accumulated Depreciation                         $67,500.00    $92,870.00
154                                                 -----------   -----------
155 Net Plant, Property, and Equipment          (35) $171,990.00   $152,320.00 (36)
156
157 Other Assets                                        $450.00       $300.00
158                                                 -----------   -----------
159 Total Assets                                (37) $673,195.00   $644,364.00 (38)
160                                                 ===========   ===========
161
```

```
         1          2      3      4          5            6              7
162 ==========================================================================
163 BALANCE SHEET - LIABILITIES (Continues to row 199)            Sheet 6.1
164 ==========================================================================
165                              Any Company
166                              Balance Sheet
167
168
169                 Liabilities and Stockholders' Equity
170
171                                                         Any Day
172                                                 ----------------------
173                                                   19XX           19XY
174                                                 --------       --------
175 Current Liabilities
176  Current Portion Long-Term Debt                 $23,567.00     $23,567.00
177  Taxes Payable                                   $9,055.00     $12,366.00
178  Accounts Payable                               $39,890.00     $42,700.00
179  Accrued Expense                                $29,900.00     $24,540.00
180  Other Current Liabilities                         $700.00          $0.00
181                                                -----------    -----------
182 Total Current Liabilities                 (39) $103,112.00    $103,173.00 (40)
183
184 Noncurrent Liabilities
185  Long-Term Debt                                $245,822.00    $135,744.00
186                                                -----------    -----------
187 Total Noncurrent Liabilities              (41) $245,822.00    $135,744.00 (42)
188
189 Other Liabilities                                $7,000.00      $2,500.00
190                                                -----------    -----------
191 Total Liabilities                         (43) $355,934.00    $241,417.00 (44)
192
193 Stockholders' Equity
194  Common Stock                             (45) $100,000.00    $100,000.00 (46)
195  Retained Earnings                        (47) $217,261.00    $302,947.00 (48)
196                                                -----------    -----------
197 Total Stockholders' Equity                (49) $317,261.00    $402,947.00 (50)
198                                                -----------    -----------
199 Total Liabilities and Equity              (51) $673,195.00    $644,364.00 (52)
200                                                ===========    ===========
201
202 ==========================================================================
203 INSTRUCTIONS                                                   Sheet 7.1
204 ==========================================================================
205
206                   1) Enter carefully, data into each area
207                   2) Recalculate by typing: F4 or !
208                   3) Check the data carefully
209                   4) SAVE the date by typing: TSB:FINSTATE (CR)
210                   5) PRINT by typing: PP
```

PRODUCING A COMPREHENSIVE FINANCIAL STATEMENT (FINSTATE)

NUMBER	LOCATION(S)	FORMULA
27	R138C1	" Less Doubtful accounts of $"&FIXED(23000,2)" in"
28	R139C1	" 19XX and $"&FIXED(19400,2)&" in 19XY"
29	R140C6	R57C6
30	R140C7	R57C7
31	R144C6	SUM(CURASSETSY1)
32	R144C7	SUM(CURASSETSY2)
33	R151C6	SUM(PPEY1)
34	R152C7	SUM(PPEY2)
35	R155C6	TOTPPEY1-ACCDEPRY1
36	R155C7	TOTPPEY2-ACCDEPRY2
37	R159C6	R144C6+R155C6+R157C6
38	R159C7	R144C7+R155C7+R157C7
39	R182C6	SUM(R176C6:R180C6)
40	R182C7	SUM(R176C7:R180C7)
41	R187C6	LONGTERMDEBTY1
42	R187C7	LONGTERMDEBTY2
43	R191C6	R182C6+R187C6+R189C6
44	R191C7	R182C7+R187C7+R198C7
45	R194C6	R115C5
46	R194C7	R119C5
47	R195C6	R115C7
48	R195C7	R119C7
49	R197C6	R194C6+R195C6
50	R197C7	R194C7+R195C7
51	R199C6	R191C6+R197C6
52	R199C7	R191C7+R197C7
53	R33C7	R153C7-R153C6
54	R51C7	R57C6

Ending inventory for both years appears on both statements. Beginning inventory in 19XY on the Statement of Cost of Goods Sold equals the ending inventory in year 19XX on the same schedule.

Cost of Goods Sold	Statement of Cost of Goods Sold Statement of Income

The total from the Statement of Cost of Goods Sold is entered on the income statement.

Operating Expenses	Statement of Operating Expenses Statement of Income

The total from the Statement of Operating Expenses is entered on the income statement.

Net Income	Statement of Income Statement of Retained Earnings

Net income for the income statement is entered in the Statement of Stockholders' Equity.

Common Stock	Statement of Retained Earnings
Retained Earnings	Balance Sheet

Totals for these two items are computed on the Statement of Stockholders' Equity and transferred to the Balance Sheet.

The STATEMENT OF OPERATING EXPENSES begins at row 11. Notice that the cells in columns 6 and 7, rows 20 through 36, are input cells. Use them to post your operating expenses to the model. The only exception is cell R33C7, which computes depreciation expense by subtracting year 19XX accumulated depreciation from year 19XY accumulated depreciation using the formula

```
R33C7 F2 = +R153C7-R153C6
```

or

```
R33C7 F2 = ACCDEPRY2-ACCDEPRY1
```

The STATEMENT OF COST OF GOODS SOLD begins at row 42. Cells R51C6 and R51C7 show each year's beginning inventory. Although this number must be entered manually for 19XX (column 6), in 19XY (column 7) the beginning inventory can be computed by drawing on the ending balance in 19XX. This computation is performed by defining cell R51C7 as

```
R51C7 $ = R57C6
```

Rows 52 and 53 should be used to input purchase data. Enter the ending inventory for the two years in cells R57C6 and R57C7. The direct materials expense represents the cost of the materials in the finished goods sold during the period and is determined by subtracting the ending inventory from the total materials available. Cell R59C7, for example, contains the formula

```
R59C7 F2 = R55C7-R57C7
```

Direct labor expense and factory overhead are entered in rows 61 and 63, respectively. Row 65 computes the total cost of goods sold by adding the three component costs: materials, labor, and overhead. For example, cell R65C6 contains the formula

R65C6 $ = R59C6+R61C6+R63C6

The STATEMENT OF INCOME, which begins on row 68, draws information from the Statement of Operating Expenses and the Statement of Cost of Goods Sold. Gross sales and returns and allowances information, however, must be entered in rows 78 and 80, respectively. The cost of goods sold is pulled from that schedule to cells R84C6 and R84C7 by a direct cell reference. For example, the formula in cell R84C6 is

R84C6 F2 = R65C6

Operating expense information is similarly drawn from the operating expense detail schedule. The formula in cell R88C6 is

R88C6 F2 = R38C6

Interest expense and other income or expense amounts are displayed in rows 90 and 92. Any income tax expense incurred in the two years should be entered in row 96.

The net income for both years is computed in cells R98C6 and R98C7, using, for example, the formula

R98C6 $ = R94C6-R96C6

The next section of the model, STATEMENT OF RETAINED EARNINGS, begins at row 102. Notice that this schedule contains data from year 19XW, the year immediately preceding 19XX. This schedule details the activity in the common stock and retained earnings accounts for the two years. Cell R113C7, which shows the net income earned by the company in 19XX, and cell R117C7, which shows the same data for 19XY, automatically pull their data from the Statement of Income. For example, cell R113C7 contains the formula

R113C7 $ = R98C6

The BALANCE SHEET begins at row 123 and is split into two parts: assets, and liabilities and equity. Notice that the totals computed in row 159 equal those in row 199; in other words, assets equal liabilities plus equity. Always check your Balance Sheets to make sure these numbers agree.

Rows 136, 138, 139, 140, 141, and 142 are used to enter the amounts in the current assets accounts. Cells R140C6 and R140C7 show the inventory at the end of each year. The data in these cells come from the Statement of Cost of Goods Sold. Cell R140C7, for example, contains the formula

R140C7 F2 = R57C7

All other asset accounts, except accounts receivable, must be entered from the keyboard.

At row 138 accounts receivable takes into consideration the fact that there will be a percentage of the accounts receivable that will be of a doubtful nature and that the amount of doubtful accounts receivable must be subtracted from the accounts receivable figure. To show the amount of doubtful accounts for each year, R138C1 and R139C1 contain a special Multiplan function, Fixed Function.

The Fixed Function is used in combination with text; combining text and numbers in the same cell is called concatenation. In cell R138C1, type V for Value. This entry calls forth the formula

R138C1 = " Less Doubtful Accounts of $"&FIXED(23000,2)&" in"

Multiplan will not consider the characters between the right and left quotation marks to be numbers. The characters between the ampersands (&) contain the formula that Multiplan will evaluate and concatenate into the cell. The formula fixes the number of significant digits that will be displayed.

The formula in cell R139C1 continues

R139C4 =" 19XX and $"&FIXED(19400,2)&" in 19XY"

The total current assets for year 19XX are derived by the formula in cell R144C6

R144C6 $ = SUM(R136C6:R143C6)

or

R144C6 $ = SUM(CURASSETSY1)

In the same way the total current assets for year 19XY are derived by the formula in cell R144C7

R144C7 $ = SUM(R136C7:R143C7)

or

R144C7 $ = SUM(CURASSETSY2)

Rows 176 through 180, 185, and 187 are used to enter the amounts for current liabilities, long-term debt, and other liabilities. Cells R194C6 and R195C6, and R194C7 and R195C7 relate to the firm's stockholders' equity. Because the figures needed for these cells have already been computed on the Schedule of Stockholders' Equity, we can use a simple formula to repeat them here. For example, cell R194C6 contains the relationship

R194C6 $ = +R115C5

Cell R195C7 is defined as

R195C7 $ = +R119C7

SUBTOTALS AND TOTALS IN THE MODEL

Row	Label	Range
38	Total Operating Expenses	20:36
55	Total Materials Available	51+52-53
59	Direct Materials Expense	55-57
65	Total Cost of Goods Sold	59+61+63
82	Net Sales	78-80
86	Gross Margin	82-84
94	Profit before Taxes	86-88-90-92
98	Net Income	94-96
115	Balance at Any Day, 19XX	111+113
119	Balance at Any Day, 19XY	115+117
144	Total Current Assets	136:142
151	Total Plant, Property, and Equipment	146:149
155	Net Plant, Property, and Equipment	151-153
159	Total Assets	144+155+157
182	Total Current Liabilities	176:180
187	Total Noncurrent Liabilities	184
191	Total Liabilities	182+187+189
197	Total Stockholders' Equity	194+195
199	Total Liabilities and Equity	191+197

Using the Model

Begin using this model by entering the required data in the financial statements. Notice that you do not need to enter any subtotals or totals—the model computes these for you—nor do you need to enter numbers in any of the cells, such as R88C7 or R113C8, that contain formulas referring to other cells. Once you have entered the appropriate data, type F4 or ! to recalculate the model.

Before you print the model, save it by typing **TSB:FINSTATE** (CR). You can print the entire model by typing **PP**, or you can print each section separately by changing the default portion of the **P**rint **O**ptions to one of each area:

Operating Expenses	R11:40
Cost of Goods Sold	R44:66
Statement of Income	R70:100
Retained Earnings	R104:121
Assets	R125:161
Liabilities	R165:201

Once your statements are printed, review them carefully for possible errors. For example, compare your total assets to your total liabilities plus equity. These numbers should always be equal. Are they? Does the retained earnings line on your Balance Sheet agree with your Statement of Retained Earnings? A few minutes of review can prevent costly errors and a great deal of embarrassment.

You will discover another benefit of this model after you start using it. When you update your statements, you can easily set up your previous period column by copying the contents of column 8 in the previous month's model into column 7 of the new model. To copy the contents, use a partial load (if you are using a fresh spreadsheet to set up the new month) or the copy command (if you are building the new model on top of the old one). Be sure to choose the V parameter in the copy command so that you copy into the new cells only the values, not the formulas.

Modifications

The advantage of this model for financial statements is that it provides a standard format that can be used again and again. Because your statements are probably different from the samples shown here, modify the format to meet your needs. This can be done easily enough by simply adding or deleting rows (or in some cases columns) from the the basic format. Be sure to save a master copy of your version for future use.

Performing Ratio Analysis

Ratios are some of the most commonly used financial analysis tools. A few standard ratios computed from a company's balance sheet and income statement can indicate the financial health, stability, and performance of that company. Comparing a company's ratios against a set of budget figures or industry averages can be an important part of measuring its operating success. Ratios do not give a complete picture of a company's financial position, but they do quickly provide information about a firm's significant strengths and weaknesses.

The Ratio Analyzer model is an example of a ratio calculator that can be built into any spreadsheet model of an income statement and balance sheet. The financial statements in this model are only examples—each business will use a different format.

By making ratio analysis an integral part of an Income Statement and Balance Sheet model, or a model of your own, you can add new insight to your analysis of company operations. Keep in mind, however, that the cell references you put in the formulas for ratio calculations must be correct. The references used in the formulas here fit the particular format used in the model's financial statements.

The Model

This model has three sections: INCOME STATEMENT, BALANCE SHEET, and RATIO ANALYSIS.

The INCOME STATEMENT and BALANCE SHEET sections, which begin at cells R10C1 and R35C1, respectively, hold the assumptions used to calculate the ratios. Column 1 contains the labels for the accounts shown on the statements, and column 5 contains the

```
        1           2           3           4            5            6          7
 1 ==========================================================================
 2 RATIO ANALYZER                              Copyright (C) QUE Corp. 1983
 3 ==========================================================================
 4
 5           For INCOME STATEMENT, (G)o (N)ame 'INCOME'
 6           For BALANCE SHEET, (G)o (N)ame 'BALANCE'
 7           For RATIOS ANALYSIS, (G)o (N)ame 'RATIOS'
 8           For Directions, (G)o (N)ame 'INSTRUCTIONS'
 9 ==========================================================================
10 INCOME STATEMENT (Continues to row 32)                          Sheet 1.1
11 ==========================================================================
12                                                   Amount     Percent
13                                                 ---------  ---------
14 Sales                                         $100000.00        100% (12)
15 Cost of Goods Sold                             $72400.00         72% (13)
16                                                ---------      ------
17 Gross Margin                                   $27600.00 (1)     28% (14)
18 Selling, General, and
19    Administrative Expenses                      $7500.00          8% (15)
20 Depreciation                                    $1000.00          1% (16)
21                                                ---------      ------
22 Profit before Interest and Taxes               $19100.00 (2)     19% (17)
23 Interest                                        $2550.00          3% (18)
24                                                ---------      ------
25 Profit before Taxes                            $16550.00 (3)     17% (19)
26 Income Taxes                                    $7050.00          7% (20)
27                                                ---------      ------
28 Profit after Taxes                              $9500.00 (4)     10% (21)
29 Dividends                                       $3500.00          4% (22)
30                                                ---------      ------
31 Retained Earnings                               $6000.00 (5)      6% (23)
32                                                =========       =====
33
```

```
      1         2         3         4         5          6         7
34 ========================================================================
35 BALANCE SHEET (Continues to row 69)                  .         Sheet 2.1
36 ========================================================================
37
38                                               Amount      Percent
39                                             ---------     -------
40 Assets
41  Cash and Marketable Securities              $9000.00          4%  (24)
42  Accounts Receivable                        $24000.00          9%  (25)
43  Inventories                                $18000.00          7%  (26)
44                                              --------      ------
45   Total Current Assets                      $51000.00 (6)     20%  (27)
46
47  Gross Fixed Assets                        $250000.00         98%  (28)
48  Accumulated Depreciation                   $45000.00         18%  (29)
49                                              --------      ------
50   Net Fixed Assets                         $205000.00 (7)     80%  (30)
51                                              --------      ------
52 Total Assets                               $256000.00 (8)    100%  (31)
53                                              ========      ======
54
55 Current Liabilities
56  Bank Loans and Notes Payable               $25000.00         10%  (32)
57  Accounts Payable                           $11000.00          4%  (33)
58                                              --------      ------
59   Total Current Liabilities                 $36000.00 (9)     14%  (34)
60
61  Long-Term Debt                            $100000.00         39%  (35)
62
63  Common Stock                               $75000.00         29%  (36)
64  Retained Surplus                           $45000.00         18%  (37)
65                                              --------      ------
66   Total Stockholders' Equity               $120000.00 (10)    47%  (38)
67                                              --------      ------
68 Total Liabilities and Equity               $256000.00 (11)   100%  (39)
69                                              ========      ======
70
71
72
73
```

```
 74 ======================================================================
 75 RATIO ANALYSIS (Continues to row 101)                        Sheet 3.1
 76 ======================================================================
 77
 78 INDICATORS OF SOLVENCY
 79  Debt/Equity Ratio                                        1.13 (40)
 80  Times Interest Earned                               (41) 6.49  Times
 81
 82 INDICATORS OF LIQUIDITY
 83  Net Working Capital                                 $15000.00 (42)
 84  Net Working Capital/Assets                               0.06 (43)
 85  Current Ratio                                            1.42 (44)
 86  Quick Ratio                                              0.92 (45)
 87  Cash Ratio                                               0.25 (46)
 88
 89 FUNDS MANAGEMENT RATIOS
 90  Receivables/Sales                                        0.24 (47)
 91  Days Sales Outstanding                              (48)   88 Days
 92  Payables/Cost of Goods Sold                              0.15 (49)
 93  Days Purchases in Payables                          (50)   55 Days
 94  Inventory Turnover                                       4.02 (51)
 95  Days Sale in Inventory                              (52)   91 Days
 96  Sales/Fixed Assets                                       0.49 (53)
 97
 98 PROFITABILITY RATIOS
 99  Return on Sales                                           10% (54)
100  Return on Total Assets                                     4% (55)
101  Return on Stockholders' Equity                             8% (56)
102
103
104 ======================================================================
105 INSTRUCTIONS                                                 Sheet 4.1
106 ======================================================================
107
108          1) Enter INCOME STATEMENT and BALANCE SHEET data
109          2) Recalculate by typing: F4 or !
110          3) Review RATIOS
111          4) SAVE by typing: TSB:RATIOS
112          5) PRINT the model by typing: PP
```

PERFORMING RATIO ANALYSIS

NUMBER	LOCATION	FORMULA
1	R17C5	SALES-CGS
2	R22C5	GM-SGAEXP-DEPR
3	R25C5	PBIT-INTEREST
4	R28C5	PBT-TAXES
5	R31C5	PAT-DIVIDENDS
6	R45C5	SUM(CA)
7	R50C5	GFA-ACCDEPR
8	R52C5	NFA+TCA
9	R59C5	SUM(CURLIAB)
10	R66C5	STOCK+RS
11	R68C5	TCL+LTD+EQUITY
12	R14C6	SALES/SALES
13	R15C6	CGS/SALES
14	R17C6	R14C6-R15C6
15	R19C6	SGAEXP/SALES
16	R20C6	DEPR/SALES
17	R22C6	R17C6+R19C6-R20C6
18	R23C6	INTEREST/SALES
19	R25C6	R22C6-R23C6
20	R26C6	TAXES/SALES
21	R28C6	R25C6-R26C6
22	R29C6	DIVIDENDS/SALES
23	R31C6	R28C6-R29C6
24	R41C6	CA/TA
25	R42C6	R42C5/TA
26	R43C6	R43C5/TA
27	R45C6	R45C5/TA
28	R47C6	R47C5/TA
29	R48C6	R48C5/TA
30	R50C6	R47C6-R48C6
31	R52C6	R50C6+R45C6
32	R56C6	R56C5/R68C5
33	R57C6	R57C5/R68C5
34	R59C6	R56C6+R57C6
35	R61C6	R61C5/R68C5
36	R63C6	R63C5/R68C5
37	R64C6	R64C5/R68C5
38	R66C6	R63C6+R64C6
39	R68C6	R59C6+R61C6+R66C6
40	R79C6	(TCL+LTC)/EQUITY
41	R80C6	PBT/INTEREST
42	R83C6	TCA-TCL
43	R84C6	NWA/TA
44	R85C6	TCA/TCL
45	R86C6	(TCA-R43C5)/TCL
46	R87C6	CASH/TCL
47	R90C6	R42C5/SALES
48	R91C6	R90C6*365
49	R92C6	ACCPAY/CGS
50	R93C6	R92C6*365
51	R94C6	CGS/R43C5
52	R95C6	(R43C5/CGS)*365
53	R96C6	SALES/NFA
54	R100C6	PAT/SALES
55	R101C6	PAT/TA
56	R102C6	PAT/EQUITY

balance in each account. The entire label, located in column 1, can be shown by changing the **F**ormat **D**efault to **C**ontinuous.

These two sections, however, are used for entering more than assumptions. Notice the series of percentages in column 6 next to each account balance. These percentages are the Income Statement and Balance Sheet Ratios.

RATIOS: Locations of Named Cells and Ranges

Description	Location	Name
INCOME STATEMENT	R11C1	INCOME
Sales	R14C5	SALES
Cost of Goods Sold	R15C5	CGS
Gross Margin	R17C5	GM
Selling, General, and Administrative Expense	R19C5	SGAEXP
Depreciation	R20C5	DEPR
Profit before Interest and Taxes	R22C5	PBIT
Interest	R23C5	INTEREST
Profit before Taxes	R25C5	PBT
Income Taxes	R26C5	TAXES
Profit after Taxes	R28C5	PAT
Dividends	R29C5	DIVIDENDS
Retained Earnings	R31C5	RE
BALANCE SHEET	R36C1	BALANCE
Cash and Marketable Securities	R41C5	CASH
Total Current Assets	R45C5	TCA
Gross Fixed Assets	R47C5	GFA
Accumulated Depreciation	R48C5	ACCDEPR
Net Fixed Assets	R50C5	NFA
Total Assets	R52C5	TA
Current Liabilities	R55:57C5	CURLIAB
Bank Loans and Notes Payable	R56C5	BLANPAY
Accounts Payable	R57C5	ACCPAY
Total Current Liabilities	R59C5	TCL
Long-term Debt	R61C5	LTD
Common Stock	R63C5	STOCK
Retained Surplus	R64C5	RS
Total Stockholders' Equity	R66C5	EQUITY

RATIOS ANALYSIS	R76C1	RATIOS
Net Working Capital	R83C6	NWC
INSTRUCTIONS	R106C1	INSTRUCTIONS

Income Statement Ratios measure the relationship between sales and each expense item on the income statement. In the example, the ratios are presented in column 6, rows 14 through 31. For example, cell R15C6 measures the ratio between sales and cost of goods sold. This cell is defined as

R15C6 % = R15C5/R17C5

or

R15C6 % = CGS/SALES

Imagine that these percentages are data for a pie chart. The "whole pie" equals the amount of sales. Each expense is a slice. Cost of goods sold would be nearly three-quarters of the pie. Earnings after taxes would be only a sliver.

These ratios are useful because they quickly provide information about business performance. Since they can easily be added to any income statement, they should become a part of all your profit and loss analyses.

In much the same way, *Balance Sheet Ratios* measure the relationship between each asset account and total assets, or between each liability and total liabilities. For example, cell R41C6 contains the formula

R41C6 % = R41C5/R52C5

or

R41C6 % = CA/TA

The result of this calculation, 4%, indicates that cash represents about 1/25th of this company's total assets.

The RATIO ANALYSIS section begins at row 75. Financial ratios can be divided into four major categories:

1. Indicators of Solvency
2. Indicators of Liquidity
3. Funds Management Ratios
4. Profitability Ratios

Each ratio is explained in detail in the following text.

Indicators of Solvency

These ratios measure the long-term financial health of a company by providing information about its capital structure and the management of its current debt burden.

The *Debt/Equity Ratio* is calculated by dividing total debt (both current and long term) by owners' equity (capital stock plus retained earnings). A result greater than one indicates that more long-term financing is being provided by outside creditors than by the owners. This situation is not necessarily cause for alarm, because high levels of debt are common in certain industries, but it does have implications for future financing. A company with a high debt/equity ratio may not be able to obtain more outside debt financing to take advantage of business opportunities or weather a downturn in sales or profits.

Debt/Equity Ratio

R79C6 F2 = (R59C5+R61C5)/R66C5

or

R79C6 F2= (TCL+LTD)/EQUITY

Times Interest Earned indicates how well a company's interest obligations are met by its earnings. If a company's interest payments can be covered several times over by its earnings, then there is little risk of defaulting on a loan if earnings drop. If interest payments are barely being met, however, the chance of default is greater.

Times Interest Earned

R80C6 F2 = R22C5/R23C5

or

R80C6 F2 = PBT/INTEREST

Indicators of Liquidity

These ratios provide signals of a firm's short-term financial health. They show how well a company is able to meet immediate financial obligations, such as bills owed or loan repayments due.

Net Working Capital is not a ratio, but a dollar amount that is determined by subtracting current liabilities from current assets. To think of it another way, net working capital represents the liquid, unencumbered resources of the company.

To say that an asset is "liquid" is to say that it can be easily converted into cash and spent. Cash is the most liquid asset because it does not need to be converted to be spent. Fixed assets (buildings, machines, and so forth) are not liquid because they cannot be converted to cash quickly.

Similarly, unencumbered assets are not offset by current liabilities. In the example, our company has $51,000 of current assets, $36,000 of current liabilities, and therefore a net working capital of $15,000. This $15,000 is unencumbered, or free to be invested or spent at the discretion of the company's management.

Because current liabilities are those obligations due for payment in a year or less, current assets (cash and items that will soon be converted into cash, such as accounts receivable) should be greater than current liabilities. Net working capital, therefore, should be positive.

Net Working Capital

R83C6 $ = R45C5-R59C5

or

R83C6 $ = TCA-TCL

Net Working Capital/Assets equals net working capital divided by total assets. This ratio indicates the percentage of a firm's assets that are liquid and unencumbered.

Net Working Capital/Assets

R84C6 F2 = R83C6/R52C5

or

R84C6 F2 = NWC/TA

The *Current Ratio* is determined by dividing current assets by current liabilities. Like net working capital, current ratio is an indicator of how well a firm can meet its short-term obligations given its current assets. In an ideal situation, where current assets exceed current liabilities, this ratio will have a value greater than one.

Current Ratio

R85C6 F2 = R45C5/R59C5

or

R85C6 F2 = TCA/TCL

The *Quick Ratio,* sometimes called the *Acid Test Ratio,* is calculated by subtracting inventories (the least liquid current asset) from total current assets and dividing the result by current liabilities. The quick ratio is a good indicator of how well current obligations can be met without the difficult task of liquidating inventories.

Quick Ratio

R86C6 F2 = (R45C5-R43C5)/R59C5

or

R86C6 F2 = (TCA-R43C5)/TCL

A firm's *Cash Ratio,* figured by dividing cash and near-cash items (marketable securities) by current liabilities, gives an indication of how well the firm can meet its current obligations with the cash and securities it now holds. This ratio shows what percentage of current liabilities could be paid if all short-term creditors demanded *immediate* payment. In the example, cash and marketable securities total $9,000, and current liabilities are $36,000, giving a cash ratio of .25. This ratio indicates that 25% of all current obligations can be met with the cash and marketable securities the firm now holds.

Cash Ratio

R87C6 F2 = R41C5/R59C5

or

R87C6 F2 = CASH/TCL

Funds Management Ratios

Funds Management Ratios measure the amount of cash that is tied up in a business as a result of operations.

Receivables/Sales is calculated by dividing accounts receivable by total sales for the reporting period. The resulting figure shows what percentage of sales has not been paid. For example, if accounts receivable are $24,000 and sales for the year are $100,000, then the receivables/sales ratio is .24, indicating that 24% of the current period's sales have not been collected. This ratio is one indication of how extensively a company is lending money to its customers by extending trade credit.

Receivables/Sales

R90C6 F2 = +R42C5/R14C5

or

R90C6 F2 = +R42C5/SALES

Days Sales Outstanding is another way of expressing the percentage of sales in accounts receivable. This ratio is computed by dividing accounts receivable by sales and multiplying the result by the number of days in the reporting period. Like the receivables/ sales example, dividing receivables by sales gives the percentage of sales for which payments have not been collected. In our example, the receivables/sales ratio is .24, and the reporting period is one year; therefore .24 x 365 or 88 days' sales are still unpaid. If customer payments are due in 30 days, this shows a pretty poor collection record!

Day Sales Outstanding

R91C6 I = R90C6*365

or

R91C6 I = R[-1]C*365

Payables/Cost of Goods Sold is figured by dividing accounts payable by the cost of goods sold for the reporting period. This ratio indicates the percentage of the current period's cost of goods sold that has not been paid. In the example, we assume that all accounts payable represent purchases of items eventually included in cost of goods to be sold.

Payables/Cost of Goods Sold

R92C6 F2 = R57C5/R15C5

or

R92C6 F2 = ACCPAY/CGS

Days Purchases in Payables is calculated by dividing accounts payable by the cost of goods sold for the reporting period and multiplying the result by the number of days in the period. For example, if the accounts payable/cost of goods sold ratio is .15, and the reporting period is one year, 55 days of cost of goods sold have not been paid (.15 x 365 = 55 days). If standard payment terms are 30 days, then the company is delinquent in paying its suppliers.

Days Purchases in Payables

R93C6 I = R92C6*365

or

R93C6 I = R[-1]C*365

Inventory Turnover measures the average number of times that inventories were replenished during the reporting period. This ratio is calculated by dividing cost of goods sold by inventory currently on hand. High inventory turnover indicates a relatively low level of inventory on hand at any one time. Because stocking inventory ties up funds, most managers prefer to have minimal inventory on hand.

Inventory Turnover

R94C6 F2 = +CGS/R43C5

or

R94C6 F2 = +R15C5/R43C5

Days Sales in Inventory is calculated by dividing inventory by cost of goods sold and multiplying the result by the number of days in the reporting period. In the example, inventory is $18,000, and cost of goods sold for the year is $72,400. Therefore, 91 days of inventory is on hand (calculated as 18,000/72,400 x 365 = 91 days). The target number of days sales in inventory ratio varies widely from industry to industry. Because a low inventory is preferred, 91 days of sales in inventory can be a sign of poor inventory management.

Days Sales in Inventory

R95C6 I = (R43C5/R15C5)*365

or

R95C6 I = (R43C5/CGS)*365

The *Sales/Fixed Assets* ratio is calculated by dividing sales by net fixed assets. Fixed assets can be thought of as the fixed, long-term investment in the business. The sales/fixed assets ratio measures the revenue generated by this investment. A low ratio indicates a capital intensive business, where large amounts of equipment are needed to generate sales. A higher ratio suggests a business with low capital requirements. This ratio, like all of the others, is significant only when compared to a budget, or to the ratios generated by competitors.

Sales/Fixed Assets

R96C6 F2 = R15C5/R50C5

or

R96C6 F2 = SALES/NFA

Profitability Ratios

Profitability ratios measure the dollar return (profit) generated by the resources invested in a business. This return is expressed in relation to sales, assets, and stockholders' equity. These important indicators of business performance provide more useful information than dollar figures alone.

Return on Sales compares a business' profit to the sales required to generate that profit. Return on sales equals earnings after taxes divided by sales. A ratio lower than the industry average may indicate poor expense management or operational inefficiency.

Return on Sales

R99C6 %= R28C5/R14C5

or

R99C6 % = PAT/SALES

The *Return on Total Assets* is calculated by dividing earnings after taxes by total assets. Because assets represent the amount invested in a business, it is important to determine what return is being realized on them. If a business consistently produces returns on assets that are below what could be earned if the assets were employed in a different capacity, management may want to consider shifting to a different product or service.

Return on Total Assets

R100C6 %= R28C5/R52C5

or

R100C6 % = PAT/TA

Return on Stockholders' Equity equals earnings after taxes divided by total stockholders' equity. This ratio is perhaps the most important profitability ratio because it measures the return the owners of the company are earning on their investment. They may compare this return to other potential investments—real estate, money markets, stock in other companies, etc.—to determine whether their investment in the company is worthwhile. If the return on equity is below the rate that may be earned on other similar investments, the stockholders of a publicly traded company may try to bid down the price of the company's stock. The owners of a small business caught in this situation may consider closing up shop.

Return on Stockholders' Equity

R101C6 % = R28C5/R66C5

or

R101C6 % = PAT/EQUITY

Using the Model

This model is not only easy to use, but it is also one of the most valuable models in the book. To use it, fill in the INCOME STATEMENT and BALANCE SHEET sections and type F4 or ! to recalculate. You can save the model by typing **TSB:RATIOS** (CR) and print it by typing **PP**.

Interpreting the results of the model is more difficult. Individual financial ratios have little meaning until they are compared to the industry's historical data. The importance and acceptable range for some ratios can vary widely among industries. In fact, authorities do not even agree on the definition of some ratios! The moral of this paragraph is to be sure to interpret the results of your model carefully.

Modifications

Although the financial statement formats in this model have been designed to be as widely applicable as possible, you may need to make some changes to meet your particular needs. This can be done easily enough, but be certain to review all of the ratio formulas after you make any changes.

These ratios can be added to your financial statement models. They are a tool for saving time and yet improving your analysis. You can also add other ratios to the model. Perhaps you measure your expenses as a percentage of gross margin or dividends as a percentage of earnings after taxes. Use whatever measures you believe will help you manage your business better.

Using Interactive Financial Statements

Could your planning be improved if you had the time to make detailed financial statement projections? Unfortunately, preparing a financial statement is a tedious, time-consuming, and error-prone chore that overworked small-business managers tend to put off. Multiplan, however, can help you develop financial statements quickly and easily.

The Interactive Income Statement and Balance Sheet model is useful for both normal reporting and the development of pro forma analyses. This model is called "interactive" because the Balance Sheet and Income Statement share data (interact). Interactive financial statement models reflect the relationships between the numbers reported in the Income Statement and those in the Balance Sheet.

Principles

An Income Statement represents financial events over some period, usually reporting revenues and expenses over several months or one year. A Balance Sheet, on the other hand, represents a company's financial situation as of a particular date. The Balance Sheet is a "snapshot" of the company's financial condition at that time.

The conditions reported on a Balance Sheet always depend on the events reported in the Income Statement for the previous period. For example, sales made during the year generate cash and accounts receivable, which will be reported on the year-end Balance Sheet. If enough cash is generated, the company may pay off some of its debt, again affecting the year-end Balance Sheet. As earnings boost owners' equity, a company may find that it has greater borrowing

```
       1         2         3         4         5         6         7         8         9
 1 ========================================================================================
 2 INTERACTIVE INCOME STATEMENT AND BALANCE SHEET          (C) QUE Corp. 1983
 3 ========================================================================================
 4
 5                   For ASSUMPTIONS (G)oto (N)ame 'ASSUMPTIONS'
 6                   For BALANCE SHEET (G)oto (N)ame 'BALANCE'
 7                   For INCOME STATEMENT (G)oto (N)ame 'INCOME'
 8                   For INSTRUCTIONS (G)oto (N)ame 'INSTRUCTIONS'
 9 ========================================================================================
10 ASSUMPTIONS (Continued through row 25)                                        Sheet 1.1
11 ========================================================================================
12
13 Interest (Income) Rate:                           18%
14   Earned on Cash Balance Over:           $      5000
15 Interest (Expense) Rate:                          18%
16 Cost of Goods Sold:                               75%
17 Payroll Taxes:                                    10%
18 Income Tax Rate:                                  25%
19
20 Depreciable Life of Assets:                        60  Months
21 Beginning Accumulated Depreciation:      $      5000
22 Days Sales in Accounts Receivable:                 45  Days
23 Days Cost of Goods Sold in Inventory:              30  Days
24 Days Cost of Goods Sold in Payables:               45  Days
25 Beginning Retained Earnings:             $      4200
26
27
```

Row	1–4		5	6	7	8	9	
28	======================							
29	INCOME STATEMENT (Continues through row 71)						Sheet 2.1	
30	======================							
31			Qtr 1	Qtr 2	Qtr 3	Qtr 4	Total	
32			------	------	------	------	------	
33	Gross Income							
34	Product Sales		50,000	55,000	60,000	70,000	235,000	
35	Income from Services		25,000	32,000	35,000	40,000	132,000	①
36	Other Sales		1,500	1,500	1,500	1,500	6,000	
37	Interest Income	③	1,111	1,795	2,699	3,801	9,406	
38			------	------	------	------	------	
39	Total Gross Income	④	77,611	90,295	99,199	115,301	382,406	
40								
41	Cost of Goods Sold	⑤	37,500	41,250	45,000	52,500	176,250	
42			------	------	------	------	------	
43	Gross Margin	⑥	40,111	49,045	54,199	62,801	206,156	②
44								
45	Operating Expenses							
46	Salaries and Wages		9,000	9,000	9,000	9,000	36,000	
47	Benefits		300	300	300	300	1,200	
48	Health Insurance		495	495	495	495	1,980	
49	Payroll Taxes	⑦	900	900	900	900	3,600	
50	Office Rent		1,842	1,842	1,842	1,842	7,368	
51	Supplies		400	400	400	400	1,600	
52	Postage		120	120	120	120	480	
53	Telephone		1,050	1,050	1,050	1,050	4,200	
54	Insurance		75	75	75	75	300	
55	Dues and Subscriptions		120	120	120	120	480	
56	Advertising and Promotion		3,000	3,000	3,000	3,000	12,000	
57	Travel and Entertainment		1,500	1,500	1,500	1,500	6,000	
58	Professional Fees		750	750	750	750	3,000	
59	Depreciation	⑧	1,700	1,700	1,700	1,700	6,800	①
60	Maintenance		400	400	400	400	1,600	
61	Interest	⑨	900	810	720	630	3,060	
62	Equipment Rental		900	900	900	900	3,600	
63	Other		400	400	400	400	1,600	
64			------	------	------	------	------	
65	Total Operating Expenses	⑩	23,852	23,762	23,672	23,582	94,868	
66			------	------	------	------	------	
67	Profit before Taxes	⑪	16,259	25,283	30,527	39,219	111,288	
68								
69	Income Taxes	⑫	4,065	6,321	7,632	9,805	27,822	
70			------	------	------	------	------	
71	Net Income	⑬	12,194	18,962	22,895	29,414	83,466	
72			======	======	======	======	======	
73								
74								

	1–4	5	6	7	8	9
75	====================	=======	=======	=======	=======	=======
76	BALANCE SHEET (Continues to row 123)					Sheet 3.1
77	====================	=======	=======	=======	=======	=======
78		Qtr 1	Qtr 2	Qtr 3	Qtr 4	
79		------	------	------	------	
80	Current Assets					
81	Cash	29,693	44,895	64,974	89,460 (14)	
82	Accounts Receivable	38,805	45,147	49,599	57,650 (15)	
83	Inventory	12,500	13,750	15,000	17,500 (16)	
84		------	------	------	------	
85	Total Current Assets	80,998	103,792	129,573	164,610 (17)	
86						
87	Fixed Assets					
88	Plant, Property, and Equipment					
89	Leasehold Improvements	10,000	10,000	10,000	10,000	
90	Furniture and Fixtures	12,500	12,500	12,500	12,500	
91	Equipment	7,500	7,500	7,500	7,500	
92	Office Equipment	4,000	4,000	4,000	4,000	
93		------	------	------	------	
94	Gross P, P, & E	34,000	34,000	34,000	34,000 (18)	
95	Accumulated Depreciation	(19) 6,700	8,400	10,100	11,800 (20)	
96		------	------	------	------	
97	Net P, P, & E	27,300	25,600	23,900	22,200 (21)	
98						
99	Deposits	611	611	611	611	
100	Other Assets	300	300	300	300	
101		------	------	------	------	
102	Total Fixed Assets	28,211	26,511	24,811	23,111 (22)	
103		------	------	------	------	
104	Total Assets	109,209	130,303	154,384	187,721 (23)	
105		=======	=======	=======	=======	
106						
107						
108	Current Liabilities					
109	Accounts Payable	18,750	20,625	22,500	26,250 (24)	
110	Income Taxes Payable	4,065	6,321	7,632	9,805 (25)	
111		------	------	------	------	
112	Total Current Liabilities	22,815	26,946	30,132	36,055 (26)	
113						
114	Noncurrent Liabilities					
115	Long-Term Debt	20,000	18,000	16,000	14,000	
116		------	------	------	------	
117	Total Liabilities	42,815	44,946	46,132	50,055 (27)	
118						
119	Common Stock	50,000	50,000	50,000	50,000	
120						
121	Retained Earnings	(28) 16,394	35,357	58,252	87,666 (29)	
122		------	------	------	------	
123	Total Liabilities and Equity	109,209	130,303	154,384	187,721	TRUE (30)
124		=======	=======	=======	=======	

(31)

```
        1        2        3        4        5        6        7        8        9
125 ==========================================================================
126 INSTRUCTIONS                                                     Sheet 4.1
127 ==========================================================================
128
129                   1) Enter ASSUMPTIONS
130                   2) Enter other INCOME STATEMENT and BALANCE
131                      SHEET data
132                   3) Recalculate by typing: F4 or !
133                   4) SAVE by typing: TSB:BSINC (CR)
134                   5) PRINT by typing: PP
```

USING INTERACTIVE FINANCIAL STATEMENTS (BSINC)

NUMBER	LOCATION(S)	FORMULA
1	R34:37,39, 41,46:63,65C9	SUM(RC[-4]:RC[-1])
2	R43C9	R39C9-R41C9
3	R37C5:8	IF(CASH>IECBO,(INCRATE/4)*(CASH-IECBO),0)
4	R39C5:8	SUM(R[-5]C:R[-2]C)
5	R41C5:8	CGSPCNT*SALES
6	R43C5:8	GROSSINC-CGS
7	R49C5:8	PAYROLL*PAYROLLTAX
8	R59C5:8	INT(GPPE/LIFE*3)
9	R61C5:8	INT(EXPRATE/4*LTD)
10	R65C5:8	SUM(R[-19]C:R[-2]C)
11	R67C5:8	GM-OPEXP
12	R69C5:8	IF(PBT>0,TAXRATE*PBT,0)
13	R71C5:8	PBT-INCOMETAXES
14	R81C5:8	R[+42]C-R[+21]C-R[+2]C-R[+1]C
15	R82C5:8	INT(DAYSALES/90*GROSSINC)
16	R83C5:8	INT(DAYSINV/90*CGS)
17	R85C5:8	SUM(R[-4]C:R[-1]C)
18	R94C5:8	SUM(R[-5]C:R[-1]C)
19	R95C5	BEGACCDEPR+DEPR
20	R95C6:8	RC[-1]+DEPR
21	R97C5:8	GPPE-ACCUMDEPR
22	R102C5:8	OTHER+DEPOSITS+NETPPE
23	R104C5:8	TCA+FA
24	R109C5:8	DAYSPAY/90*CGS
25	R110C5:8	INCOMETAXES
26	R112C5:8	SUM(R[-4]C:R[-1]C)
27	R117C5:8	TCL+LTD
28	R121C5	BEGRE+PAT
29	R121C6:8	R[-50]C+RC[-1]
30	R123C9	IF(OR(DELTA()<0.1,ITERCNT()=25),TRUE(),FALSE())
31	R123C5:8	TL+CS+RE

capacity, which, if utilized, will increase the amount of debt reported on the Balance Sheet.

A Balance Sheet may also reflect management's expectations about events that will be reported on the next period's Income Statement. For example, the amount of inventory shown on the Balance Sheet in one period is related to the expectation of sales volume for the near future. The inventory will be expensed on a future Income Statement as cost of goods sold.

The events reported on the Income Statement are also related to the conditions reported on the Balance Sheet. Depreciation expense is related to a company's fixed assets, and interest expense is based on the amount of debt. If a company has excess cash, it may earn additional revenue from interest.

Any relationship between an Income Statement and a Balance Sheet can be reflected in an interactive spreadsheet model like this one. If you want to build pro forma statements to cover several years, the relationships can be stated once and then replicated to later periods. This feature saves a tremendous amount of set-up time. If "what if" analysis is performed at a later date, the model will automatically compute the effect of any change on all the interrelationships.

The relationships built into a pro forma model are usually based on either past performance or future objectives. For example, if the cost of goods sold has always been approximately 55% of sales, then this relationship would be expected to hold true in future periods. If management believes that inventory can be held realistically at two months of cost of goods sold, then this relationship will be built into the pro forma analysis. When a company's results are reported, they can be analyzed by comparing the actual relationships to those expected.

The Model

This model has three sections: ASSUMPTIONS, INCOME STATEMENT, and BALANCE SHEET. The ASSUMPTIONS section begins at row 10. The first two assumptions compute interest income on excess cash. The interest rate paid on the excess cash invested is entered in cell R13C6. The cash amount that will *not* be invested to earn interest is entered in cell R14C6. In the example, 5000 is entered in cell R14C6. If the balance in the cash account goes over $5000, then 18% annual interest will be earned on the excess amount.

BSINC: Locations of Named Cells and Ranges

Description	Location	Name
ASSUMPTIONS	R11C1	ASSUMPTIONS
Interest (Income) Rate	R13C6	INCRATE
Earned on Cash Balance Over	R14C6	IECBO
Interest (Expense) Rate	R15C6	EXPRATE
Cost of Goods Sold (Percent)	R16C6	CGSPCNT
Payroll Taxes (Percent)	R17C6	PAYROLLTAX
Income Tax Rate (Percent)	R18C6	TAXRATE
Depreciable Life of Assets (Months)	R20C6	LIFE
Beginning Accumulated Depreciation	R21C6	BEGACCDEPR
Days Sales in Accounts Receivable	R22C6	DAYSALES
Days Cost of Goods Sold in Inventory	R23C6	DAYSINV
Days Cost of Goods Sold in Payables	R24C6	DAYSPAY
Beginning Retained Earnings	R25C6	BEGRE
INCOME STATEMENT	R30C1	INCOME
Product Sales	R34C5:8	SALES
Total Gross Income	R39C5:8	GROSSINC
Cost of Goods Sold (Dollar)	R41C5:8	CGS
Gross Margin	R43C5:8	GM
Salaries and Wages	R46C5:8	PAYROLL
Depreciation	R59C5:8	DEPR
Total Operating Expenses	R65C5:8	OPEXP
Profit before Taxes	R67C5:8	PBT
Income Taxes	R69C5:8	INCOMETAXES
Net Income	R71C5:8	PAT

BSINC: Locations *(cont.)*

Current Assets (Year 19XY)	R136:142C7	CURASSETSY2
Plant, Property, and Equipment 19XX	R147:149C6	PPEY1
Plant, Property, and Equipment 19XY	R147:149C7	PPEY2
Total Plant, Property, and Equipment 19XX	R151C6	TOTPPEY1
Total Plant, Property, and Equipment 19XY	R151C7	TOTPPEY2
Accumulated Depreciation (Year 19XX)	R153C6	ACCDEPRY1
Accumulated Depreciation (Year 19XY)	R153C7	ACCDEPRY2
BALANCE SHEET - LIABILITIES	R164C1	LIABILITIES
Long-Term Debt (Year 19XX)	R185C6	LONGTERMDEBTY1
Long-Term Debt (Year 19XY)	R185C7	LONGTERMDEBTY2
INSTRUCTIONS	R204C1	INSTRUCTIONS

Most of the formulas in this model are simple totals and subtotals; these calculations are summarized in the chart at the end of this section. The more complex relationships are discussed below.

FINANCIAL STATEMENT RELATIONSHIPS

Account	**Appears on**
Depreciation	Statement of Operating Expenses Balance Sheet

Depreciation expense in 19XY equals the difference between 19XX and 19XY accumulated depreciation on the balance sheet.

Inventory	Statement of Cost of Goods Sold Balance Sheet

BALANCE SHEET	R77C1	BALANCE
Cash (Current Assets)	R81C5:8	CASH
Accounts Receivable	R82C5:8	AR
Inventory	R83C5:8	INVENTORY
Total Current Assets	R85C5:8	TCA
Gross P, P, & E	R94C5:8	GPPE
Accumulated Depreciation	R95C5:8	ACCUMDEPR
Net P, P, & E	R97C5:8	NETPPE
Deposits	R99C5:8	DEPOSITS
Other Assets	R100C5:8	OTHER
Total Fixed Assets	R102C5:8	FA
Total Current Liabilities	R112C5:8	TCL
Long-Term Debt	R115C5:8	LTD
Total Liabilities	R117C5:8	TL
Common Stock	R119C5:8	CS
Retained Earnings	R121C5:8	RE
INSTRUCTIONS	R127C1	INSTRUCTIONS

The third assumption, the rate of interest paid on long-term debt, is entered in cell R15C6, EXPRATE. Cell R16C6, CGSPCNT, contains the percentage of product sales put toward cost of goods sold. Payroll taxes, in cell R17C6, PAYROLLTAX, are assumed to be a percentage of the salaries and wages expense. Cell R18C6, TAXRATE, displays the percentage of income tax paid on earnings.

Cells R20C6, LIFE, and R21C6, BEGACCDEPR, contain assumptions related to fixed assets. The average depreciable life of the company's property, plant, and equipment (PP&E), expressed in months, is entered in cell R20C6, LIFE. Cell R21C6, BEGACCDEPR, holds the depreciation accumulated to date on PP&E (that is, the depreciation prior to the periods reported in these financial statements).

In cell R22C6 enter the number of days' sales represented by accounts receivable. (See the Ratio Analyzer model for a discussion of days' sales in accounts receivable.) Cells R23C6 and R24C6, DAYSINV and DAYSPAY, respectively, display the days of cost of goods sold in inventory and days of cost of goods sold in accounts payable. The final assumption, beginning retained earnings, is entered in cell R25C6, BEGRE.

The INCOME STATEMENT begins at row 29. Under the heading Gross Income, you will see a list of revenue categories. For Product Sales, Income from Service, and Other Sales, you should enter the expected quarterly figures. The category Interest Income is derived from the balance in the cash account. If cash exceeds the amount input in cell R14C6, IECBO, then the excess funds are invested at the annual interest rate given in cell R13C6, INCRATE. If the cash balance is less than or equal to the amount in cell R14C6, IECBO, then no interest income will be realized. For the calculation of interest income, the interest rate, shown in cell R13C6, INCRATE, is converted to a quarterly rate by dividing by four. The formula for this calculation is

R37C5 I = IF(R81C5>R14C6,(R13C6/4)*(R81C5-R14C6,0)

or

R37C5 I = IF(CASH>IECBO,(INCRATE/4)*(CASH-IECBO),0)

Total gross income, displayed in row 39, is computed by totaling all income from the various sources, using the formula

R39C5 I = SUM(R34C5:R37C5)

Cost of goods sold is computed by multiplying only product sales revenue by the percentage entered in cell R16C6, CGSPCNT, using the formula

R41C5 I = R34C5*R16C6

or

R41C5 I = CGSPCNT*SALES

Gross margin is computed by subtracting cost of goods sold from total gross income. In this example, the formula for gross margin is

R43C5 I = R39C5-R41C5

or

R43C5 I = GROSSINC-CGS

The next category on the Income Statement is operating expenses. Some of these figures must be entered manually, but others are computed by Multiplan. The expenses that must be keyed in are

Supplies
Dues and Subscriptions
Advertising and Artwork
Maintenance

Payroll taxes are calculated by multiplying salaries and wages by the percentage assumed in cell R17C6, PAYROLLTAX,

R49C5 I = R46C5*R17C6

or

R49C5 I = PAYROLL*PAYROLLTAX

Depreciation expense is based on a straight-line schedule and the depreciable life assumed in cell R20C6, LIFE. To calculate depreciation expense, divide gross plant, property, and equipment (from cell R94C5, PPE) by the number of months in the life of the assets. Then multiply the result by three to obtain the depreciation for one quarter. The formula for computing depreciation expense is

R59C5 I = INT(R94C5/R20C6*3)

or

R59C5 I = INT(GPPE/LIFE*3)

Interest expense is based on both the annual interest rate entered in cell R15C6, EXPRATE, and the outstanding long-term debt in cell R115C5, LTD. To compute interest expense, convert it to a quarterly rate by dividing by four. Multiply the result by the long-term debt balance to obtain the interest expense. The formula for this calculation is

R61C5 I = INT(R15C6/4*R115C5)

or

R61C5 I = INT(EXPRATE/4*LTD)

After all operating expenses have been keyed in or computed, Multiplan totals them, using the SUM function, and displays the total in cell R65C5, OPEXP, using the formula

R65C5 I = SUM(R46C5:R63C5)

Profit before taxes is computed by subtracting total operating expenses from gross margin, using the formula

R67C5 I = R43C5-R65C5

or

R67C5 I = GM-OPEXP

Next, income taxes are computed, using the tax rate entered in cell R18C6, TAXRATE. Because cell R69C6, INCOMETAXES, contains a conditional statement, no tax will be paid unless income is earned. Tax expense is computed by the formula

R69C6 I = IF(R67C5>0,R18C6*R67C6,0)

or

R69C6 I = IF(PBT>0,TAXRATE*PBT,0)

The final figure on the Income Statement—net income, or profit after tax—is computed by subtracting income taxes from profit before taxes, using the formula

R71C5 I = R67C5-R69C5

or

R71C5 I = PBT-INCOMETAXES

Column 9 displays the totals for each Income Statement category. All of these totals are calculated using Multiplan's SUM function to add the figures in columns 5 through 8. For example, total product sales for the four quarters is computed by this formula

R34C9 I = SUM(RC[-4]:RC[-1])

The BALANCE SHEET begins at row 76 and continues through row 123. The first account balance, cash, is defined in terms of several other cells in the Balance Sheet. An examination of these cells will help explain the cash formula.

Accounts receivable is based on the assumption made in cell R22C6. This number is first converted to a quarterly number by dividing the number by 90 (the number of days in a quarter), then multiplying by the total gross income for the quarter to obtain an accounts receivable balance. These computations are contained in the formula

R82C5 I = INT(R22C6/90*R39C5)

or

R82C5 I = INT(DAYSALES/90*GROSSINC)

The balance in the inventory account is based on the assumption made in cell R23C6 about the number of days of cost of goods sold in inventory. In our example, inventory is equal to 30 days. This figure is converted to one-fourth by dividing it by 90 (days). The inventory balance at the end of the first quarter is similarly computed with the formula

R83C5 I = INT(R23C6/90*R41C5)

or

R83C5 I = INT(DAYSINV/90*CGS)

Total current assets—equal to the sum of cash, accounts receivable, and inventory—are computed in the first quarter by the formula

R85C5 I = SUM(R81C5:R84C5)

The depreciable assets—property, plant, and equipment—are listed under the heading Fixed Assets. The amounts in each fixed asset account appear in rows 89 through 92. Gross PP&E in the first quarter is computed by the formula

R94C5 I = SUM(R89C5:R93C5)

Net PP&E equals gross PP&E less accumulated depreciation. Cell R95C5 computes the new accumulated depreciation balance with the formula

R95C5 I = R21C6+R59C5

or

R95C5 I = BEGACCDEPR+DEPR

This balance is then subtracted from the gross PP&E in cell R94C5 to arrive at net PP&E.

R97C5 I = R94C5-R95C5

or

R97C5 I = GPPE-ACCUMDEPR

There are two other fixed asset accounts in this example: deposits and other assets. The balances for both of these accounts must be entered manually, then added to net PP&E to obtain total fixed assets, computed by the formula

R102C5 I = R100C5+R99C5+R97C5

or

R102C5 I = OTHER+DEPOSITS+NETPPE

Finally, total assets are figured by adding total current assets and total fixed assets, as follows:

R104C5 I = R85C5+R102C5

or

R104C5 I = TCA+FA

The first liability account, accounts payable, is determined by the current period's cost of goods sold and the assumption entered in cell R24C6, DAYSPAY. The number of days is divided by 90 to convert it to a quarterly amount, then multiplied by the cost of goods sold for the quarter. For example, in cell R109C5, ACCPAY, accounts payable for the first quarter is computed by the formula

R109C5 I = R24C6/90*R41C5

or

R109C5 I = DAYSPAY/90*CGS

Income taxes payable are assumed to be equal to the income tax expense for the current quarter and are obtained by referring to the taxes computed on the Income Statement in the formula

R110C5 I = R69C5

or

R110C5 I = INCOMETAXES

Total current liabilities, which is the sum of all current liabilities, is computed in the first period with the formula

R112C5 I = SUM(R108C5:R111C5)

In this example, noncurrent liabilities have only one account: long-term debt. This number is entered when the model is built.

Noncurrent and current liabilities are added to obtain total liabilities, using the formula

R117C5 I = R112C5+R115C5

or

R117C5 I = TCL+LTD

The amount of common stock outstanding should be entered in cell R119C5, CS. The new retained earnings balance is then computed by adding the prior balance to net income (profit after taxes) for the period.

R121C5 I = R25C6+R71C5

or

R121C5 I = BEGRE+PAT

This figure becomes the prior retained earnings balance for the following period.

The last figure on the Balance Sheet, total liabilities and equity, equals the sum of total liabilities, common stock, and retained earnings. This value must equal the value in row 104, total assets, in order for the figures to balance.

R123C5 I = R117C5+R119C5+R121C5

or

R123C5 I = TL+CS+RE

Now, skip back up to row 81, which is labeled Cash. The cash balance is computed by subtracting accounts receivable, inventory, and total fixed assets from total liabilities and equity. If you study this relationship closely, you will see that cash becomes the "plug" that balances the Balance Sheet. Notice, however, that the plug is an accurate one. The sum of total liabilities and equity can be thought of as all of the cash that has flowed into a company, while accounts receivable, inventory, and total fixed assets represent the cash obligations. Netting these inflows and outflows will yield the cash balance, which is calculated by the formula

R81C5 I = +R[+42]C-R[+21]C-R[+2]C-R[+1]C

Using the Model

This model is easy to use. You need only to determine the numerical relationships that exist in your business between the Balance Sheet and the Income Statement and enter the numbers, either actual or pro forma, in the statements for the period you are modeling.

Some relationships in the model are circular references; that is, the contents of one cell determine the formula in another cell, and so on through the model until the first cell is influenced again. For example, in this model, cash balance determines interest income, which affects net income, which affects retained earnings, which determines total liabilities and equity. Because cash is defined, in part, by total liabilities and equity, an increase in cash will lead eventually to an increase in retained earnings, which will lead to another increase in cash, and so on.

To overcome the circular reference problem, the formula

```
IF(OR(DELTA()<0.1,ITERCNT()=25),TRUE(),FALSE())
```

is placed in cell R123C9. This cell is then identified as the location of the completion test for Multiplan's iterative recalculation command by typing

Options(TAB) (TAB)**Y**(TAB)**R123C9**

Each time you instruct Multiplan to recalculate when the program is in the iterative mode, the program will begin recalculating and will continue until the completion test becomes TRUE. Thus, in the case above, the program will continue to recalculate until either the total change of all the values in the model from one recalculation to the next is less than 0.1 (the DELTA test) or until 25 complete recalculations have been made. Because of the iterative abilities of Multiplan, the circular references in this model are no problem.

After the recalculations are finished you can save the model by typing **TSB:BSINC** (CR) and print it by typing **PP**.

By using this Multiplan model to plan your business, you can save a tremendous amount of time that may otherwise be spent tracking the flow of funds. The effects of increases or decreases in sales and expenses, fixed asset purchases and sales, and changes in the collection or payment cycles will be calculated automatically by the model. Be sure to take advantage of this feature by performing extensive "what if" analysis on your projections.

Modifications

This model was designed to accommodate the financial statements of an average company. Most of the concepts included in it probably apply to your business. You can modify the model to fit special needs by changing the labels and inserting or deleting a few rows.

7

Planning and Budgeting

Performing Statistical Analysis

Managers use statistics regularly to analyze their business situation and to facilitate the decision-making process. For example, in analyzing the past year's sales, a manager may want to know the average sales per month per salesperson, or may want to study the relationship between advertising and sales. Statistics can also be used to study production processes and to analyze both equipment and employee performance.

Multiplan has some built-in functions that can help you do basic statistical analysis on a series of numbers. The Statistics Calculator model shows you how to perform the analysis.

Principles

Statistics summarize and organize data in a meaningful and useful way. The *mean,* or average, is a commonly used statistic that marks the midpoint, or norm, of a group of data. It is calculated by adding the items in a group and dividing the total by the number of items.

A moving average is one of a series of averages calculated for a group of numbers. Moving averages are computed for data that represent observations made over a certain period. For example, many businesses track sales on a monthly basis and construct moving averages from this data. Every month, an average of the last three months' sales is computed, called the three-month moving average. Moving averages can be computed for other periods, such as 2 weeks, 6 months, 12 months, and so on.

Statistics can be used to indicate the dispersion of values in a group of numbers, or how much the numbers, as a group, vary from the average. Two of these statistics, the *minimum* and the *maximum,* represent the smallest and largest numbers in a group. Another

```
       1          2          3          4          5          6          7
 1 ========================================================================
 2 STATISTICS CALCULATOR                         Copyright (C) QUE Corp. 1983
 3 ========================================================================
 4
 5           For DATA TABLE and MOVING AVERAGES, (G)oto (N)ame 'TABLE'
 6           For SOLUTIONS, (G)oto (N)ame 'SOLUTIONS'
 7           For INSTRUCTIONS, (G)oto (N)ame 'INSTRUCTIONS'
 8
 9 ========================================================================
10 DATA TABLE AND MOVING AVERAGES (Continues to row 42)          Sheet 1.1
11 ========================================================================
12                 Data            3-Period  6-Period 12-Period
13                 Item    Value    Moving    Moving    Moving
14                  (X)     (Y)     Average   Average   Average
15                 ----   -------   -------   -------   -------
16                    1     2500
17                    2     3467
18                    3     4335   3434.00
19                    4     6554   4785.33
20                    5     2333   4407.33
21                    6     5789   4892.00   4163.00
22                    7     3445   3855.67   4320.50
23                    8     2467   3900.33   4153.83
24                    9     4568   3493.33   4192.67
25                   10     9777   5604.00   4729.83
26                   11     8666   7670.33   5785.33
27                   12    10995   9812.67   6653.00   5408.00
28             (1)   13    10540  10067.00   7835.50   6078.00
29                   14     7656   9730.33   8700.33   6427.08
30                   15    10444   9546.67   9679.67   6936.17
31                   16    11025   9708.33   9887.67   7308.75
32                   17     9555  10341.33  10035.83   7910.58
33                   18    10678  10419.33   9983.00   8318.00
34                   19    11934  10722.33  10215.33   9025.42
35                   20    12450  11687.33  11014.33   9857.33
36                   21    11777  12053.67  11236.50  10458.08
37                   22    12017  12081.33  11401.83  10644.75
38                   23    12698  12164.00  11925.67  10980.75
39                   24    13000  12571.67  12312.67  11147.83
40               -------  -------
41    Totals     (2) 300  198670 (3)   (4)       (5)       (6)
42               =======  =======
43
```

SCRATCH PAD

Row	Difference from Mean	Difference Squared	X Times Y	X Squared
16	5778	33384321	2500	1
17	4811	23144919	6934	4
18	3943	15546592	13005	9
19	1724	2971889	26216	16
20	5945	35342034	11665	25
21	2489	6194706	34734	36
22	4833	23357084	24115	49
23	5811	33766753	19736	64
24	3710	13763482	41112	81
25	-1499	2247251	97770	100
26	-388	150609	95326	121
27	(14) -2717	7382542 (15)	131940 (16)	144 (17)
28	-2262	5117021	137020	169
29	622	386780	107184	196
30	-2166	4691917	156660	225
31	-2747	7546467	176400	256
32	-1277	1630942	162435	289
33	-2400	5760400	192204	324
34	-3656	13366945	226746	361
35	-4172	17406279	249000	400
36	-3499	12243584	247317	441
37	-3739	13980744	264374	484
38	-4420	19537137	292054	529
39	-4722	22298071	312000	576
41		321218468	3028447	4900
		(18)	(19)	(20)

```
        1         2         3         4         5         6         7
44 =======================================================================
45 SOLUTIONS                                                    Sheet 2.1
46 =======================================================================
47          Number of Items:                          24.00 (7)
48          Maximum Value                       (8) 13000.00
49          Minimum Value:                          2333.00 (9)
50          Range:                             (10) 10667.00
51          Mean:                                   8277.92 (11)
52          Standard Deviation:                (12)  3737.11
53          Linear Regression:
54            Data Item:                                 26
55            Estimated Value:                     14676.59 (13)
56
57
58
59
60
61 =======================================================================
62 INSTRUCTIONS                                                 Sheet 3.1
63 =======================================================================
64
65
66          1) Enter data in column headed "Values"
67          2) RECALCULATE by typing: F4 or !
68          3) SAVE by typing: TSB:STAT (CR)
69          4) Print by typing: PP
```

STATISTICS (STAT)

NUMBER	LOCATION(S)	FORMULA
1	R17:39C2	R[-1]C+1
2	R41C2	SUM(X)
3	R41C3	SUM(Y)
4	R18:39C4	AVERAGE(R[-2]C[-1]:RC[-1])
5	R21:39C5	AVERAGE(R[-5]C[-2]:RC[-2])
6	R27:39C6	AVERAGE(R[-11]C[-3]:RC[-3])
7	R47C5	COUNT(Y)
8	R48C5	MAX(Y)
9	R49C5	MIN(Y)
10	R50C5	MAX-MIN
11	R51C5	AVERAGE(Y)
12	R52C5	STDEV(Y)
13	R55C5	(((((TI*TV)/COUNT)-TXY)/(((TI^2/COUNT)-T2))*R54C5)+((TV/COUNT)-(((((TV*TI)/COUNT)-TXY)/(((TI^2)/COUNT)-T2))*(TI/COUNT))))
14	R16:39C10	MEAN-Y
15	R16:39C11	DIFFERENCE^2
16	R16:39C12	X*Y
17	R16:39C13	X^2
18	R41C11	SUM(DIFFSQ)
19	R41C12	SUM(XY)
20	R41C13	SUM(XSQ)

statistic, the *range,* is the difference between the minimum and the maximum.

The *variance* and the *standard deviation* are related dispersion statistics. To calculate the variance, subtract the mean of the numbers from each number in the group and square each result. Add the squares, and divide the total by the number of figures in the group. To compute the standard deviation, take the square root of the variance.

What does the standard deviation tell you? As a general rule, about 68% of the items in a normally distributed population will fall in a range between the mean plus the standard deviation, and the mean minus the standard deviation. That is, 68% of the numbers in the group are no more than one standard deviation from the mean.

Some statistical methods can be used to make predictions. One such method, *linear regression,* is based on the study of the relationship between two variables. For example, suppose a business manager wants to study the relationship between company sales and advertising expenditures. The two variables involved are sales dollars and advertising dollars. In this case, advertising is the "independent" variable, or the variable that can be changed—for example, more or less can be spent on advertising, as the manager decides. Sales is the "dependent" variable, or the variable that depends on the value of the independent variable.

Let's assume that the manager wants to know what sales for the next quarter will be if advertising expenditures are doubled. This figure can be determined by using linear regression to define the relationship between the sales for the past quarter and the corresponding advertising expenditures. With this relationship, a prediction can be made about next quarter's sales given a certain amount of advertising.

If you are familiar with regression analysis, you know that it is more complex than this brief explanation implies. This example is used to show how Multiplan can perform a simple linear regression based on one independent variable.

The Model

The Statistics Calculator model has two sections: DATA TABLE AND MOVING AVERAGES and SOLUTIONS. The DATA TABLE, beginning at row 10, contains the numbers to be analyzed and the moving averages for the series of numbers.

STATS: Locations of Named Cells and Ranges

Description	Location	Name
TABLE	R11C1	TABLE
SCRATCH PAD	R14C9	
Data Item (X)	R16:39C2	X
Value (Y)	R16:39C3	Y
Difference from Mean	R16:39C10	DIFFERENCE
Difference Squared	R16:39C11	DIFFSQ
Value Times Data Item	R16:39C12	XY
X Squared	R16:39C13	XSQ
Total of Items	R41C2	TI
Total of Values	R41C3	TV
Total of Sums of X and Y	R41C12	TXY
Total of X Squared	R41C13	T2
SOLUTIONS	R46C1	SOLUTIONS
Number of Items	R47C5	COUNT
Maximum Value	R48C5	MAX
Minimum Value	R49C5	MIN
Range	R50C5	RANGE
Mean	R51C5	MEAN
INSTRUCTIONS	R63C1	INSTRUCTIONS

Numbers are entered in rows 16 through 39 under the Value (Y) heading, then totaled in cell R41C3 by the formula

R41C3 I = SUM(R16C3:R39C3)

or

R41C3 I = SUM(Y)

Each cell in column 2 contains a number for each item in the series. For example, cell R16C2, X, contains the number 1. Cell R17C2 is then defined as

R17C2 = +R[-1]C+1

Cells are numbered using the automatic numbering method of adding one to the immediately preceding cell. For example, cell R27C2 is defined as

R27C2 = +R[-1]C+1

The numbers in column 2 will be used later as the independent variable in the linear regression. If you do not want to use the automatic numbering method, you can enter the actual values for the independent variable on which your regression will be based.

After all of the data has been entered, moving averages are computed in columns 4 through 6. The first 3-period moving average is displayed in cell R18C4. It calculates the average of cells R16C3 through R18C3, X, using the formula

R18C4 F2 = AVERAGE(R[-2]C[-1]:RC[-1])

This formula is **C**opied with relative references through cell R39C4.

The first 6-period moving average appears in cell R21C5, using the formula

R21C5 F2 = AVERAGE(R[-5]C[-2]:RC[-2])

Cell R27C6 holds the first 12-period moving average, which is defined as

R27C6 F2 = AVERAGE(R[-11]C[-3]:RC[-3])

The SOLUTIONS section of the model provides several statistics for the series of numbers being analyzed. The following formulas calculate these statistics:

Number of Items

R47C5 I = COUNT(Y)

or

R47C5 I = COUNT(R17C3:R39C3)

Maximum Value

R48C5 F2 = MAX(Y)

or

R48C5 F2 = MAX(R17C3:R39C3)

Minimum Value

R49C5 F2 = MIN(Y)

or

R49C5 F2 = MIN(R17C3:R39C3)

Range

R50C5 F2 = MAX-MIN

or

R50C5 F2 = R48C5-R49C5

Mean

R51C5 F2 = AVERAGE(Y)

or

R51C5 F2 = AVERAGE(R17C3:R39C3)

Before the standard deviation or the linear regression can be computed, the model must make some intermediate calculations in the SCRATCH PAD that begins at R14C9.

Under the heading, Difference from Mean, each number in column 3 is subtracted from the mean, as calculated in cell R51C5, MEAN. For example, the formula in cell R25C10 is

R25C10 I = R51C5-R25C3

or

R25C10 I = MEAN-Y

Each figure from column 10 is squared in column 11 (which has a range name of DIFFSQ). This can be done either by raising the number to the power of 2 (for example, R25C10^2) or by multiplying each number by itself, the method used in this model.

R25C11 I = R25C10^2

or

R25C11 I = DIFFERENCE^2

Column 12 contains the result of multiplying the figures in column 2, X, by the corresponding values in column 3, Y. For example

R25C12 I = R25C2*R25C3

or

R25C12 I = X*Y

The range R16:39C12 bears the name XY. The results are totaled in cell R41C12.

R41C12 I = SUM(R17C12:R19C12)

or

R41C12 I = SUM(XY)

The figures from column 2 are squared in column 13; the range name of the column is XSQ. For example, cell R25C13 contains the formula

R25C13 I = X^2

or

R25C13 I = R25C2^2

These results are totaled in cell R41C13.

R41C13 I = SUM(R17C13:R39C13)

or

R41C13 I = SUM(XSQ)

After these calculations have been performed, the model can compute the remaining statistics. The standard deviation is computed by the formula

R52C5 F2 = STDEV(R17C4:R39C4)

or

R52C5 F2 = STDEV(Y)

To perform the linear regression, select a value for the independent variable and enter it in cell R54C5 (26 was chosen for this example).

Then the value of the dependent variable can be calculated in cell R55C5 using the rather lengthy formula

R55C5 F2 = (((((TI*TV)/COUNT)-TXY)/(((TI^2/COUNT)-T2))*R54C5)+((TV/COUNT)-(((((TV*TI)/COUNT)-TXY)/(((TI^2)/COUNT)-T2))*(TI/COUNT))))

Using the Model

To use this model, enter the data items you want to evaluate in column 3. When they are all in place, type F4 or ! to recalculate.

To perform a regression analysis, enter a target data item in cell R54C5 and recalculate. You may want to perform this operation several times to evaluate the expected values at a number of different data points.

You can save the model by typing **TSSTATS** (CR) and print it by typing **PP**.

If you track statistics on a regular basis, a model like this one can be valuable. If you keep monthly sales records for each salesperson, you can use this model to build another one that will allow you to enter the latest numbers and adjust the statistical formulas to compute updated statistics.

Modifications

You can evaluate more or fewer data items than the 24 presented in the example by inserting or deleting rows. Be sure to adjust the cell references in the formulas in the SOLUTIONS cells to reflect your changes.

Calculating Growth Capacity

How fast can your business grow? The growth potential of any business depends on many factors, including the availability of outside financing, profitability, and the percentage of profits paid out in dividends. One way to analyze the growth capacity of your business is to develop financial projects based on realistic assumptions about the factors that constrain growth. This Multiplan Growth Capacity Calculator model can help you do that.

Principles

A company's sales cannot grow without the necessary financial resources. In other words, "You have to spend money to make money." Before sales can increase, a company must obtain enough working capital (cash) to hire more workers, buy additional raw materials, or invest in new equipment. Higher sales also lead to higher accounts receivable balances that must be financed. In most cases, the increased expenses will be incurred before the first dollar of increased revenue comes through the door. This is true for both service and manufacturing firms.

Building a financial growth model involves making projections about future financing based on the following factors:

1. The debt-to-equity ratio (See the Ratio Analyzer in Chapter 6 for more information.)
2. The interest rate paid on long-term debt
3. The company's profitability
4. The tax rate on the company's earnings
5. The percentage of earnings distributed as dividends

```
        1         2         3        4        5        6        7        8
 1 ==========================================================================
 2 GROWTH CAPACITY CALCULATOR                       Copyright (C) QUE Corp 1983
 3 ==========================================================================
 4
 5          For CAPITALIZATION (G)oto (N)ame 'CAPITALIZATION'
 6          For PROFITABILITY (G)oto (N)ame 'PROFITABITLITY'
 7          For EARNINGS AND DIVIDENDS (G)oto (N)ame 'EARNINGS'
 8          For INSTRUCTIONS, (G)oto (N)ame 'INSTRUCTIONS'
 9 ==========================================================================
10 CAPITALIZATION               Year 1    Year 2    Year 3    Year 4    Year 5
11 ========================== ======== ======== ======== ======== ========
12                                          (2)
13 Accepted Debt/Equity Ratio (1) 0.80    [0.80      0.80]     1.00      1.00
14 * Equity               $    5,000 (3) 5,717 (4) 6,495 (5) 7,411 (6) 8,551
15 * Total Debt           $    4,000     4,574     5,196     7,411     8,551 (7)
16                             ------    ------    ------    ------    ------
17 Total Capitalization   $    9,000    10,291    11,691    14,821    17,103 (8)
18                             ======    ======    ======    ======    ======
19
20 * Interest Rate (Percent)     13%       15%       13%       12%       11%
21                             ======    ======    ======    ======    ======
22
23 ==========================================================================
24 PROFITABILITY               Year 1    Year 2    Year 3    Year 4    Year 5
25 ==========================  ======    ======    ======    ======    ======
26 * Profit before Interest
27     and Taxes          $      1700     1,944     2,208     2,800     3,231 (9)
28 Interest Expense       $       520       663       675       889       941 (10)
29                             ------    ------    ------    ------    ------
30                        $     1,180     1,281     1,533     1,910     2,290 (11)
31 Tax Rate (Percent)       (12) 35%     [35%       35%       35%       35%] (13)
32                             ------    ------    ------    ------    ------
33 * Tax Expense                  414       449       538       670       803 (14)
34                             ------    ------    ------    ------    ------
35 Profit after Tax               766       831       995     1,240     1,486 (15)
36                             ======    ======    ======    ======    ======
37
```

```
38 ==========================================================================
39 EARNINGS AND DIVIDENDS          Year 1   Year 2   Year 3   Year 4   Year 5
40 ======================== ======== ======== ======== ======== ========
41
42 Target Dividend Payout (%)     (16) 6%  (17) 6%       8%  (17) 8%  (17) 8%
43 * Dividends Paid                   49       53       80       99      119 (18)
44                                ------   ------   ------   ------   ------
45 Earnings Reinvested               717      778      915    1,141    1,368 (19)
46                                ======   ======   ======   ======   ======
47
48 Net Return on Equity (%)       15.32%   14.54%   15.32%   16.73%   17.38% (20)
49                                ======   ======   ======   ======   ======
50
51
52 ==========================================================================
53 INSTRUCTIONS
54 ==========================================================================
55
56          1) Enter data in the positions marked with a '*'
57          2) Recalculate by typing: F4 or !
58          3) Review PROFITABILITY results
59          4) SAVE by typing: TSB:GROWTH (CR)
60          5) PRINT by typing: PP
```

CALCULATING GROWTH CAPACITY

NUMBER	LOCATION(S)	FORMULA
1	R13C4	TOTALDEBT/EQUITY
2	R13C5:6,8	RC[-1]
3	R14C5	R14C4+R45C4
4	R14C6	R14C5+R45C5
5	R14C7	R14C6+R45C6
6	R14C8	R14C7+R45C7
7	R15C5:8	DERATIO*EQUITY
8	R17C4:8	EQUITY+TOTALDEBT
9	R27C5:8	RC[-1]/R[-10]C[-1]*R[-10]C
11	R28C4:8	INTERESTRATE+TOTALDEBT
12	R30C4:8	PBIT-INTERESTEXP
13	R31C4	(TAXEXP/(PBIT-INTERESTEXP))
14	R31C5:8	TAXRATE
15	R33C5:8	((PBIT-INTERESTEXP)*TAXRATE)
16	R35C4:8	PBIT-INTERESTEXP-TAXEXP
17	R42C4	DIVIDENDS/PAT
18	R42C5,7,8	RC[-1]
19	R43C5:8	TARGETPAY*PAT
20	R45C4:8	PAT-DIVIDENDS
21	R48C4:8	PAT/EQUITY

Sales growth financing can come from three sources: selling stock, borrowing from a bank or other outside lender, or reinvesting profits earned by the firm. Each alternative has its strengths and weaknesses. Because you don't have to pay dividends or interest on stock, it is a cheap way to raise money. But selling stock takes some of the control over the business away from the owners. In addition, new stock issues are feasible only if the company can offer real value for each share. Borrowing does not require sacrificing ownership interest, but can become unsafe or impossible when debt begins to exceed a certain percentage of a firm's total capitalization. Reinvestment of earnings is the least expensive way to raise money, but requires both profitability *and* investors who are willing to forgo high dividends.

Typically, a firm begins its life with a combination of stock and debt, which, as time passes, is supplemented by retained earnings.

Occasionally, a company will be capitalized exclusively with stock. Let's examine why this is not always the best policy.

The term "leverage" describes the advantages of careful borrowing. Here's an example of how leverage works. Joe Smith starts Company A by investing $100 of his hard-earned cash. In its first year of operations, Company A makes a profit of $10. Joe Jones, another budding entrepreneur, starts company B at the same time, investing $50 of his own money and borrowing $50 from his bank. Jones' business also makes a profit (in this case, before interest) of $10. After he pays his interest of $4, he is left with $6, or $4 less than Smith. But notice that Smith has $100 invested in Company A, whereas Jones has only $50 in Company B. Smith's $10 profit represents a 10% return on his investment, but Jones' $6 is a 12% return on his smaller investment. Jones has used a lever—the bank loan—to increase the earning power of his investment.

If Jones had invested only $1 and had borrowed $99, his return would have been even higher. But would you lend money to Jones under those circumstances? Probably not. Most lenders want a "cushion" of stock to protect their loan from any losses the borrower may incur. The realities of borrowing can constrain a company from realizing the maximum leverage on its investment.

Debt creates an expense—interest—that affects the third source of financing, the firm's profits. In general, debt is advantageous as long as the company earns a rate of return that is higher than the interest rate it pays on the loan. This is the case in our example. If the loan does not create a positive net return, then the excess interest expense will reduce the amount of earnings that can be plowed back into the firm.

Taxes and dividends also affect the amount of profit that can be retained in the business because they drain cash from the business that could be used to finance growth. As a result, growing firms frequently pay no dividends. Taxes are unavoidable, but every attempt should be made to minimize and defer as much of the tax burden as possible under the law.

The Model

All of the factors discussed above are included in the financial growth model. This model analyzes the growth capacity of a business over a five-year period, given certain assumptions about the company's debt-to-equity ratio, its profitability, the tax rate, and the dividend payout percentage. The model has three sections: CAPITALIZATION, PROFITABILITY, and EARNINGS AND DIVIDENDS.

GROWTH: Locations of Named Cells and Ranges

Description	**Location**	**Name**
CAPITALIZATION	R11C1	CAPITALIZATION
Accepted Debt/Equity Ratio	R13C4:8	DERATIO
Equity	R14C4:8	EQUITY
Total Debt	R15C4:8	TOTALDEBT
Interest Rate (Percent)	R20C4:8	INTERESTRATE
PROFITABILITY	R25C1	PROFITABILITY
Profit before Interest and Taxes	R27C4:8	PBIT
Interest Expense	R28C4:8	INTERESTEXP
Tax Rate (Percent)	R31C4:8	TAXRATE
Tax Expense	R33C4:8	TAXEXP
Profit after Tax	R35C4:8	PAT
EARNINGS AND DIVIDENDS	R40C1	EARNINGS
Target Dividend Payout (%)	R42C4:8	TARGETPAY
Dividends Paid	R43C4:8	DIVIDENDS
Earnings Reinvested	R45C4:8	REINVESTED
INSTRUCTIONS	R54C1	INSTRUCTIONS

The CAPITALIZATION section begins at row 10. Columns 1 through 3 contain labels that define the cells in each row. The rows that begin with an asterisk (*) indicate where you should enter your assumptions about each factor. This model has been formatted to show commas by the **F**ormat **O**ptions(TAB)**Y**es (for commas) command. If you use a dollars and cents format, you will be unable to show 80 columns on the screen at one time.

Cell R14C4, EQUITY, shows the current amount of equity invested in our sample business, including stock and any profits retained from past years' operations. Cell R15C4, TOTALDEBT, contains the amount of debt owed by the firm.

Multiplan uses the inputs in cells R14C4, EQUITY, and R15C4, TOTALDEBT, to compute the company's accepted debt-to-equity ratio in cell R13C4, using the formula

R13C4 F2 = R15C4/R14C4

or

R13C4 F2 = TOTALDEBT/EQUITY

Cell R17C4 contains the formula

R17C4 I = R14C4+R15C4

or

R17C4 I = EQUITY+TOTALDEBT

which represents the total capitalization of the sample firm.

The cells in row 20 show the interest rates to be paid on the company's debt in each of the next five years. You must enter a rate for each year. If you have loans at several different rates, these cells should contain a weighted average of all the loan rates.

The next section of the model, PROFITABILITY, begins at row 24. Cell R27C4, PBIT, shows the profit earned for the past year, before interest and taxes.

Multiplan computes the annual interest expense in row 28 by multiplying total debt by the interest rate. For example, cell R28C4, INTERESTEXP, contains the formula

R28C4 I = R20C4*R15C4

or

R28C4 I = INTERESTRATE*TOTALDEBT

Cell R30C4 subtracts the interest expense from the profit before interest and taxes using the formula

R30C4 I = R27C4-R28C4

or

R30C4 I = PBIT-INTERESTEXP

Cell R33C4, TAXEXP, is also an input cell. It displays the amount of income tax paid by our sample business during the current year. Multiplan uses this amount to compute the actual tax rate. This calculation is performed in cell R31C4, TAXRATE, by the formula

R31C4 % = (R33C4/(R27C4-R28C4))

or

R31C4 % = (TAXEXP/(PBIT-INTERESTEXP))

Cell R35C4, PAT, shows the profit after both interest and taxes have been deducted, which is computed as

R35C4 I = R30C4-R28C4-R33C4

or

R35C4 I = PBIT-INTERESTEXP-TAXEXP

The next section of the model, EARNINGS AND DIVIDENDS, begins at row 39. Cell R43C4, DIVIDENDS, holds the dividend amount paid out to the firm's stockholders during the current year. Multiplan computes the target dividend payout percentage in cell R42C4, TARGETPAY,

R42C4 % = R43C4/R35C4

or

R42C4 % = DIVIDENDS/PAT

Cell R45C4, REINVESTED, calculates the amount of income reinvested in the firm during the current year. This amount equals net income after interest, dividends, and taxes have been deducted. Cell R45C4, REINVESTED, is defined as

R45C4 I = R35C4-R43C5

or

R45C4 I = PAT-DIVIDENDS

The final row in this section, row 48, computes the net return on equity for each of the five years by dividing the profit after tax, but before dividends (row 35), by the company's total equity (row 15). For example, cell R48C4 contains the formula

R48C4 % = R35C4/R14C4

or

R48C4 % = PAT/EQUITY

Row 48 helps measure the effect any changes made to the model will have on the return earned by the stockholders.

Now move back up the worksheet to cell R13C5. Notice that this cell is defined as

R13C5 F2 = +RC[-1]

Cell R13C6, is also defined as

R13C6 F2 = R13C5

or

R13C6 F2 = +RC[-1]

In fact, each cell in row 13 is defined as equal to the ratio calculated in the preceding cell in that row. Unless you change it, Multiplan will assume that the same debt-to-equity ratio will be used for each year in the future.

This scheme is used to define rows 31 (effective tax rate) and 42 (target dividend payout percentage). The formulas in each cell refer to the cells immediately to their left, keeping these target relationships constant until you decide to change them.

A similar relationship used in row 27 (PBIT) is

R27C5 I = +RC[-1]/R[-10]C[-1]*R[-10]C

Cell R27C6 is also defined as

R27C6 I = RC[-1]/R[-10]C[-1]*R[-10]C

The formula takes the prior year's profit before interest and taxes, divides it by the prior year's capitalization, and multiplies the result by this year's capitalization.

Move the cursor to cell R14C5, EQUITY, which displays the equity invested in the business at the beginning of the second year. This cell contains the formula

R14C5 I = R14C4+R45C4

or

R14C5 I = -RC[-1]+R[+31]C[-1]

In other words, the equity in one year equals the equity from the previous period plus any earnings retained in the business from that year. Therefore, the equity in cell R14C5 is $717 more than that in cell R14C4. The $717 represents new capital, which can be used to finance sales growth. It also qualifies the business for additional debt financing. Assuming that the debt-to-equity ratio is maintained at .8, $717 of new equity will allow the company to borrow $574 of new debt. In the real world, this borrowing would not take place all at once on the first day of the new year. But if a company were attempting to "grow" its sales as fast as possible, it would certainly want to consider maintaining its debt at the highest acceptable level by borrowing more money. Cell R15C5, TOTALDEBT, reflects this assumption with the formula

R15C5 I = R13C5*R14C5

or

R15C5 I = DERATIO*EQUITY

Columns 6, 7, and 8 repeat the same relationships.

Using the Model

Let's review what this model does. The model calculates various percentages from actual first-year data that you enter in column 4. These percentages are then used to compute projections for sales, dividends, and taxes in columns 5, 6, 7, and 8. Retained earnings from each year carry over to the equity line in the next year, thus increasing the company's level of indebtedness to the degree specified by the debt-to-equity ratio.

To use the model, enter your data in the following cells:

Current Equity	R14C4
Current Debt	R15C4
Interest Rates on Debt	R20C4:8
Current Year Tax Expense	R33C4
Current Year Dividend Payout	R43C4

As you review the formulas in this model, you will notice that there are several "forward references"—cells that depend on other cells that are either below them or to their right. Unlike SuperCalc, Multiplan offers a natural method of recalculation that can handle forward references.

Recalculate the model by typing F4 or ! and review the results. You can save the model by typing **TSB:GROWTH** (CR) and print it by typing **PP**.

Be sure to play with the model to see what effect each variation has on your assumptions. For example, look at cell R13C4, DERATIO. This value should be your present actual debt-to-equity ratio. Is this number as high as you would like? Can you take advantage of leverage by increasing the amount of debt on your books? Or is the number too high? Do you feel overburdened by the amount of debt you are carrying? If so, make changes in the future periods to adjust this figure.

The projection can be altered either by changing the assumptions computed the first year or by altering one of the model's "constants"—the debt-to-equity ratio, the tax rate, or the dividend payout percentage. Changing any of these assumptions is easy. Move the cursor to the appropriate cell and enter your new number. For example, suppose that you want to increase your debt-to-equity ratio from .8 to 1 in the fourth year. Move the cursor to cell R13C7, DERATIO, and enter a 1. Now recalculate the model. Notice that the ratio in cell R13C8, DERATIO, is now also 1.00. If you want a different ratio in column 8, you must make the change manually.

Managing Queues

Every company deals with waiting lines, or queues, at some point in its operations. When you think of a waiting line, you may picture people waiting for a service, such as the line at a bank teller's window, but there are other kinds of queues: machines waiting to be repaired, products waiting to be packaged, programs waiting to be run on a computer, and so on.

As a manager, your goal is to keep waiting time in the queue to a minimum without sacrificing the efficiency of the service system. Queuing theory, as used in this book, can help you evaluate your current queuing system and decide when to increase service capacity to meet growing demand. Queuing theory can answer such questions as: Do my customers wait too long for service? What is the typical backlog of orders waiting to be processed? Should I hire extra workers during the busy season? If so, how many?

The *two* models in this section can help you evaluate many different alternatives for queue management to decide which one is best for your business.

Principles

The waiting time in a queue depends on two factors:

1. Demand—How many people or items require service in a given period
2. Capacity—How many people or items can be serviced in a given period

To use queuing theory, you will need the demand and capacity information for the system you want to evaluate. For example, if you are the manager of a customer service department that handles telephone calls from people placing orders and asking about products, you will need to know the average number of calls received in an hour, as well as the average number of calls that can be handled by your department in an hour. You may want to collect separate data for peak service hours and other special times.

Some businesses consider queuing management from a different standpoint. For example, a frame shop may want to find out how many pictures, on average, are brought in each week for framing and how many can be framed in a week given the current staff and facilities.

After the demand and capacity information has been collected, you can use queuing theory to find the average waiting time for your queue, its average length, the average service time, and what percentage of the service system is being utilized. Using this information, you can vary some of the factors and study the effect on the overall system.

Returning to the customer service example, suppose that you want to cut down the average waiting time for each caller. You may want to consider two possibilities: adding another person to take calls, or streamlining call-handling procedures so that the current number of employees can answer more calls per hour. Either or both of these possibilities can be incorporated into this Multiplan model to allow you to study their effect on waiting time.

The Models

These models evaluate queue management for two basic types of systems: a single-station service system and a multistation service system. One example of a single-station service system is a dentist's office where a single dentist handles all patients. A multistation service system may be a fast-food restaurant where several people take orders and collect money. Because the formulas for multiple stations are more complex than those for a single station, the two models will be explained separately.

MSQUEUE and SSQUEUE: Locations of Named Cells and Ranges

Description	SSQUEUE	MSQUEUE	Names
ASSUMPTIONS	R11C1	R11C1	ASSUMPTIONS
FACTORIAL TABLE	N/A	R6C12	FACTORIALTABLE
Average Number of Arrivals/Hour	R14C7	R14C7	ARRIVALS
Average Service Capacity/Hour	R15C7	R15C7	CAPACITY
Number of Service Facilities	N/A	R16C7	FACILITIES
SOLUTIONS	R23C1	R31C1	SOLUTIONS
Idle Time Percentage	R24C7	R34C7	IDLETIME
Expected Number in Queue	R28C7	R37C7	EXPECTED
Total Factorial	N/A	R6:30C14	TOTALFACTOR
INSTRUCTIONS	R42C1	R46C1	INSTRUCTIONS

Each model has two sections: ASSUMPTIONS and SOLUTIONS. The ASSUMPTIONS section begins at cell R10C1. Cell R14C7, ARRIVALS, contains the first assumption, the average number of arrivals per hour, which is equivalent to the demand for service that will be placed on the system in a given period. Although one hour is the period used in these models, it can be changed to minutes, quarter hours, days, weeks, or whatever best fits your queuing situation.

The second assumption, entered in cell R15C7, CAPACITY, is the average service capacity per hour, which is the number of individuals who can receive service during the given period. For the multistation model, this figure should indicate the hourly service capacity of each service station. For example, in a fast-food restaurant, the number of customers handled by each cashier in an hour would be entered here.

```
         1         2         3         4         5         6         7         8
 1 ===============================================================================
 2 QUEUE ANALYSIS (SINGLE-STATION SERVICE FACILITY)      (C) QUE Corp. 1983
 3 ===============================================================================
 4
 5                    For ASSUMPTIONS, (G)oto (N)ame 'ASSUMPTIONS'
 6                    For SOLUTIONS, (G)oto (N)ame 'SOLUTIONS'
 7                    For INSTRUCTIONS, (G)oto (N)ame 'INSTRUCTIONS'
 8
 9 ===============================================================================
10 ASSUMPTIONS                                                          Sheet 1.1
11 ===============================================================================
12
13
14          Average Number of Arrivals per Hour:                   25
15          Average Service Capacity per Hour:                     30
16
17
18
19
20
21 ===============================================================================
22 SOLUTIONS                                                            Sheet 2.1
23 ===============================================================================
24          Idle Time Percentage:                                  17% (1)
25          Utilization Percentage:                                83% (2)
26          Average Service Time:                           (3)  2.00 Minutes
27          Expected Number in System:                              5 (4)
28          Expected Number in Queue:                               4 (5)
29          Average Waiting Time In Queue:                  (6) 10.00 Minutes
30          Probability That Number in System
31            Is Greater Than:         5                           48% (7)
32
33
34
35
36
37
38
39
40 ===============================================================================
41 INSTRUCTIONS                                                         Sheet 3.1
42 ===============================================================================
43
44
45                    1) Enter ASSUMPTIONS
46                    2) Recalculate by typing: F4 or !
47                    3) SAVE by typing: TSB:SSQUEUE (CR)
48                    4) PRINT by typing: PP
```

MANAGING QUEUES SINGLE STATION (SSQUEUE)

NUMBER	LOCATION(S)	FORMULA
1	R24C7	(1-(ARRIVALS/CAPACITY))
2	R25C7	1-IDLETIME
3	R26C7	60/CAPACITY
4	R27C7	ARRIVALS/(CAPACITY-ARRIVALS)
5	R28C7	(ARRIVALS^2)/(CAPACITY*(CAPACITY-ARRIVALS))
6	R29C7	(EXPECTED/ARRIVALS)*60
7	R31C7	((ARRIVALS/CAPACITY)^(R31C4-1))

In the multistation model only, the number of stations providing service must be entered in cell R16C7, FACILITIES. The term "station" in this model refers to an individual service provider; it may be a teller window in a bank or a checkout counter in a grocery store.

Caution: The average number of arrivals in a period must always be less than the average number that can be served in that period. That is, the number input in cell R14C7, ARRIVALS, must always be less than the number input in R15C7, CAPACITY (or in the multistation model, less than the value in cell R15C7, CAPACITY, times the value in R16C7, FACILITIES). Otherwise, the queue would grow longer and longer as time passed, until it finally (at least in theory) reached infinity.

Single-Station Facility Model

Let's look at the SOLUTIONS section, cell R22C1, in the single-station facility model. The first two figures in this section, idle time percentage and utilization percentage, indicate how efficiently the service system is being used. The idle time percentage is the percentage of time that nothing or no one is waiting in the queue or being serviced. It is computed by the formula

R24C7 % = (1-(R14C7/R15C7))

or

R24C7 % = (1-(ARRIVALS/CAPACITY))

Utilization percentage is calculated by subtracting the idle time percentage from 1, using the formula

R25C7 % = 1-R24C7

or

R25C7 % = 1-IDLETIME

Cell R26C7 holds the average amount of time required to service each person or item in the queue. This amount is computed by dividing the 60 minutes in an hour by the hourly service capacity. Therefore, the formula for cell R26C7 is

R26C7 F2 = 60/R15C7

or

R26C7 F2 = 60/CAPACITY

The next figure, expected number in system, represents the average number of people or items being serviced and waiting for service at any time. This figure is computed by the formula

R27C7 I = R14C7/(R15C7-R14C7)

or

R27C7 I = ARRIVALS/(CAPACITY-ARRIVALS)

The expected number in the queue, as displayed in cell R28C7, represents the expected length of the waiting line and is computed as

R28C7 I = (R14C7^2)/(R15C7*(R15C7-R14C7))

or

R28C7 I = (ARRIVALS^2)/(CAPACITY*
(CAPACITY-ARRIVALS))

The average waiting time is computed by dividing the length of the queue by the number of arrivals per hour. The result of this computation was multiplied by 60 to express the waiting time in minutes rather than as a fraction of an hour.

R29C7 F2 = (R28C7/R14C7)*60

or

R29C7 F2 = (EXPECTED/ARRIVALS)*60

The last computation made for a single-station system is the probability of whether the number in the system will be greater than some figure you enter. Remember that the number in the system equals the sum of the number receiving service and the number waiting in the queue. Enter the number that you want to evaluate in cell R31C4. In this example, we used 5. Cell R27C7 tells us that the expected number in the system at any time is 5. If we want to know what the chances are of having more than this number, we use the formula

R31C7 % = ((R14C7/R15C7)^(R31C4-1))

or

R31C7 % = ((ARRIVALS/CAPACITY)^(R31C4-1))

The result tells us that there is a 48% chance of having more than 5—the expected number—waiting in the queue or being serviced.

Multistation Facility Model

The FACTORIAL TABLE, located at cell R6C12 contains LOOKUP tables that allow Multiplan to solve formulas which contain a factorial expression (like some of the multistation queuing formulas). A factorial, denoted by an exclamation point (!) after a number, is interpreted as the product of the number multiplied by each positive integer less than that number. For example, 5 factorial would be denoted by 5! and interpreted as 5*4*3*2*1 = 120.

Because Multiplan has no built-in factorial function, a table of factorial values was created for the numbers 1 through 25. This table is very easy to construct. In one column, list the numbers for which you want factorial values. In this example, the numbers 1 through 25 are listed in cells R6C12 through R30C12.

Each factorial value can be based on the factorial for the number that immediately precedes it. For example, four factorial (4!) is equal to 4 x 3! We can begin computing the factorial values by entering a 1 in cell R6C13. Then, in cell R7C13, we use the formula

R7C13 I = +R[-1]C*RC[-1]

```
        1         2         3         4         5         6         7         8
 1 ==========================================================================
 2 QUEUE ANALYSIS (MULTISTATION SERVICE FACILITY)        (C) Que Corp. 1983
 3 ==========================================================================
 4
 5                   For ASSUMPTIONS (G)oto (N)ame `ASSUMPTIONS'
 6                   For SOLUTIONS (G)oto (N)ame `SOLUTIONS'
 7                   For INSTRUCTIONS (G)oto (N)ame `INSTRUCTIONS'
 8
 9 ==========================================================================
10 ASSUMPTIONS                                                      Sheet 1.1
11 ==========================================================================
12
13
14          Average Number of Arrivals per Hour:                  75
15          Average Service Capacity per Hour:                    30
16          Number of Service Facilities:                          3
17
18
19
20
21
22
23
24
25
26
27
28
29 ==========================================================================
30 SOLUTIONS                                                        Sheet 2.1
31 ==========================================================================
32
33
34          Idle Time Percentage:                         ①  4.49%
35          Utilization Percentage:                       ② 95.51%
36          Average Service Time:                         ③  2.00   Minutes
37          Expected Number in Queue:                     ④     4
38          Average Waiting Time in Queue:                ⑤     3   Minutes
39
40
41
42
43
44 ==========================================================================
45 INSTRUCTIONS                                                     Sheet 3.1
46 ==========================================================================
47
48                   1) Enter ASSUMPTIONS
49                   2) Recalculate by typing: F4 or !
50                   3) Review SOLUTIONS
51                   4) SAVE by typing: TSB:MSQUEUE (CR)
52                   5) PRINT by typing: PP
```

	9	10	11	12	13	14
1						
2					FACTORIAL	
3					TABLE	
4						
5						
6				1	1 (6)	2.5
7				2	2	3.125
8				3	6	0
9				4	24	0
10				5	120	0
11				6	720	0
12				7	5040	0
13				8	40320	0
14				9	362880	0
15				10	3628800	0
16				11	39916800	0
17				12	4.79E+08	0
18				13	6.23E+09 (7)	0 (8)
19				14	8.72E+10	0
20				15	1.31E+12	0
21				16	2.09E+13	0
22				17	3.56E+14	0
23				18	6.4E+15	0
24				19	1.22E+17	0
25				20	2.43E+18	0
26				21	5.11E+19	0
27				22	1.12E+21	0
28				23	2.59E+22	0
29				24	6.2E+23	0
30				25	1.55E+25	0
31						--------
32						5.625 (9)
33						========

MANAGING QUEUES MULTISTATION (MSQUEUE)

NUMBER	LOCATION(S)	FORMULA
1	R34C7	(((ARRIVALS/CAPACITY)^FACILITIES)/(LOOKUP (FACILITIES,R6C12:R30C13)*(1-((ARRIVALS/ CAPACITY)/FACILITIES)))+1+R32C14)^(-1)
2	R35C7	1-IDLETIME
3	R36C7	60/CAPACITY
4	R37C7	(((ARRIVALS/CAPACITY)^(FACILITIES+1))/ (FACILITIES*(LOOKUP(FACILITIES,R6C12:R30C13))* (1-((ARRIVALS/CAPACITY)/FACILIITES))^2))*IDLETIME
5	R38C7	(EXPECTED/ARRIVALS)*60
6	R6C13	RC[-1]
7	R7:30C13	R[-1]C+RC[-1]
8	R6:30C14	IF((FACILITIES-1)>=RC[-2],((ARRIVALS/CAPACITY)^ RC[-2])/RC[-1],0)
9	R33C14	SUM(TOTALFACTOR)

This formula makes the value for 2! appear in cell R7C13. Using relative values, you can replicate the formula down through cell R30C13. Because the factorial values become large quickly, many of them will appear in scientific notation.

The numbers in cells R6C14 through R30C14 of the table are used to compute the idle time percentage, on which some of the other formulas for multistation queues are based. The formula contains the expression

$$\frac{(A/C)^1}{1!} + \frac{(A/C)^2}{2!} + \ldots + \frac{(A/C)^{S-1}}{(S-1)!}$$

where

A = average number of arrivals per hour
C = average service capacity per hour
S = number of service stations

Clearly, this expression cannot be handled by Multiplan's built-in functions. Column 14 of the table computes a sum based on this expression and the number of service stations as given in cell R16C7, FACILITIES. To build this part of the table, the following formula is entered in cell R14C6:

```
R6C14= IF(R16C7-1)>RC[-2],((R14C7/R15C7)^RC[-2]/
       RC[-1],0)
```

or

```
R6C14= IF((FACILITIES-1)>=RC[-2],((ARRIVALS/
       CAPACITY)^RC[-2])/RC[-1],0)
```

The same formula is copied through cell R30C14, TOTALFACTOR. Cell R32C14 displays the total of cells R6C14 through R30C14, TOTALFACTOR, using the formula

```
R32C14= SUM(R6C4:R30C14)
```

or

```
R32C14= SUM(TOTALFACTOR)
```

The first calculation in the SOLUTIONS section of the model, which begins at cell R30C1, is the idle time percentage in cell R34C7, IDLETIME. It is computed by the formula

R34C7 % = (((R14C7/R15C7)^R16C7)/(LOOKUP(R16C7,
R6C12:R30C13)*(1-((R14C7/R15C7)/R16C7)))+1
+R32C14)^(-1)

or

R34C7 % = (((ARRIVALS/CAPACITY)^FACILITIES) /
(LOOKUP(FACILITIES,R6C12:R30C13)*(1-
((ARRIVALS/CAPACITY)/FACILITIES)))+1
+R32C14)^(-1)

The result is subtracted from 1 to obtain the utilization percentage. This percentage is displayed in cell R35C7, which contains the formula

R35C7 % = 1-R34C7

or

R35C7 % = 1-IDLETIME

The formula for computing average service time is the same for both the multi- and the single-station models and is entered in cell R36C7 as

R36C7 F2 = 60/R15C7

or

R36C7 F2 = 60/CAPACITY

The expected number in the queue is displayed in cell R37C7 and computed by the formula

R37C7 I =(((R14C7/R15C7)^(R16C7+1))/(R16C7*LOOKUP
(R16C7,R6C12:R30C13))*(1-((R14C7/R15C7)/
R16C7)^2))*R34C7

or

R37C7 I =(((ARRIVALS/CAPACITY)Δ(FACILITIES+1))/
(FACILITIES*LOOKUP(FACILITIES,
R6C12:R30C13))*(1-((ARRIVALS/CAPACITY)/
FACILITIES))^2))*IDLETIME

The result of this calculation is used to compute the average waiting time in the queue. This figure appears in cell R38C7, which contains the formula

R38C7 I = (R37C7/R14C7)*60

or

R38C7 I = (EXPECTED/ARRIVALS)*60

Using the Model

The instructions for the single-station and the multistation models are similar. To start, enter the ASSUMPTIONS in the appropriate cells and type F4 or ! to recalculate. Save the model by typing **TSB:MSQUEUE** (CR) or **TSB:SSQUEUE** (CR) and print by typing **PP**.

You can use both of these models to determine the effects of increasing your service capacity. For example, if you now have one person handling phone-in orders, the single-station model will evaluate the service being provided by this one person. You can then use the multistation model to see what would happen to callers' waiting time if two people were receiving phone-in orders.

Modifications

This model can be modified to evaluate queue information using a basis other than one hour. To do the modification, change the assumptions at the top of your model to reflect the new basis. For example, to analyze the number of machines brought in for repair each day, your assumptions should read: Average Number of Arrivals per Day and Average Service Capacity per Day. Then change the average service time and average waiting time to an hourly or daily basis.

Budgeting for a New Venture

New venture budgets are used frequently by product managers, sales managers, and entrepreneurs to analyze the potential of a new product or business. New venture budgets are also used by venture capitalists to determine investment potential.

Unfortunately, developing such a budget can be a complex process. The budget must include all revenues and expenses associated with the new venture and calculate expected profits and retained earnings over a certain period. Because expectations about these factors can vary widely and change rapidly, start-up budgets are usually changed many times before they are finalized. With Multiplan and this budget model, however, you can build and modify budget projections quickly and easily.

Principles

The profit potential of any new product or business depends on two factors: how much money is expected to flow in and how much is expected to flow out. The level of inflows and outflows depends on the number of units sold of a product or service, unit price, unit cost, selling costs, the overhead level that must be maintained to support the sales effort, and so on. Let's take a look at some important relationships that affect the profitability of a new product.

The gross margin of a product equals its sale price minus its cost and direct selling expenses. If the product is purchased and resold, both the cost and sales price are easily measured. Estimating the true cost for manufactured goods, however, is more difficult. The gross margin equals the real income (the value added, so to speak) that is gained by selling a product. All expenses must be paid out of this amount. Anything left over after expenses is profit.

The direct selling cost of a product, which may include sales commissions and shipping and handling costs, varies from product to product. In general, the direct selling cost is estimated as a percentage or a fixed dollar amount per unit sold.

Overhead expenses can also be linked to sales. Selling more units requires more support staff, more space to house that staff, and so on. These relationships are not as closely linked to the level of sales as the gross margin, but an accurate model will find the "stepping points" where these expenses increase, and include them.

The goal of this model is to determine the profit level a product will generate. Profit is the net income (sales minus expenses) generated in a period. Retained earnings equals the accumulated profit earned by a product across many periods. Naturally, both numbers vary with revenues and expenses.

To build a new venture budget, you must analyze the relationships between cash inflows and outflows. In an ideal world, all interrelationships would be incorporated into the model. Unfortunately, not even Multiplan can include every relationship, although the following model does include all those discussed above.

The Model

This model makes projections for a product that consists of two components sold together as a single package. You might think of it as a specialized computer system where the two components are hardware and software. Where unit sales are projected, each unit is composed of these two separate components. Commas are used in this model by typing **F**ormat **O**ptions(TAB)**Y**es.

```
        1        2        3         4          5          6          7          8
 1 ==========================================================================
 2 NEW VENTURE BUDGET                             Copyright (C) QUE Corp. 1983
 3 ==========================================================================
 4
 5        For PRODUCT PRICE AND COST DATA (G)oto (N)ame `PRICECOST'
 6        For EXPENSE DATA (G)oto (N)ame `EXPENSE'
 7        For PROJECTIONS (G)oto (N)ame `PROJECTIONS'
 8        For INSTRUCTIONS (G)oto (N)ame `INSTRUCTIONS'
 9 ==========================================================================
10 PRODUCT PRICE AND COST DATA                                      Sheet 1.1
11 ==========================================================================
12                                 Sales      Unit     Gross    Percent
13                                 Price      Cost     Margin    Margin
14                               --------   --------  --------  --------
15  Component 1                     9745       5450      4295       44%
16  Component 2                     7000       1100      5900 (1)   84% (2)
17                               --------   --------  --------  --------
18                            (3)  16745  (4)  6550     10195       61%
19                              =========  =========  =========  =========
20
21 ==========================================================================
22 EXPENSE DATA                                                     Sheet 2.1
23 ==========================================================================
24 Sales Commission                   8%
25 Base Salary                    17000  per Quarter
26   to Be Increased by            6250  after            20   Sales
27 Wage Overhead                    30%   of Salaries
28
29 Office Expenses                10000
30   to Be Increased by            2000  after            20   Sales
31
32 Advertising Expense              10%   of Sales  and        50000   in Year 1
33
```

```
          1        2        3        4         5         6         7         8
34 ===========================================================================
35 PROJECTIONS (Continues to the right)                              Sheet 3.1
36 ===========================================================================
37
38                               Year 1                    Year 2
39                              --------   ------------------------------------
40                               Total    1st Qtr   2nd Qtr   3rd Qtr   4th Qtr
41                              --------  --------  --------  --------  --------
42 Unit Sales                         0         7         9        11        12
43 Dollar Sales                       0   117,215   150,705   184,195   200,940 (5)
44
45 Cost of Goods Sold                 0    45,850    58,950    72,050    78,600 (7)
46 Direct Sales Expenses              0     9,377    12,056    14,736    16,075 (8)
47                               ------    ------    ------    ------    ------
48 Gross Margin                       0    61,988    79,699    97,409   106,265 (9)
49
50 Operating Expenses
51  Salaries                 (10) 68,000 (11)17,000 (12)17,000 (13)23,250 (14)23,250
52  Wage Overhead            (19) 81,600 (20) 5,100     5,100     6,975     6,975
53  Office Expenses          (21) 40,000 (22)10,000 (23)10,000 (24)12,000 (25)12,000
54  Advertising              (30) 50,000 (31)11,722    15,071    18,420    20,094
55                               ------    ------    ------    ------    ------
56 Total Operating Expenses(32) 239,600    43,822    47,171    60,645    62,319 (32)
57                               ------    ------    ------    ------    ------
58 Net Income                  -239,600    18,166    32,528    36,765    43,946 (33)
59                              =======   =======   =======   =======   =======
60 Retained Earnings       (34) -239,600  -221,434  -188,906  -152,141  -108,195 (35)
61                              =======   =======   =======   =======   =======
62
63
64 ===========================================================================
65 INSTRUCTIONS                                                      Sheet 4.1
66 ===========================================================================
67
68                  1) Enter PRODUCT PRICE and COST DATA
69                  2) Enter EXPENSE DATA
70                  3) Enter UNIT SALES projection
71                  4) Recalculate by typing: F4 or !
72                  5) SAVE by typing: TSB:STARTUP
73                  6) PRINT by typing: PP
```

	9	10	11	12	13	14	15
34							
35							
36							
37							
38				Year 3			
39		--------	--------	--------	--------		
40	Total	1st Qtr	2nd Qtr	3rd Qtr	4th Qtr	Total	Totals
41	--------	--------	--------	--------	--------	--------	--------
42	39	14	14	14	14	56	95
43	653,055	234,430	234,430	234,430	234,430 (5)	937,720	1,590,775
44	(6)						
45	255,450	91,700	91,700	91,700	91,700 (7)	366,800	622,250
46	52,244	18,754	18,754	18,754	18,754 (9)	75,018	127,262
47	------	------	------	------	------	------	------
48	345,361	123,976	123,976	123,976	123,976	495,902	841,263
49							
50			(9)			(36)	(37)
51	80,500	(15) 23,250	(16) 23,250	(17) 23,250	(18) 23,250	93,000	241,500
52	24,150	(20) 6,975	6,975	6,975	6,975	27,900	133,650
53	44,000 (6)	(26) 12,000	(27) 12,000	(28) 12,000	(29) 12,000	48,000	132,000
54	65,306	(31) 23,443	23,443	23,443	23,443	93,772	209,078
55	------	------	------	------	------	------	------
56	213,956	65,668	65,668	65,668	65,668 (32)	262,672	716,228
57	------	------	------	------	------	------	------
58	131,405	58,308	58,308	58,308	58,308 (33)	233,230	125,036
59	=======	=======	=======	=======	=======	=======	=======
60		-49,887	8,420	66,728	125,036		
61		=======	=======	=======	=======		
62							
63							
64							

BUDGETING FOR A NEW VENTURE (STARTUP)

NUMBER	LOCATION(S)	FORMULA
1	R15:16,18C6	SALESPRICE-UNITCOST
2	R15:16,18C7	GROSSMARGIN/SALESPRICE
3	R18C4	COMP1SP+COMP2SP
4	R18C5	COMP1UC+COMP2UC
5	R43C4:8,10:13	R[-1]C*R18C4
6	R42,43,45,46, 51,52,53,54,56C9	SUM(RC[-4]:RC[-1])
7	R45C4:8,10:13	R[-3]C*R18C5
8	R46C4:8,10:13	R[-3]C*R24C4
9	R48C5:13	R[-5]C-R[-3]C-R[-2]C
10	R51C4	(BASESALARY+IF(R42C4>BASESALES,BASEINCREASE,0))*4
11	R51C5	(BASESALARY+IF(SUM(R42C4:R42C5)>BASESALES,BASEINCREASE,0))
12	R51C6	(BASESALARY+IF(SUM(R42C4:R42C6)>BASESALES,BASEINCREASE,0))
13	R51C7	(BASESALARY+IF(SUM(R42C4:R42C7)>BASESALES,BASEINCREASE,0))
14	R51C8	(BASESALARY+IF(SUM(R42C4:R42C8)>BASESALES,BASEINCREASE,0))
15	R51C10	(BASESALARY+IF(SUM(R42C9:R42C10)>BASESALES,BASEINCREASE,0))
16	R51C11	(BASESALARY+IF(SUM(R42C9:R42C11)>BASESALES,BASEINCREASE,0))
17	R51C12	(BASESALARY+IF(SUM(R42C9:R42C12)>BASESALES,BASEINCREASE,0))
18	R51C13	(BASESALARY+IF(SUM(R42C9:R42C13)>BASESALES,BASEINCREASE,0))
19	R52C4	WAGEOH*SALARIES*4
20	R52C5:8,10:13	WAGEOH*SALARIES
21	R53C4	(OFFEXP+IF(R42C4>OFFEXPINCSALES,OFFEXPINC,0))*4
22	R53C5	(OFFEXP+IF(SUM(R42C4:R42C5)>OFFEXPINCSALES,OFFEXPINC,0))
23	R53C6	(OFFEXP+IF(SUM(R42C4:R42C6)>OFFEXPINCSALES,OFFEXPINC,0))
24	R53C7	(OFFEXP+IF(SUM(R42C5:R42C7)>OFFEXPINCSALES,OFFEXPINC,0))
25	R53C8	(OFFEXP+IF(SUM(R42C5:R42C8)>OFFEXPINCSALES,OFFEXPINC,0))
26	R53C10	(OFFEXP+IF(SUM(R42C9:R42C10)>OFFEXPINCSALES,OFFEXPINC,0))
27	R53C11	(OFFEXP+IF(SUM(R42C9:R42C11)>OFFEXPINCSALES,OFFEXPINC,0))
28	R53C12	(OFFEXP+IF(SUM(R42C9:R42C12)>OFFEXPINCSALES,OFFEXPINC,0))
29	R53C13	(OFFEXP+IF(SUM(R42C9:R42C13)>OFFEXPINCSALES,OFFEXPINC,0))
30	R54C4	ADEXPPLUS
31	R54C5:8,10:13	DOLLARSALES*ADEXP
32	R56C4:8,10:13	SUM(R[-5]C:R[-2]C)
33	R58C4:8,10:13	R[-10]C-R[-2]C
34	R60C4	R58C4
35	R60C5:8,10:13	R[-2]C+RC[-1]
36	R42,43,45,46,48,51:54,56,58C14	SUM(RC[-4]:RC[-1])
37	R42,43,45,46,48,51:54,56,58C15	RC[-1]+RC[-6]+RC[-11]

PRODBUD: Locations of Named Cells and Ranges

Description	Location	Name
PRODUCT PRICE AND COST DATA	R11C1	PRICECOST
Component 1 Sales Price	R15C4	COMP1SP
Component 2 Sales Price	R16C4	COMP2SP
Component 1 Unit Cost	R15C5	COMP1UC
Component 2 Unit Cost	R16C5	COMP2UC
Sales Price	R15:18C4	SALESPRICE
Unit Cost	R15:18C5	UNITCOST
Gross Margin	R15:18C6	GROSSMARGIN
EXPENSE DATA	R23C1	EXPENSE
Base Salary	R25C4	BASESALARY
Base Salary Increase Amount	R26C4	BASEINCREASE
Base Salary Toggle	R26C6	BASESALES
Wage Overhead	R27C4	WAGEOH
Office Expenses	R29C4	OFFEXP
Office Expenses Increase Amount	R30C4	OFFEXPINC
Office Expenses Increase Toggle	R30C6	OFFEXPINCSALES
Advertising Expense	R32C4	ADEXP
Advertising Expense Lump Sum	R32C7	ADEXPPLUS
PROJECTIONS	R36C1	PROJECTIONS
Unit Sales	R42C4:15	UNITSALES
Dollar Sales	R43C4:15	DOLLARSALES
Salaries	R51C4:15	SALARIES
INSTRUCTIONS	R66C1	INSTRUCTIONS

The model has three sections: PRODUCT PRICE AND COST DATA, EXPENSE DATA, and PROJECTIONS. The PRODUCT PRICE section, which begins at cell R10C1, contains data about the variable costs and sales price for the product being analyzed. The unit costs of components 1 and 2 equal either the total variable manufacturing costs or the total purchase costs of the components.

These figures are entered, respectively, in cells R15C5 and R16C5, UNITCOST. Cells R15C4 and R16C4, SALESPRICE, contain the selling price for each component even though the parts will be sold together as a single package. The package price is calculated in cell R18C4 by the formula

R18C4 I = R15C4+R16C4

or

R18C4 I = COMP1SP+COMP2SP

Cell R18C5 shows the total cost of the product:

R18C5 I = R15C5+R16C5

or

R18C5 I = COMP1UC+COMP2UC

Cells R15C6 and R16C6, GROSSMARGIN, compute the gross margin earned on each component by subtracting the cost of the part from its sale price. For example, cell R16C6 contains the formula

R16C6 I = R16C4-R16C5

or

R16C6 I = SALESPRICE-UNITCOST

Cells R15C6 and R16C6, GROSSMARGIN, convert these dollar margins into percentages by dividing the dollar amounts by the components' prices. For example, cell R16C7 is defined as

R16C7 % = R16C6/R16C4

or

R16C7 % = GROSSMARGIN/SALESPRICE

The Percent Margin column from rows 16 through 18 is Formatted to display percentages (%).

The second section of the model, EXPENSE DATA, begins at row 22, and shows the assumptions about payroll, office, and advertising expenses that will be used later in the model. The first expense, sales commissions, is expressed as a percentage of the total unit price. In this example, an 8% commission will be paid for each unit sold, so .08 is entered in cell R24C4.

Assumptions about salary and wage overhead expenses are located in cells R25C4, R26C4, R27C4, and R26C6. Cell R25C4, BASESALARY, contains the base quarterly salary expense. Cell R26C4, BASEINCREASE, shows the increase in salary that is anticipated after the sale of a certain number of units, which is displayed in cell R26C6, BASESALES. Finally, cell R27C4, WAGEOH, contains the assumed wage overhead rate. Wage overhead includes such items as payroll taxes and employee benefits.

Office expense assumptions are entered in a similar way in cells R29C4, R30C4, and R30C6. Cell R29C4, OFFEXP, holds the base office expenses number, and cell R30C4, OFFEXPINC, shows the expected increase in these expenses. The number of units that must be sold before this increase can take effect is shown in cell R30C6, OFFEXPINCSALES.

Implicit in our estimates for salaries and office expenses is the assumption that expenses will increase when our new product begins to sell. The increased salary may be used to hire a customer service representative or more order entry clerks; the increased office expenses reflect the extra rent and supplies needed to support these people.

The last expense item, advertising, is defined as a percentage of sales. The assumed percentage should be entered in cell R32C4, ADEXP. We have also included a first-year lump sum advertising expense in cell R32C7, ADEXPLUS.

The PROJECTIONS section of the model, beginning at cell R35C1, uses the assumptions to build sales and expense projections for the new product. Because the first year is the development and start-up year, these projections assume that no units are sold and that no variable costs are incurred. Significant overhead costs, however, are incurred. After the first year, projections of revenues and expenses are made on a quarterly basis for two more years.

The first step in making projections is to estimate unit sales for each quarter. These amounts are entered in row 42, Unit Sales. For the second and third years, Multiplan totals the quarterly unit sales to obtain annual unit sales. Total unit sales for the second year appear in cell R42C9, which contains the formula

R42C9 I = SUM(R42C5:R42C8)

or

R42C9 I = SUM(RC[-4]:RC[-1])

A similar formula is used in cell R42C14 to total unit sales for the third year.

R42C14 I = SUM(RC[-4]:RC[-1])

In row 43, unit sales are converted to dollar sales by multiplying the unit sales projections by the sales price per unit as given in cell R18C4, SALESPRICE. For example, dollar sales for the second quarter of the second year, which appear in cell R43C6, are calculated by the formula

R43C6 = R[-1]C*R18C4

Row 45 displays the cost of goods sold. These figures are calculated by multiplying unit sales by the total cost per unit from cell R18C5, UNITCOST. For example, the cost of goods sold for the second quarter of the second year is displayed in cell R45C6 by the formula

R45C6 I = R[-3]C*R18C5

Direct sales expenses, as displayed in row 46, are calculated by multiplying the sales commission percentage from cell R24C4 by the dollar sales figure in row 43. For the second year, second quarter, these expenses are calculated by the formula

R46C6 I = +R[-3]C*R24C4

Next, Multiplan computes the gross margin, in row 48, by subtracting direct sales expenses and cost of goods sold from dollar sales. For example, for the first quarter of year 2, gross margin is calculated by the formula

R48C5 I = +R[-5]C-R[-3]C-R[-2]C

Operating expenses, listed in rows 51 through 54, are based on the estimates entered in the EXPENSE DATA section. For example, cell

R51C4, which displays total salary expenses for the first year, contains the formula

R51C4 I = (R25C4+(IF(R42C4>R26C6,R26C4,0))*4

or

R51C4 I = (BASESALARY+IF(R42C4>BASESALES, BASEINCREASE,0))*4

(Multiplying by four converts the number from a quarterly to an annual amount.)

Salary expenses for the first quarter of the second year are computed by the formula

R51C5 I = R25C4+(IF(SUM(R42C4:R42CG58)>R26C6, R26C4,0))

or

R51C5 I = (BASESALARY+IF(SUM(R42C4:R42C5)> BASESALES,BASEINCREASE,0))

These formulas mean that the salary expense for the period equals the base salary shown in cell R25C4, BASESALARY, plus the amount shown in cell R26C4, BASEINCREASE, if the total number of units sold to date exceeds the number in cell R26C6, BASESALES. Whenever the cumulative number of units sold exceeds the number in cell R26C6, BASESALES, the additional salary will be posted automatically to the cells in row 51.

The total salary expense for the first year is shown in cell R51C9:

R51C9 I = SUM(RC[-4]:RC[-1])

Cells R52C9, R53C9, and R54C9 use the same formula to compute annual totals for wage overhead, office expenses, and advertising costs.

Wage overhead is computed by multiplying the total salary expense in each period by the wage overhead percentage shown in cell R27C4.

For example, cell R52C5 is defined as

R52C5 I = R27C4*R51C5

or

R52C5 I = WAGEOH*SALARIES

The office expenses in row 53 are also related to our expense assumptions. For example, in the first quarter of the second year, the formula for computing office expenses is

R53C5 I = (R29C6+IF(SUM(R42C4:R42C5)>R30C6,R30C4,0))

or

R53C5 I = (OFFEXP+IF(SUM(R42C4:R42C5)>
OFFEXPINCSALES,OFFEXPINC,0))

This formula is almost identical to the one used to compute salary expense and works the same way.

Advertising expense for the first year equals the first-year lump sum specified in cell R32C7. The formula in cell R54C4 is

R54C4 I = R32C8

or

R54C4 I = ADEXPPLUS

Quarterly advertising expense in each of the following periods is based on the sales volume for that period and the percentage found in cell R32C4. For example, cell R54C5 contains the formula

R54C5 I = R43C5*R32C4

or

R54C5 I = DOLLARSALES*ADEXP

Total operating expenses, shown in row 56, are computed as the sum of the individual operating expenses. For example, the formula for total operating expenses for the first quarter of the second year is

R56C5 I = SUM(R51C5:R54C5)

Net income is calculated by subtracting total operating expenses from gross margin. The formula for calculating net income for the first quarter of the second year is

R58C5 I = R48C5-R56C5

The retained earnings figures in row 60 represent the cumulative net income generated by the product being analyzed. In the first year retained earnings equal net income. For the following periods retained earnings are computed by adding the net income for the current period to the previous period's retained earnings. For example, retained earnings for the first quarter of the second year are calculated by the formula

R60C5 I = R60C4+R58C5

or

R60C5 I = +R[-2]C+RC[-1]

Column 15 shows the three-year total for each income and expense item. For example, cell R42C15 is defined as

R42C15 I = +RC[-1]+RC[-6]+RC[-11]

Cell R58C15 computes the total net income for the three-year period with the same formula

R58C15 I = +RC[-1]+RC[-6]+RC[-11]

Using the Model

To use this model, you must first develop your own assumptions for sales and expenses and then enter them in the appropriate cells in the PRODUCT DATA and EXPENSE DATA sections. Your projected quarterly unit sales figures should be entered in row 41.

After the data is entered, type F4 or ! to recalculate the model. You can save the model by typing **TSB:STARTUP** (CR) and print it by typing **P**rint**M**arginsR10:R61(CR)**P**rinter.

Be sure to take advantage of Multiplan's "what if" powers when using this model. Change your price, cost, and expense assumptions; then examine the changes in net income and retained earnings. Some of the "what if" questions you may want to consider are

1. What if unit sales are not as high as I expect?
2. What if I raise the price and sell fewer units? What if I lower the price?
3. What if fixed and variable costs increase by 10% each year?

4. What if start-up and development costs in the first year are much higher than I expect?
5. What if it takes more than one year to get the product to market?

Analyzing these and other scenarios will make this model a more effective and valuable planning tool for your business.

Modifications

This model can be modified to provide more information on product profitability. For example, the net present value of the net income figures can be calculated using Multiplan's NPV function.

In our example, no tax effects are considered. Because of loss carry-forward, taxes would not be paid until the fourth quarter of the third year, when they would begin to reduce the amount of the retained earnings account shown in the example. You may want to include a tax table in your version of the model.

Determining Price-Volume Relationships

What price should I charge for my product? Almost every business-person faces that tough decision at some point. Generally, there is a trade-off between charging a high price, with the risk of losing sales volume, and charging a low price to gain market volume, with the chance that you will not be able to cover costs. When a new product is introduced, the pricing decision can be particularly difficult because of the uncertainty about how well the product will sell and what price the market will bear.

Sometimes the price-volume relationship for a particular product can be determined by test marketing. In most cases, however, assumptions must be made about what the relationship will be. Examining numerous assumptions to come up with the "most likely" price-volume scenario can be accomplished quickly and easily with Multiplan.

Principles

The ideal price for a product, one that maximizes profits, will be different under different market conditions and cost structures. Unfortunately, the relationship between price and profit is not linear. Raising the price of a product will sometimes increase profit, but at other times reduce it. Even if price and volume move up and down together, they rarely move in direct proportion to each other.

A demand curve represents the price-volume relationship. In most markets, as the price increases, fewer people buy the product. Of course, each market has characteristics that help shape the price-volume relationship, including the amount and intensity of com-

```
        1           2           3          4                 5                 6                 7                  8
 1 =================================================================================
 2 PRICE-VOLUME ANALYSIS                              (C) QUE CORPORATION 1983
 3 =================================================================================
 4
 5                       For INSTRUCTIONS (G)oto (N)ame 'INSTRUCTIONS'
 6                       For ASSUMPTIONS (G)oto (N)ame 'ASSUMPTIONS'
 7                       For SOLUTIONS, (G)oto (N)ame 'SOLUTIONS'
 8 ====================================================================================================================
 9 ASSUMPTIONS                                                                     Sheet 1.1
10 ====================================================================================================================
11
12 Fixed Costs                          $600,000.00
13
14 Per Unit Variable Costs                    $0.35
15
16 Sales Price/Unit                           $1.00             $1.10             $1.24             $1.50             $2.00
17
18 Expected Sales Volume                    920,000           900,000           825,000           625,000           400,000
19
20 ====================================================================================================================
21 SOLUTIONS                                                                       Sheet 2.1
22 ====================================================================================================================
23 Total Dollar Sales                (1) $920,000.00       $990,000.00     $1,023,000.00       $937,500.00       $800,000.00
24 Variable Costs                    (2) $322,000.00       $315,000.00       $288,750.00       $218,750.00       $140,000.00
25 Fixed Costs                       (3) $600,000.00       $600,000.00       $600,000.00       $600,000.00       $600,000.00
26                                       -----------       -----------       -----------       -----------       -----------
27 Net Income                            ($2,000.00)       $75,000.00       $134,250.00       $118,750.00        $60,000.00
28                                       ===========       ===========       ===========       ===========       ===========
29                                                                         (4)
30 Return on Sales (Percent)                    -0%                8%               13%               13%                8%
31                                       ===========       ===========       ===========       ===========       ===========
32
33                                                                         (5)
34
35 ====================================================================================================================
36 INSTRUCTIONS                                                                                          Sheet 3.1
37 ====================================================================================================================
38
39
40                       1) Enter ASSUMPTIONS
41                       3) Recalculate by typing: F4 or !
42                       3) SAVE by typing: TSB:PV (CR)
43                       4) PRINT by typing: PP
```

PRICE-VOLUME ANALYSIS

NUMBER	LOCATION(S)	FORMULA
1	R23C4	PRICE*VOLUME
2	R24C4	UNITVAR*VOLUME
3	R25C4	FIXEDCOSTS
4	R27C4	GROSSSALES-VARIABLE-FIXEDCOSTS
5	R30C4:8	NET/GROSSSALES

petition, the financial resources of the customers, the relative importance of the product to them, and their ability to perceive significant differences among competitive products. The classic demand curve demonstrates this price-volume relationship.

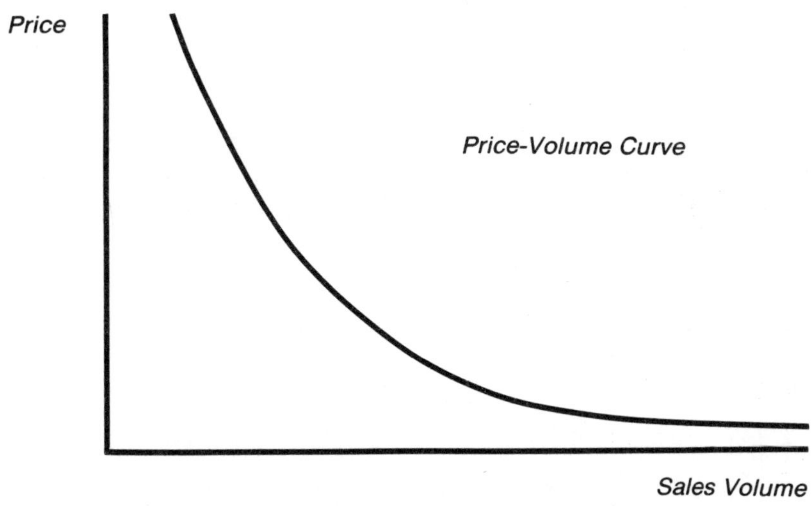

As unit price increases, the number of units sold decreases, and vice versa. The two end points of the curve illustrate the "lowest volume" and "highest volume" cases. In most cases, however, these extreme points can be dismissed as lying outside the "relevant range" of realistic opportunities available to the seller. For example, a car dealer could sell all the cars in his inventory if he charged only $10 per car, but he would lose his shirt in the process. On the other hand, the dealer could have a tremendous profit margin if he charged $50,000 per car, but it is doubtful that he would sell even one.

Most businesses want to find the price-volume relationship that will maximize profits. That relationship usually lies within a narrow range on the demand curve. The trick is to pin down the point with a careful analysis of prices, costs, and sales volumes.

The Model

This model has two sections: ASSUMPTIONS and SOLUTIONS. The ASSUMPTIONS section begins at cell **N**ame ASSUMPTIONS.

PRICEVOL: Locations of Named Cells and Ranges

Description	**Location**	**Name**
ASSUMPTIONS	R10C1	ASSUMPTIONS
Fixed Costs	R12C4	FIXEDCOSTS
Per Unit Variable Costs	R14C4	UNITVAR
Sales Price/Unit	R16C4:8	PRICE
Expected Sales Volume	R18C4:8	VOLUME
SOLUTIONS	R22C1	SOLUTIONS
Total Dollar Sales	R23C4:8	GROSSSALES
Variable Costs	R24C4:8	VARIABLE
Net Income	R27C4:8	NET
INSTRUCTIONS	R37C1	INSTRUCTIONS

The numbers in this model have been formatted with commas by typing **F**ormat **O**ptions **Y**es(CR) and with embedded dollar signs by typing **F**ormat **D**efault **C**ells (TAB)**$**(CR). Cell R12C4, FIXEDCOSTS, is used to enter the estimated fixed costs associated with a product. Because fixed costs do not vary with changes in sales volume, only one figure for fixed costs is needed. The variable costs per unit are entered in cell R14C4, UNITVAR. This number should be expressed as a dollar amount. The sample model shows a product with per unit variable costs of $.35.

Rows 16 and 18 are used to enter the five price-volume combinations you select for testing. Notice that in the example, the expected sales volume decreases as the price increases.

In the SOLUTIONS section, which begins at row 21, Multiplan computes the total dollar sales, variable costs, net income, and return on sales for each price selected. In row 23, dollar sales for each price-volume pair are computed by multiplying the sales price by the expected volume. The row has a range name of GROSS-SALES. For example, cell R23C4 contains the formula

R23C4 $ = R16C4*R18C4

or

R23C4 $ = PRICE*VOLUME

The version of this formula using named cells can be repeated in cells across row 23 with Multiplan's **C**opy **R**ight command. Total variable costs are computed in range VARIABLE, row 24. This calculation is made by multiplying the expected sales volume in row 18 by the variable cost factor in cell R14C4, UNITVAR. For example, the formula for cell R24C4, VARIABLE, is

R24C4 $ = R18C4*R14C4

or

R24C4 $ = UNITVAR*VOLUME

Similarly, the formula in cell R24C8 is

R24C8 $ = R18C8*R18C4

or

R24C8 $ = UNITVAR*VOLUME

Now look at row 25. Each cell in this row is defined in terms of the fixed cost assumption made in cell R12C4, FIXED. For example, cell R25C6 is defined as

R25C6 $ = R12C4

or

R25C6 $ = FIXEDCOSTS

The variable and fixed costs are subtracted from the dollar sales figures to obtain a net income for each price point. These computations appear in row 27, which has been named NET. For example, the formula in cell R27C4 is

R27C4 $ = R23C4-R24C4-R12C4

or

R27C4 $ = GROSSSALES-VARIABLE-FIXEDCOSTS

In row 30, the model calculates the return on sales for each price-point combination. Return on sales is an expression of net income as a percentage of sales and is calculated by dividing net income (row 27) by dollar sales (row 23). For example, the formula in cell R30C4 is

R30C4 % = R27C4/R23C4

or

R30C4 % = NET/GROSSSALES

This formula is repeated, using relative references, from R30C4 to R30C8 and is **F**ormatted using the % option.

Using the Model

Before sitting down with this model, you will need to accumulate data about fixed and variable costs and select several different sets of price-volume combinations for testing. After the data has been assembled, enter it in the appropriate locations and type F4 or ! to recalculate. You can save the model by typing **TSB:PV** (CR) and print it by typing **PP**.

The key to success with this model is the extensive use of "what if" analysis. By raising and lowering your expectations for sales volume at each price, you can measure the effects of changes in your sales volume on your return on sales.

If you have a graphics program, consider plotting several sets of price-volume pairs using a line chart.

8
Quote Preparation

Preparing Quotations

Preparing Quotations

In your business, do you prepare quotations? If you do, then you probably will welcome help with this time-consuming task. Developing a quotation can be a complicated procedure that involves three steps: looking up price and cost data, manipulating the data to arrive at the appropriate price for each item being quoted, and typing the quote itself. Although this process may require a great deal of time, this Multiplan model can save time by combining all three steps into one.

The Model

Any business that needs to prepare quotations can use this model. You can not only write and track as many as 10 quotes with the model, but also maintain cost and price data for 26 parts. This model consumes a great deal of RAM. Very little free memory will exist after the model is entered, and if your computer has less than 64K of memory, the model will not work. If you have added, or can add, additional memory that Multiplan will recognize, the model may be expanded easily.

QUOTATIONS: Locations of Named Cells and Ranges

Description	Location	Name
QUOTE FORM	R11C1	QUOTE
Quote Number (Form)	R12C3	THISQN
Name of Customer	R14C1	NAME
Customer Number (Form)	R14C9	CUSTNO
Quantity (Form)	R26:33C1	QTY
Part Number (Form)	R26:33C2	PART
Quoted Price	R26:33C6	QUOTED
Extended Price (Form)	R26:33C7	EXTPR

QUOTATIONS: Locations of Named Cells and Ranges *(cont.)*

Unit Cost	R26:33C9	COST
Extended Cost	R26:33C11	EXTCOST
Dollar Margin	R26:33C12	DOLMARGIN
Subtotal of Extended Costs	R35C7	SUBT
Total Quote Extended Cost	R35C11	SUMEX
Shipping (Form)	R36C7	SHIPPING
Net Quotation	R38C7	NETQUOTE
State Sales Tax	R39C7	SALESTAX
QUOTE TRACKER	R45C1	TRACKER
Quote Number (Quote Tracker)	R49:58C1	TRACKQN
Quote Subtotal (Quote Tracker)	R49:58C3	QSUBT
Total Cost (Quote Tracker)	R49:58C4	TOTCOST
Margin (Quote Tracker)	R49:58C5	TMARGIN
UNIT COST AND PRICE TABLES	R64C1	TABLES
Part Numbers (Lookup Table)	R68:94C1	PARTNO
Unit Cost (Lookup Table)	R68:94C2	UNITCOST
List Price (Lookup Table)	R68:94C3	LIST
Minimum Price (Lookup Table)	R68:94C4	MINPRICE
Description/Part Name	R68:94C5	NAMES
INSTRUCTIONS	R97C1	INSTRUCTIONS

The Quote Generator has three sections: QUOTE FORM, QUOTE TRACKER, and UNIT COST AND PRICE TABLES. The central feature of the model is the QUOTE FORM, which begins at row 10 and continues to row 42. The upper part of the form includes space for a quote number (R12C3) and an address heading. The quote number is very important because the model uses this number to retain information about the quote. Notice also that cell R14C9 contains a number that identifies the customer to whom the quote is being sent. This optional entry does not appear on the final printed quote.

Rows 23 and 24 contain headings for the other columns in the form. Column 1 is an input column for the number of units for each part included in the quote. For example, our sample quote specifies one unit of part number 101.

Part numbers are entered in column 2. Our sample quote includes parts 101, 201, 422, 211, 402, 601, 704, and 611.

Multiplan gives us the capability of filling in the description of the items when the part number cell at R27C2, PART, is supplied. The formula

R27C3 = IF(PART=LOOKUP(PART,PARTNO),LOOKUP(PART, PARTNO:NAMES,"ERROR")

or

R27C3 = IF(R27C2=LOOKUP(R27C2,R68C1:R94C1), LOOKUP(R27C2,R68C1:R94C5), "ERROR")

looks up the part number in the multicolumn table and returns the description located in column 5. If the part number is not in the table, Multiplan will place the ERROR message in the cell. This search feature allows you to use nonconsecutive part numbers.

Column 6 shows the quoted price for each item. Our example contains several quotes at list price and several discounted quotes. If this example were an actual quotation, the salesperson would decide how much discount, if any, was needed to get the sale. The quoted price can be varied until the ideal margin-price combination is reached.

Column 7 computes the extended price for each item in the quote. The formula in R27C7, EXTPR, is

R27C7 $R = IF(R27C6>LOOKUP(R27C2,R68C1:R94C4), R27C1*R27C6,999999)

or

R27C7$R = IF(QUOTED>LOOKUP(PART,PARTNO: MINPRICE),QTY*QUOTED,999999)

The extended price is calculated by multiplying the quoted price per unit by the number of units quoted. This formula contains an interesting check against quotation errors. If the quoted price is less than the minimum price entered in the range R68:94C7, MINPRICE, then 999999 is returned. It is not the 9s themselves, but the number of 9s, that is important. Notice that the width of column K is set to 10 characters—too narrow to accommodate the entire string of 9s. When this problem is encountered, Multiplan displays a series of #

```
        1         2         3         4         5         6         7
 1 ===========================================================================
 2 QUOTE GENERATOR                             Copyright (C) QUE Corp. 1983
 3 ===========================================================================
 4
 5          For QUOTE FORM, (G)oto (N)ame `QUOTE'
 6          For QUOTE TRACKER, (G)oto (N)ame `TRACKER'
 7          For UNIT COST AND PRICE TABLES (G)oto (N)ame `TABLES'
 8          For INSTRUCTIONS, (G)oto (N)ame `INSTRUCTIONS'
 9 ===========================================================================
10 QUOTE FORM                                                      Sheet 1.1
11 ===========================================================================
12 Quote Number:            1003
13
14 Mr. Larry Framer
15 Any Corporation
16 9000 Keystone Crossings
17 Indianapolis, Indiana 46240
18
19 Dear Mr. Framer:
20
21 We are pleased to submit the following quotation:
22
23                Part                                     Quoted   Extended
24  Quantity    Number  Description                         Price     Price
25  --------  --------- -----------------------------    --------- ---------
26        1       101   No. 303 Cabinet                  $1895.00  $1895.00
27        3       201   ARIES Fireplace Module           $1825.00  $5475.00
28        4       422   COLESON Replacement 220 VAC        $14.00    $56.00
29       20       211   Blower for ARIES Models       (1)   $95.00  $1900.00
30        1       402   COLESON Home Heat/AC Plant       $3200.00  $3200.00 (2)
31        1       601   BARGER BROS. Fuse Ass'y             $5.00     $5.00
32        1       704   BARGER BROS. Kickplate Kit         $32.00    $32.00
33       10       611   BARGER BROS. Faceplate              $6.00    $60.00
34                                                                  --------
35                      Subtotal:                                 $12623.00 (9)
36                      Shipping and Handling:                      $155.00
37                                                                  --------
38                      Net Quotation:                            $12778.00 (10)
39                      State Sales Tax:                            $638.90 (11)
40                                                                  --------
41                      Total Quotation:                          $13416.90 (12)
42                                                                  ========
```

CUSTNO. 104

8	9	10	11	12	13
List Price	Unit Cost	Unit Margin	Extended Cost	Dollar Margin	Percent Margin
1540.00	1155.00	740.00	1155.00	740.00	39%
1995.00	1695.00	130.00	5085.00	390.00	7%
14.00	7.00	7.00	28.00	28.00	50%
100.00	45.00	50.00	900.00	1000.00	53%
3200.00	2300.00	900.00	2300.00	900.00	28%
5.00	2.50	2.50	2.50	2.50	50%
45.00	25.00	7.00	25.00	7.00	22%
6.00	3.00	3.00	30.00	30.00	50%
			9525.50		
(3)	(4)	(5)	(6) (7)	(7)	(8)

```
        1         2          3          4          5          6         7           8          9
43 ===============================================================================
44 QUOTE TRACKER (Continues to row 61)                                Sheet 2.1
45 ===============================================================================
46   Quote    Customer     Quote     Total                  Percent   Buyer's                TRUE (20)
47   Number   ID Number   Subtotal   Cost        Margin     Margin      Name
48  --------  --------   --------  --------    --------   --------  ------------
49      1001       116   12183.00   9525.50     2657.50        22%  Dr. Michael Ravell
50      1002       338   12623.00  10065.50     2557.50        20%  Ms. Luann Johnson
51      1003       104   12623.00   9525.50     3097.50        25%  Mr. Larry Framer
52      1004         0       0.00      0.00        0.00         0%
53      1005         0       0.00      0.00        0.00         0%
54      1006 (13)    0 (14)  0.00 (15) 0.00 (16)   0.00 (17)    0% (18)                  (19)
55      1007         0       0.00      0.00        0.00         0%
56      1008         0       0.00      0.00        0.00         0%
57      1009         0       0.00      0.00        0.00         0%
58      1010         0       0.00      0.00        0.00         0%
59                         ------     ------      ------     -------
60 Totals:               37429.00   29116.50     8312.50        22%
61                          (21)       (22)        (23)        (24)
62 ===============================================================================
63 UNIT COST AND PRICE TABLES (Continues to row 94)                   Sheet 3.1
64 ===============================================================================
65     Part       Unit       List     Minimum  Description/
66    Number      Cost       Price     Price   Part Name
67    -----      -----      -----      -----   -----------
68       101   1155.00    1540.00    1350.00  No. 303 Cabinet
69       111     95.00     150.00     135.00  No. 919 Support Struts
70       112     75.00     145.00     125.00  No. Support Struts
71       123   1895.00    2595.00    2200.00  RM71 9 Ton A.C.
72       131    125.00     235.00     200.00  Heat Exchanger Module
73       132    175.00     299.00     225.00  Heat Exchanger Module (wired)
74       133    450.00     800.00     650.00  Dehumidifier Module
75       201   1695.00    1995.00    1800.00  ARIES Fireplace Module
76       211     45.00     100.00      55.00  Blower for ARIES Models
77       221     60.00     100.00      80.00  ARIES Blower (wired)
78       231    550.00     995.00     675.00  SANTALLA Franklin Stove
79       310    175.00     300.00     225.00  MORGAN Fireplace Blower
80       311    150.00     325.00     275.00  MORGAN Fireplace Blower Wired
81       401   1600.00    2300.00    1800.00  COLESON Home Heat Plant
82       402   2300.00    3200.00    2600.00  COLESON Home Heat/AC Plant
83       411      4.00       8.00       6.00  COLESON Replacement Glass 9X12
84       412      4.00       8.00       6.00  COLESON Replacement Glass 12X13
```

```
          8        9         10        11       12        13
 85      422      7.00     14.00     10.00 COLESON Replacement 220 VAC
 86      501    450.00    650.00    575.00 BARGER BROS. Fireplace Insert
 87      502    850.00   1250.00   1000.00 BARGER BROS. Heating Plant
 88      511      6.00     10.00     10.00 BARGER BROS. Replacement Glass
 89      521     15.00     35.00     25.00 BARGER BROS. 220 VAC Module
 90      601      2.50      5.00      4.00 BARGER BROS. Fuse Ass'y
 91      602      4.50      7.50      6.50 BARGER BROS. 220 VAC Fuse Ass'y
 92      611      3.00      6.00      5.00 BARGER BROS. Faceplate
 93      612      6.00      9.00      8.00 BARGER BROS. Hinges
 94      704     25.00     45.00     30.00 BARGER BROS. Kickplate Kit
 95 ========================================================================
 96 INSTRUCTIONS                                                  Sheet 4.1
 97 ========================================================================
 98
 99           1) Enter the following data: Quantities, Part Numbers,
100              and Quoted Price
101           2) Recalculate by typing: F4 or !
102           3) To PRINT Quotation only, type: POR11C1:R43C7(CR)P
103           4) To PRINT entire model, type: PP
104           5) SAVE by typing: TSB:QUOTE (CR)
```

QUOTE GENERATOR

NUMBER	LOCATION(S)	FORMULA
1	R26:33C3	IF(PART=LOOKUP(PART,PARTNO), LOOKUP(PART,PARTNO:NAMES),"ERROR")
2	R26:33C7	IF(QUOTED>LOOKUP(PART,PARTNO: MINPRICE),QTY*QUOTED,999999)
3	R26:33C8	LOOKUP(PART,PARTNO:LIST)
4	R26:33C9	LOOKUP(PART,PARTNO:UNITCOST)
5	R26:33C10	QUOTED-COST
6	R26:33C11	COST*QTY
7	R26:33C12	EXTPR-EXTCOST
8	R26:33C13	DOLMARGIN/EXTPR
9	R35C7	SUM(EXTPR)
10	R38C7	SHIPPING+SUBT
11	R39C7	0.05*NETQUOTE
12	R41C7	SALESTAX+NETQUOTE
13	R50:58C1	R[-1]C+1
14	R49:58C2	IF(TRACKQN=THISQN,CUSTNO,IF (TRACKQN<THISQN,RC,0))
15	R49:58C3	IF(TRACKQN=THISQN,SUBT,IF (TRACKQN<THISQN,RC,0))
16	R49:58C4	IF(TRACKQN=THISQN,SUMEX,IF (TRACKQN<THISQN,RC,0))
17	R49:58C5	QSUBT-TOTCOST
18	R49:58C6	IF(QSUBT>0,RC[-1]/RC[-3],0)
19	R49:58C7	IF(TRACKQN=THISQN,""&MID(NAME, 1,19),IF(TRACKQN<THISQN,RC,""))
20	R46C9	TRUE()
21	R61C3	SUM(QSUBT)
22	R61C4	SUM(TOTCOST)
23	R61C5	SUM(TMARGIN)
24	R61C6	SUM(TMARGIN)/SUM(QSUBT)

symbols in the cell. If the quoted price is too low, the extended price will appear as ##########. This provides a quick, visual safeguard against error in pricing.

Column 9 displays the unit cost of each part listed in column 2. These cells look up the amounts automatically from the UNIT COST AND PRICE TABLES, which begin at row 68. Cell R27C9, COST, is an example of the formulas in this range.

R27C9 F2 = LOOKUP(PART,PARTNO:UNICOST)

or

R27C9 F2 = LOOKUP(R27C2,R68C1:R94C2)

No matter which part number you enter in R27C2, PART, its cost will automatically be returned in cell R27C9 (assuming the part number has been described in the UNIT COST AND PRICE TABLES). Using the named ranges, you can quickly copy this formula with the **C**opy command.

The cells in column 8 use the same automatic technique to display the list price for each product. For example, cell R30C8 contains the formula

R30C8 = LOOKUP(PART,PARTNO:LIST)

or

R30C8 = LOOKUP(R30C2,R68C1:R94C3)

The total for the extended price column, in cell R37C7, will also display the # message. This check also helps ensure that no quote will include an unacceptably low price, thus preventing costly errors.

Column 11 computes the extended cost for each product in the quote by multiplying the unit cost in column 9 by the number of units in column 1. Cell R30C11, EXTCOST, is typical of the formulas in this range:

R30C11 F2 = R30C9*R30C1

or

R30C11 F2 = COST*QTY

Finally, columns 12 and 13 compute the dollar and percentage margins on the quote, using extended prices and costs. Column 12 computes the dollar margin at list price for each product unit being quoted by subtracting the unit cost from the list price. Cell R27C12, DOLMARGIN, for instance, is defined as

R27C12 F2 = R27C7-R27C11

or

R27C12 F2 = EXTPR-EXTCOST

Column 13 displays the percentage retail margin at list price. This figure is calculated by dividing the margin, computed in column 9, by the price of the product. The formula for cell R27C13 is

R27C13 % = R27C12/R27C7

or

R27C13 % = DOLMARGIN/EXTPR

A quote subtotal is computed in cell R35C7, SUBT, by adding the range of cells from R26C7 to R33C7. Shipping and handling costs for the order should be entered in cell R37C6, SHIPPING. The net quotation is computed in cell R38C7, NETQUOTE, with the formula

R38C7 $ = R36C7+R35C7

or

R38C7 $ = SHIPPING+SUBT

Sales tax is computed in cell R39C7, SALESTAX. The sample model has a built-in rate of 5%. You should, of course, use a formula that calculates the sales tax for your state. If sales tax is not included in the quote, enter 0 in this cell.

The total amount of the quotation is displayed in cell R41C7, which contains the formula

R41C7 $ = R38C7+R33C7

or

R41C7 $ = SALESTAX+NETQUOTE

The second section of the model, QUOTE TRACKER, begins at cell R44C1. Rows 46 and 47 hold the column labels for the data recorded for each quote: Quote Number, Customer ID Number, Quote Subtotal, Total Cost, Margin, Percentage Margin, and Name.

Cell R49C1, TRACKQN, is used to enter the first quote number for the period. Cell R50C1 is then defined as

R50C1 = R[-1]C+1

Each cell in column 1 is defined in terms of the previous cell's number plus one. This part of the table is built automatically. It is essential to number the quotes sequentially. If you attempt to re-enter and change an earlier quote, you will lose much of the contents of the model.

Cell R49C2 retains the customer number for quote #1001. The formula in this cell is

R49C2 I = IF(R49C1=R12C3,R14C9,IF(R49C1<R12C3,
R49C2,0))

or

R49C2 I = IF(TRACKQN=THISQN,CUSTNO,IF(TRACKQN<
THISQN,RC,0))

If the quote number in cell R12C3 equals the quote number on row 49 of the table, set cell R49C2 equal to the customer number in cell R14C9. If the quote number for row 49 is less than the quote number in cell R12C3, leave cell R49C2 unchanged. This formula lets the cells in this column capture data selectively for a specific quote and retain that data. For example, cell R57C2 contains the formula

R57C2 I = IF(R57C1=R12C3,R14C9,IF(R57C1<R12C3,
R57C2,0))

or

R57C2 I = IF(TRACKQN=THISQN,CUSTNO,IF(TRACKQN<
THISQN,RC,0))

The same basic formula is used to define the cells in columns 3 and 4. These columns also compare the number of the quote being written to the quote number in each row. The row that matches the number of the quote captures either the cost or the total amount of the quote. Cells in rows with quote numbers that are less than the current quote number will not be changed. For example, cell R57C3, QSUBT, contains the formula

R57C3 F2 = IF(R57C1=R12C3,R35C7,IF(R57C1<
R12C3,R57C3,0))

or

R57C3 F2 = IF(TRACKQN=THISQN,SUBT,IF(TRACKQN<
THISQN,RC,0))

This formula captures the subtotal amount for quote #1009 and places it into this R57C3.

Cell R57C4, TOTCOST, contains the formula

R57C4 F2 = IF(R57C1=R12C3,R36C12,IF(R57C1<
R12C3,R57C4,0))

or

R57C4 F2 = IF(TRACKQN=THISQN,SUMEX,IF(TRACKQN<
THISQN,RC,0))

This formula captures the total cost of the goods in quote #1009 and places the cost into cell R57C4.

The cells in column 5 compute the margin on each quote by subtracting the cost from the amount of the net quotation. Column 6 then computes the percentage margin by dividing the dollar margin by the price. For example, cell R57C6 is defined as

R57C6 % = IF(QSUBT>0,RC[-1]/RC[-3],0)

or

R57C6 % = IF(R57C3>0,R57C5/R57C3,0)

Column 7 traps the name of the individual that each quotation was made for with the formula

R49C7 CO = IF(R49C1=R12C3," "&MID(R14C1,1,19),IF
(R49C1<R12C3,R49C7,""))

or

R49C7 CO = IF(TRACKQN=THISQN," "&MID(NAME,1,19),IF
(TRACKQN<THISQN,RC,""))

This formula uses Multiplan's exclusive MID( ) function. The MID( ) function allows a certain portion of a cell to be displayed. The first part indicates the cell or text to be used; the second part indicates the starting position (in number of characters); and the third position calls out the number of characters to be displayed, in this case 19.

The formula in R49:58C7 puts a space in front of the name of the person, in cell R14C1, NAME, if the quote numbers match. If the quote number (THISQN) is greater than the cell's TRACKQN, R49C1, then it returns its already-filled-in name, or a blank cell, indicated by the double quotation marks, "".

The cells in row 60 compute totals for the last four columns in this table. For example, cell R60C3 is defined as

R60C3 2 = SUM(R49C3:R58C3)

or

R60C3 2 = SUM(QSUBT)

Cell R60C6 is not a total, but a percentage computed by using the totals. The formula in this cell is

R60C6 = SUM(R49C5:R58C5)/SUM(R49C3:R58C3)

or

R60C6 = SUM(TMARGIN)/SUM(QSUBT)

The section of the model labeled UNIT COST AND PRICE TABLES begins at row 63 and continues through row 94. The tables in this section contain the cost, list price, minimum quote price, and name of each part. The data in these tables is the first to be entered after the model is set up. The values can be changed as often as necessary to reflect changing prices.

When entering the parts and their descriptions in the UNIT COST AND PRICE TABLES, it is not necessary to enter them in numeric order. After you have entered information about all the parts, you can arrange them by using Multiplan's **S**ort Command. To sort the parts with the **S**ort Command, using the same amount and locations, type the following:

S1(TAB)**68**(TAB)**94**(TAB)>(CR)

This string of characters puts the part numbers (rows 68 through 94, column 1) with their descriptions and rows of data in ascending order (note the > in the formula). The lookup tables function correctly *only* if the part numbers are in ascending order.

Using the Models

To prepare a quote, call up the master form and begin entering part numbers, quantities, and quoted prices. *Be sure to update the quote number before you recompute the model.* Use the list price, cost, and margin data to help you prepare the quote. You will want to retain this data with the quote for future reference, but you certainly do not want the data sent to your customers.

You can now print the quote by typing **PP**, after changing the **P**rint **O**ptions area to print to R12C1:R43C7. To make more than one copy of the form, use carbon or carbonless copy paper.

Save the quote by typing **/TSB:QUOTES** (CR). Choose a simple file name for easy identification. For example, quote #1001 might be saved under the name Q1001. If your customers bargain over prices, you can use the quotes you've saved to evaluate their counteroffers.

If you want to expand or shorten a form, simply add or delete lines, using Multiplan's built-in editing features. The models have been designed to allow you to add and delete rows for each form.

When you have filled the tracking table in a model, print a copy and store it in a safe place as the permanent record of the model's activity for that particular period.

Modifications

You can make several changes on this model; for example, you can add more items to the data tables. Unfortunately, because this model uses almost all of the available memory in a 64K CP/M computer, it is likely that you can add more items only by reducing the size of the tracking table, the number of parts, or the form.

You can also change the part numbers to suit your particular needs. Remember, however, that the numbers you use must be composed of numbers only; they cannot contain dashes, letters, or any other characters.

Finally, you can use the table-building routine to track anything that can be numbered sequentially, including checks, receiving tickets, proposal drafts, and laboratory observations. Put this tool to work in your own models.

Index

FOLD HERE

Place
20¢
Stamp
Here

que™

7960 Castleway Drive
Indianapolis, IN 46250

Affix Tape Here

FOLD HERE

NOW AVAILABLE!

The models in this book are *also* available on disk. Now, without the delay and inconvenience of entering them manually, these helpful financial tools can be put to use immediately. To order, check the disk(s) you want and return this card.

_____ copy(s) of diskette #1 @ $39.95 each = $_______
(models in chapters 2, 3, 4 and 5)

_____ copy(s) of diskette #2 @ $39.95 each = $_______
(models in chapters 6, 7, and 8)

Shipping & Handling = $ 2.50

TOTAL = $_______

Method of Payment: ☐ Check ☐ MasterCard ☐ VISA

Credit Card Number: _______________________

Exp. Date: _______________________

Check Format:

- ☐ IBM PC (PC DOS 1.1)
- ☐ 8″ SS/SD
- ☐ Osborne I
- ☐ Apple II

Name: _______________________

Address: _______________________

____

City, State, Zip: _______________________

Place
20¢
Stamp
Here

MULTIPLAN MODELS FOR BUSINESS
P.O. Box 50507
Indianapolis, Indiana 46250

FOLD HERE